Building Up To Financial Freedom

FINANCIAL & RETIREMENT PLANNING FOR DENTISTS

BUILDING UP TO FINANCIAL FREEDOM

FINANCIAL & RETIREMENT PLANNING FOR DENTISTS

JAMES B. JACKSON, DDS

PennWell Books
DENTAL ECONOMICS
PennWell Publishing Company
Tulsa, Oklahoma USA

PennWell Publishing Company
1421 South Sheridan Road/P.O. Box 1260
Tulsa, Oklahoma 74101

Library of Congress cataloging in publication data

Jackson, James B.
Building up to financial freedom
Bibliography: p.

Retirement—Economic aspects. I. Title. [DNLM:
3. Retirement. WU 77 J13b]
RK58.J33 1986 322! .0246176 85–32047
ISBN 0–87814–302–5

Printed in the United States of America

1 2 3 4 5 90 89 88 87 86

BUILDING UP TO FINANCIAL FREEDOM

FINANCIAL & RETIREMENT PLANNING FOR DENTISTS

JAMES B. JACKSON, DDS

PennWell Publishing Company
1421 South Sheridan Road/P.O. Box 1260
Tulsa, Oklahoma 74101

Library of Congress cataloging in publication data

Jackson, James B.
Building up to financial freedom
Bibliography: p.

Retirement—Economic aspects. I. Title. [DNLM:
3. Retirement. WU 77 J13b]
RK58.J33 1986 322! .0246176 85–32047
ISBN 0–87814–302–5

Printed in the United States of America

1 2 3 4 5 90 89 88 87 86

CONTENTS

SECTION IV
FINANCIAL PLANNING FOR DENTAL FAMILIES

ACKNOWLEDGMENTS

Even though I was finally ecstatic to stop staring at the screen of my word processor, my friends who have been so helpful are probably happier!

Tom Cooper, my friend and insurance agent, and Dave Dwyer, from the American Dental Association Council on Insurance, have answered questions until they probably thought I was daffy. I'll never compete as an insurance agent! I don't think I'll ever make it as an attorney, either, but I don't think my neighbor, John Von Lehe, or my childhood friend, Bill Dennis, both capable tax attorneys, are exactly worried. They both were as patient as Job, which is an excellent trait when explaining the vagaries of the law to the uninitiated.

To the numerous dentists who have shared with me the valuations and sales information of their practices, I am most grateful. I probably have more information on this timely subject than anyone, thanks to them. Ken Beacham of the Council on Dental Practice and my "boss" for the seminars I give for the ADA has been most helpful in rounding up additional information, reading my notes, and even reading my mind at times when I "couldn't get it out of my mouth." Dr. Jim Hodges shared with me his first-class method of valuing a practice and the resulting documentation. Roger Hill of Business and Professional Associates, Houston, Texas, was of invaluable help in sharing ideas, notes, etc., on bringing in an associate. His seminar on associateships formed the basis of the chapter on the subject.

Investing is such a complicated and many-faceted area that the innumerable people with whom I talked and who shared with me their methods are probably legion. Joe Sabattino and David Maynard of Fidelity Investments have been most helpful fielding questions on mutual funds—regardless of the time or effort involved.

On one of my numerous trips through Atlanta, I met Richard Whitehead of Whitehead Financial Advisors. Through discussion about the needs of dentists evolved the inside look at the financial plans of the Turner, Mitchell, and Stevens families. Barbara Naylor, an associate at Whitehead Financial and the widow of an Atlanta dentist, was most helpful in her insight into the needs of dental families. They wrote the final three chapters of the book, which bring together what financial planning for dentist ought to be about. The discussions and analysis of these three families are representative of the kind of solid, thoughtful planning provided by competent financial planners.

To my partners, who bit the bullet and took call in order for me to spend the weekends locked up with my trusty word processor, and to the staff of Children's Dentistry, whose patience with me knows no end, I am very grateful and in their debt.

Vickie Matcovich and Peggy Peters, two super ladies who have the dubious distinction of being my secretarial brigade, have worked tirelessly on this project and are equally happy it is finished. Last, but certainly not least, Dr. Joe Dunlap of PennWell Publishing Co. who has listened to all the yelling and screaming and went on with his business, and mine, unaffected by it all, a sincere thank you.

INTRODUCTION

As the title suggests, this book is concerned with helping you attain a successful retirement. That goal, quite obviously, can only be achieved if there has been adequate financial planning during your productive years. The book is organized to lead the reader through the many considerations that must be made in the journey from practicing dentist to retired dentist.

Section I deals with the basics of financial planning—the tools you must know how to use and the bare-rock questions that must be addressed. In financial planning there are three fundamental questions: (1) Where am I now? (2) Where am I going? and (3) How will I get there?

The first question is rather simply answered by having a complete net worth statement prepared. "Where am I going?" is more complicated and is best answered by a goal-setting session with your spouse. An evening with the phones disconnected and the TV turned off will get the task underway. Goals are constantly changing. Today's decisions are certain to be modified or changed tomorrow. Understand that change is normal and to be expected. As a matter of fact, flexibility is an asset—especially in financial planning. "How will I get there?" starts to become apparent as you begin the process of budgeting. Most of us think of budgets as things that people with modest incomes use. The reality, however, is that wealthy people use budgets all the time. That's part of the reason they *are* wealthy.

Section I continues with the psychology of retirement, a subject which should be considered no matter what your age. Getting your insurance portfolio properly arranged can liberate a lot of money. Most of us pay too much for insurance and tend to believe it is an inevitable expense. The inevitable part is correct because we need insurance companies to help with risks, but the expense part can be pared severely if you know the right approach. There *are* ways to pay less for better coverage. The first section concludes with a discussion of estate planning, educating your children, and/or supporting your parents. Understanding estate planning is important if you want to avoid having Uncle Sam take too large a bite from that which you intend to leave your family.

Section II deals with valuing your practice and introducing an associate either well before retirement or as part of your overall plans at the time of retirement. There are many ways to value a practice and to bring in an associate. These common-sense considerations will help you make decisions that will be to your benefit. Your practice should be valued every few years in order for you to update your net worth statement accurately.

Section III brings investing into focus. Understanding how to shelter income through deferred compensation plans and how to shelter personal money through real estate or other limited partnerships will increase your knowledge of the tax laws and, as a consequence, allow you to make them work in your favor. The best way to grow rich is s-l-o-w-l-y. As a matter of fact, the most successful investors follow a rather plodding and predictable course. With a good game plan you won't believe how easy it is to achieve a net worth that will allow you to relax and "smell the roses" as you're still practicing or to serve as the foundation for your retirement. Gaining an understanding of the time value of money will help you comprehend why Einstein said that his greatest discovery was compound interest. Problems you can work with a financial calculator such as the Texas Instruments Business Analyst II or the Hewlett Packard HP12 are offered in the Appendix. These exercises will help you start thinking about investing as an exciting and interesting hobby to pursue.

Section IV deals with financial planners and discusses the financial plans of three typical dental families. These examples will help you relate your plans to those of the Turners, Mitchells, and Stevens. For many readers, this will be the most fascinating part of the book. Seeing how other people have dealt with problems that are common to many may serve as an inspiration for the ideas you need for your own plan.

I hope you have as much pleasure reading this book as I had in writing it. And I wish you much success in all your plans—both for today and tomorrow.

James B. Jackson

TO
CAROL, STUART, AND ELEANOR

SECTION I

GETTING ORGANIZED FOR A SUCCESSFUL PLAN

Preliminary to planning, there must be organizing—the gathering of data, the assessing of the present situation, the identification of goals. From the bringing together of such information, a plan emerges. And a plan is the most fundamental essential to ultimate success.

Assembling this information requires familiarity with a few standard financial tools, an ability to look at things objectively, and a fair amount of soul-searching. Parts of the process are pleasant, parts a little less so. But the potential rewards are so grand that the discomforts will seem insignificant.

Section I will start you on the journey to your successful plan. *Let's go for it!*

CHAPTER

1

The Basic Tools of Financial Planning

To move ahead with any project, from restoring a tooth to building a house, it is necessary to get all the "tools" together and organized. There are a few things you will need to do to initiate a successful financial plan. Most Americans are trained to worry about money, but few ever do anything about it. The next few pages should be used to help you answer the three most important questions in beginning a financial plan. These are the foundation tools of any successful plan. Although completing the accompanying worksheets may not be fun, you should learn a great deal about your particular situation. "Where am I today?" will be answered when your net worth statement is completed. "Where am I going?" will be determined when you set your goals. And a look at both your net worth *and* your goals will help you realize that the "How will I get there?" aspect is a result of the interaction of the first two questions coupled with the establishment of a budget.

Setting goals or objectives will take some of the anxiety out of what you do not understand. Goals are easy to achieve if your approach is realistic. You should have short, intermediate, and long-term goals. The short, or one-year goals, can be changed as necessary. Don't be discouraged if you have to change your goals slightly. Many of us are very rigid and have difficulty using the more flexible, and productive, approach that allows us to change goals in response to changing circumstances. Intermediate goals should be in the three- to five-year range. Long-term goals should not be further in the future than ten years.

Even though some of your goals will reach beyond the suggested ten years, such as retirement in fifteen years, you should decide where you need to be in ten years and then, when you reach the tenth year, reevaluate and set another long-range goal. Setting goals too far out tends to make them lose realism and moves them into the world of dreams. Remember to keep your goals specific. Wanting to have enough money for retirement is not a goal; but having a specific amount for retirement, such as $400,000, is. Never doubt that you can reach a *reasonable goal*. Success is 20% ability and 80% attitude. It is true that "Procrastination has a devil brother named Indecision." Therefore, your first order of business is to write down your goals on 3 × 5 cards (see Fig. 1–1) and place them where you can read them daily. Let your subconscious help you attain your goals!

Your net worth statement (Table 1–1) should be realistic. It serves no purpose to overinflate the worth of your home, practice, real estate holdings, or other possessions. It is estimated that most people would get 30% to 40% less than their net worth statements indicate if they had to sell everything they owned.

Figure 1–1 3 × 5 goal-setting card

Table 1–1
NET WORTH STATEMENT

Assets	Amount	Title (if Applicable)
Cash or Equivalent		
1. Bank Accounts:		
His	$______	______
Hers	______	______
2. Savings:		
S&L	______	______
Credit union	______	______
Money market funds	______	______
3. Cash value of life insurance:	______	______
4. Monies owed you (personal or property loans, etc.):	______	______
Real Estate		
1. Home	______	______
2. Vacation	______	______
3. Other single-family homes	______	______
4. Apartments (your share if not wholly owned)	______	______
5. Farms or raw land	______	______
6. Commercial property	______	______
7. Other	______	______
Personal Possessions		
1. Jewelry	______	______
2. Clothing, furs	______	______
3. Collectibles	______	______
4. Automobiles	______	______
5. Furniture, antiques, silver	______	______
6. Other	______	______
Other Investments		
1. Stock	______	______
2. Bonds	______	______

Table 1–1 cont'd

Assets	Amount	Title (if Applicable)
3. Partnerships (other than dental)	________	________
4. Corporations (other than dental)	________	________
Retirement Funds		
1. Corporate pension plan	________	________
2. Corporate profit-sharing plan	________	________
3. Keogh	________	________
4. IRA	________	________
Practice Value	________	________
Other Special Situations in which you are involved	________	________
Total Assets	$________	

Liabilities	Amount	Title (if Applicable)
Loans (business)	________	________
Loans (personal)	________	________
All credit cards	________	________
Mortgages		
1. Home	________	________
2. Vacation home	________	________
3. Other homes	________	________
4. Apartments	________	________
5. Farm land	________	________
6. Commercial property	________	________
7. Debts	________	________
8. Other	________	________
Total Liabilities	$________	

Net worth	= Total assets	− Total liabilities
$________	= $________	− $________

Possessions are only worth what a willing buyer will pay. So it is important that you know your "working net worth" as opposed to your "total net worth" (see Table 1–2). Working net worth is the money you have invested that will bring a return. It is important to *know* who has title to real property, bank accounts, and so on when you work with your attorney on your estate plan. Be as comprehensive as possible. This net worth statement, coupled with the worksheets in Chapter 4 on estate planning, will help

Table 1–2
WORKING NET WORTH

Assets		**Current Value**
Assets Producing Neither Income nor Expense		
Paid-up life insurance		$________
Furniture, antiques		________
Collectibles, etc.		________
Art, silver, jewelry		________
Other		________
	Total	$________
Assets Requiring Expense (Upkeep)		
Home		$________
Vacation home		________
Automobiles (depreciation, insurance, maintenance, gas, etc.)		________
Other		________
	Total	$________

Summary of Total Assets

Assets Producing Income	$________
Assets Producing Neither Income nor Expense	________
Assets Requiring Expense (Upkeep)	________
Total Assets	$________

Now that you've completed these calculations, you can see that some of your funds are tied up in assets that will not produce an income for you when you are enjoying a new lifestyle. Working net worth is the amount of money that you will be able to utilize to bring in the necessary income. It may be necessary to reevaluate some of the possessions in **assets producing neither income nor expense or assets requiring expense** to raise your working net worth.

Table 1–3
PERSONAL BUDGET

Gross Income	
Salary and bonus	$________
Rental income	________
Interest, dividends, net gains	________
Other sources (trust funds, etc.)	________
Total	$________
Less Taxes	$________
Federal	________
State and local	________
Social Security	________
Total	$________
Net Income	$________
Fixed Expenses	
Housing and utilities	$________
Transportation	________
Insurance	________
Installment loans (cars, etc.)	________
Education (college or private school)	________
Investments	________
Other	________
Total	$________
Variable Expenses	
Food, household supplies	$________
Clothing, cleaning	________
Recreation	________
Household furnishings, improvements	________
Contributions	________
Education, publications	________
Savings, retirement plan	________
Investments	________
Other	________
Total Variable Expenses	$________

Total annual expenses = Total fixed expenses + Total variable expenses
$________ = $________ + $________

your attorney get an accurate total picture. This will, in turn, allow him or her to make the most beneficial recommendations to you.

Budgeting is a process with which most dentists have little familiarity. Although ideally both you and your spouse would work up a budget, it is often preferable for the family member who has been paying the bills to make the first draft. Then, with a preliminary budget in hand that is based in realism, modifications can be jointly determined. Completing Tables 1–3 and 1–4 will assist you in your budgetary planning.

Table 1–4
PROJECTED ANNUAL RETIREMENT BUDGET

Gross Income	
Retirement funds	$________
Social Security	________
Rental income	________
Interest, dividends, net gains	________
Other sources (trust funds, etc.)	________
Total Gross Income	$________
Less Taxes	
Federal	$________
State and local	________
Total Taxes	$________
Net Income	$________
Fixed Expenses	
Housing and utilities	$________
Transportation	________
Insurance	________
Installment loans (cars, etc.)	________
Investments	________
Other	________
Total Fixed Expenses	$________

Table 1–4, cont'd

Variable Expenses	
Food, household supplies	$________
Clothing, cleaning	________
Recreation	________
Household furnishings, improvements	________
Contributions	________
Savings	________
Investments	________
Other	________
Total Variable Expenses	$________

Total annual expenses = Total fixed expenses + Total variable expenses
$________ = $________ + $________

Summary

This chapter has been concerned with familiarizing yourself with the basic tools of financial planning: net worth statements, goal determinations, and budgets. If you've followed the steps recommended, you now know more about both your present situation and your future. This fundamental data is what you will build as your retirement plan takes shape.

CHAPTER

2

Thinking about Retirement

Remember the first day you went to dental anatomy class and the instructor asked you to carve a tooth? Most of us were not exactly afraid, but we did have a lot of anxiety. Well, that eventually passed and you have enjoyed dentistry ever since. Similarly, contemplating retirement may at first cause anxiety; but when you get into it, you'll probably find you really enjoy it. At my retirement seminars, I routinely distribute a questionnaire for the members of the audience to complete. I'll never forget one response that started with the words, "I wish I were still in practice . . ."—I cringed in anticipation of what was coming next—"so I could take a day off! This has been the most wonderful time of our lives. I'm glad we retired early at age 62." The best of your life *really can be* the rest of your life.

Retirement is not for everyone. This book will help you with the decisions that need to be made even if you do not retire. Many people are interested in just "being able to retire" as opposed to actually retiring. You should not allow yourself to be forced into retirement by family or friends. There are, believe it or not, "dropouts" from retirement. You have to have your emotional act together to avoid that syndrome. If you think of retirement as a new career and keep a positive mental attitude, you will come through with flying colors.

The question of when to retire is intensely personal. For some, age 60 will be desirable; for others, there never is a good time. The following questions may be helpful in making this very important decision.

1. Do you have the strength, endurance, mobility, dexterity, coordination, and sensory capacities—especially eyesight—to continue practicing?

2. Are you able to remain flexible, or do the stresses of active practice wear you down more than they did in the past?
3. Do you have a desire for more time to cultivate relationships with family or friends?
4. Do you have hobbies or interests other than dentistry that you'd like to pursue?
5. Do you want to relocate or travel and partake of the attendant new experiences while you are still physically able to so do?
6. Have your finances reached a point where retirement is more advantageous than continuing to practice?

You may or you may not subscribe to the philosophy espoused by Robert Browning in his poem "Rabbi Ben Ezra":

Grow old along with me!
The best is yet to be,
The last of life, for which the first was made.

But in any case, you have to think about the future before you can have a successful one. You are not the only person who is retiring or contemplating retirement. Every year, 300,000 people in the United States reach age 65. As the Baby Boom generation ages and our population continues to grow, so will that number. There are 23 million people in our country who are presently 65 or older. Contrary to what you may believe, only 5% of that number are in nursing homes. Approximately 85% are reported to be free from chronic disease.

Back in the nineteenth century, Otto von Bismarck arbitrarily chose 65 as the age of retirement for his civil servants. Nowhere is it carved in stone that 65 is the appropriate retirement age for everyone. I like to think of retirement as a new beginning, as a time to start a different part of life. It should be entered into when one wishes, not solely as the result of the turnings of the calendar.

Dentistry has been an important part of your life. After years of training, you devoted an entire career to helping others. Your worth, however, does not decrease just because you are contemplating retirement from active practice. You need to appreciate that the skills you learned in dental school had to be enhanced by who you were as a person. Don't be caught in the trap of allowing your identity to be defined by your profession alone. The relationships you built with your patients were based both on how you performed their dentistry *and* on the caring you brought to each case. Your passage from full-time practice should not signal an end of your importance to family and community. Rather, retirement is an opportunity to explore anew who you are—to develop new ways to express your individuality and new ways to contribute.

One of the most challenging times for your ego will be when you are no longer referred to as Dr. Jones, but rather as Mr. or Ms. Jones. For some of us, the loss of prestige associated with the title "doctor" is hardly bearable. It may surprise you to learn that spouses also enjoy the "perks" of being associated with the title, and they, too, must do some adjusting when it is no longer being used. You were a Mr. or Ms. before you were a Doctor. Don't let the change in title get to you. You are a person, not a degree. I like to make a game of it: if they don't think I'm a doctor, they may not charge me as much.

Many times, no doubt, you have heard the phrase, "Retire *to* something, not *from* something." The concept is important. Planning for such needs well before retirement will bring many rewards. People who have devoted their lives to work often find they are embarrassed being a novice at a newly acquired hobby such as photography. Look upon the development of new interests as part of the preparation for another phase of your life. You can be as good at a hobby as you were in dentistry, especially if the hobby involves dealing with people. Many dentists become experts at their hobbies and are almost forced into second careers because of their abilities.

Even though financial and investment considerations have been listed by professional advisors as the number one concern, the emotional concerns of retirement are a close second. Not uncommonly, emotional considerations are more important than money or even physical health.

Only the naíve or terminally optimistic believe you can suddenly decide to retire, step out of the office on Friday, and jump into a successful retirement on Monday. It doesn't work that way—neither financially nor emotionally. You'll need time to locate the ideal dentist to take over your practice and for you to adapt to a life of leisure—or to embark on a second career. Successful retirement is the result of sound financial planning *and* thoughtful emotional adaptation.

The adage, "For better or worse, but not for lunch," and the after-retirement joke, "I've got twice as much husband and half as much money," should alert you to the fact that planning for retirement is something that needs to be done in close consultation with your life partner. Together, you should discuss how and where you would like to spend your retirement years. It sometimes happens that the husband has been dreaming of one retirement plan while, for a similar number of years, the wife has been dreaming of another. Today, many families are composed of partners with separate professions. Sometimes this results in one partner being ready to retire while the other wants to continue working for a few more years. Even the spouse who is "employed" in the home has created a life separate from the dentist's. Communication is the key. If you have nourished your marital relationship through the years, your sudden appearance as a constant companion should not result in stress. And if you haven't, it may.

An ideal plan and timetable might look like this:

1. **Eight to ten years before retirement,** decide the *how, when,* and *where* of retirement. You will be happiest if you set a date and work toward it.

2. **Five years before retirement,** you should have established a hobby that you'll find enjoyable during retirement. A hobby you can take anywhere, such as photography, gives a lot of flexibility. Begin to "experience" retirement. Redesign your work schedule so you will have a day each week to "practice" retirement. Do not do any of the usual day-off chores on that day. You will find this simple program very helpful in reducing the anxiety that builds up before retirement.

3. **Two years before retirement,** begin to plan for the valuation of your practice and for bringing in an associate. If you have had the practice valued a few years earlier, it will help get the ball rolling in your mind. There are services

that can provide a computer's-eye view of your practice for a small fee. These should not be used as a basis for a sale, but they are good for getting organized.

4. **One year before retirement,** review all your personal, legal, and insurance needs. Get your house in order. If you have decided to move out of state, you will need to be certain that your legal and insurance needs are adequately covered in your new home state.

Home Sweet Home

Where will you live in retirement? Many dentists choose to move in their retirement years. Health is often the reason, but there are others. If you feel you will not be able to maintain your current standard of living where you are, it is sometimes a good idea to move to another area where you can establish new standards. It is difficult to accept invitations if you have misgivings about your ability to reciprocate. Such occurrences are psychologically traumatic.

But before you move, for whatever reason, think about the following:

1. It does not pay to move to be near the kids. On the contrary, pick a good resort area and you may find yourself needing to put up the "Sorry, No Vacancy" sign. Every grandchild I know loves Disney World and theme parks of all kinds.
2. The body does not have the same resilience it had in the earlier years. Adjusting to temperature extremes is difficult; therefore, a climate that is mild and sunny year-round is usually preferable.
3. Avoid moving to a retirement community at first. You may eventually decide such a place is where you would like to be, but most older people tend to do better if they are *not* surrounded by people of their own age group. Being around people of all ages keeps us young.

Before making a relocation decision, it is a good idea to look at many individual areas of concern, such as property and state taxes, cultural exposure, nonmanufacturing employment growth and unemployment rates, housing expenses, and living costs. Checking out a community is easier than you might think. Many books have been written on retirement living, and they tell you exactly what to look for. A visit to a bookstore will be very helpful.

Traditionally, Sunbelt states such as Florida, California, and Arizona have provided homes for disproportionate numbers of older adults. According to a recent report, Arizona, in the past 20 years, has shown an increase of 215% in the immigration of retired persons; however, during that same period, Texas has shown an increase of 191%. The study also showed small but increasing numbers of older adults moving to South Carolina. From this study, we can assume that some of the once-popular retirement states are now being reconsidered. This may be because they are saturated with older adult communities or because they don't offer the lifestyle that the new generation of retirees is seeking. Whatever the reason, along with the traditional retirement states, you may want to consider other states with temperate climates—or, for the adventuresome, the attractive alternatives of New England or the Rocky Mountains.

For a variety of reasons, many United States citizens are retiring abroad. More favorable climates and lower costs of living are the primary attractions. It's an idea you might wish to investigate. Before making any bridge-burning decisions, you might consider swapping your home or renting one through an agency that does this sort of thing full time. One such agency is:

Home Exchange International
22713 Ventura Blvd., Suite F
Woodland Hills, California 91364

Peter A. Dickinson has written a number of books on retirement living. One of his books, *Travel and Retirement Edens Abroad,* would be very worthwhile reading for anyone considering this alternative. Even if you do not want to live abroad on a permanent basis, you might enjoy leasing a house to use as a "headquarters" for a six-month stay. There are other ways to see a foreign country than from the windows of a hotel. Living abroad for a period of time might prove to be an exciting idea.

Competition for older adult citizens among the various states is quite keen. Many states have mounted marketing efforts and encouraged the development of retirement communities. Therefore, before making any decision, you and your spouse would be wise to visit as many communities as possible during different seasons. You may love the idea of brisk walks down wintery Vermont lanes, but your spouse may want to retire among the cacti. Arizona is a wonderful place in the winter, but during the summer months the daytime temperatures rarely drop below 110° in Phoenix. Conversely, there is nothing quite as beautiful as springtime in the Rockies; but can you live with a long winter season during which you may be snowed in? Visiting off-season is an excellent way to see an area at its worst. It's an experience that may make you realize a place is not for you.

If you are planning to move at retirement, try this proven method which has helped many middle and upper income retirees:

1. You and your spouse visit the area during the season and spend from two weeks to a month there. If you like the area and think "this is it," then go to step 2.
2. If your spouse is not working, lease an apartment for a longer period and let your spouse stay there to get used to the area. You can commute during times other than your vacation. Your spouse should know your needs and desires better than anyone. Together you can see if the criteria you both established for a retirement area are being met.
3. The first two steps should take four to five years. Only then should you buy a house. I know, you could have bought one cheaper earlier, but you might have had an albatross around your neck if the area didn't turn out as planned.

If you have decided to remain in your hometown, consider moving to a smaller home or condominium a year or two before your actual retirement. The cost of moving and getting organized can be paid out of current income rather than from retirement funds. Another advantage of this tactic is that you do not have to get used to so many "new" things all at once. A condominium is particularly nice if you like to travel. Being able to shut the door and walk away, with someone else caring for the lawn, has great appeal to many people. By the year 2000, a large part of the American population will be living in condominiums.

Today, in some areas, real estate is not continuing to rise in value as it has in the past. As a matter of fact, some places are declining and others are showing a lower rate of appreciation than ever before. Before you decide to move, know the alternatives. The Consumer Economics and Housing Department of Cornell University has a service known as "Buy or Rent." Their questionnaire is divided into six sections with a total of 32 questions that run the gamut of home ownership versus renting. For a copy of their questionnaire and more information, write to:

Buy or Rent Analysis
Consumer Economics and Housing Department
120 Rensselaer Hall
Cornell University
Ithaca, New York 14853

The following data from the Weather Service (Tables 2–1, 2–2, 2–3) may also help you narrow down your choices of locations. The underlined examples highlight the differences between two areas of the country. The United States Weather Service in Asheville, North Carolina, will supply you with copies of these tables upon request. These charts are updated every few years.

Summary

Planning is the key to successful retirement. Planning must be done not only for financial matters, but also for the intangibles that will inevitably prove to be major factors in achieving retirement success.

We must think about *when* retirement will be appropriate; *what* we will do with the free time suddenly available; and *where* would be the most desirable place to live.

With adequate anticipation of needs and desires, we can ease into retirement in transitional stages, such as more time away from the office or having a spouse conduct an extended investigation of a prospective retirement locality. The more considerations we address in advance, the greater will be our retirement success.

Table 2–1

AVERAGE PERCENT OF POSSIBLE SUNSHINE

[Airport data, except as noted. For period of record through 1979, except as noted]

STATE	STATION	Length of record (yr.)	Jan.	Feb.	Mar.	Apr.	May	June	July	Aug.	Sept.	Oct.	Nov.	Dec.	Annual
Ala.	Montgomery	29	47	54	58	65	65	66	63	66	62	67	56	50	59
Alaska	Juneau [1]	33	32	32	37	39	39	34	31	32	26	19	23	20	32
Ariz.	Phoenix	84	78	80	83	88	93	94	85	85	89	88	84	77	86
Ark.	Little Rock [2]	32	46	54	57	62	68	73	71	73	68	69	56	48	64
Calif.	Los Angeles [3]	32	69	72	73	70	66	65	82	83	79	73	74	71	73
	Sacramento	31	46	61	71	80	87	92	97	96	93	84	63	47	79
	San Francisco [3]	38	56	62	69	73	72	73	66	65	72	70	62	53	67
Colo.	Denver	30	72	72	71	67	65	71	71	73	75	73	65	69	70
Conn.	Hartford	25	57	58	57	57	58	59	62	62	59	57	46	49	58
Del.	Wilmington [4]	37	51	54	57	57	57	62	62	62	59	59	52	50	57
D.C.	Washington	31	48	52	56	58	58	64	63	63	62	59	52	48	58
Fla.	Jacksonville	29	57	61	67	72	69	63	61	59	54	58	61	56	62
	Key West [1]	19	72	76	82	85	80	73	77	77	71	70	72	73	76
Ga.	Atlanta	44	48	54	57	66	68	67	62	65	63	68	60	50	61
Hawaii	Honolulu	27	63	64	68	67	69	70	74	75	75	68	60	59	68
Idaho	Boise [1]	37	41	51	63	67	71	75	88	85	82	68	45	40	67
Ill.	Chicago	37	44	47	51	54	62	67	70	68	64	60	41	38	57
	Peoria	36	46	50	51	55	59	66	68	67	65	62	45	41	57
Ind.	Indianapolis [2]	35	41	51	51	55	62	67	67	70	67	63	43	40	56
Iowa	Des Moines	29	51	54	54	55	60	68	72	70	65	63	50	45	60
Kans.	Wichita	26	59	60	61	62	65	70	74	74	66	67	59	59	65
Ky.	Louisville	32	42	48	50	55	61	66	65	67	65	62	47	41	57
La.	New Orleans	6	46	59	56	65	59	66	56	55	58	71	57	56	59
Maine	Portland	39	55	59	56	56	56	59	65	64	61	58	47	53	58
Md.	Baltimore	29	51	56	56	56	56	62	64	61	60	59	51	49	57
Mass.	Boston	44	53	57	57	57	59	64	66	66	64	61	51	53	60
Mich.	Detroit [2]	32	32	43	49	52	59	65	70	65	61	56	35	32	54
	Sault Ste. Marie	38	35	46	54	55	57	58	63	58	46	40	23	27	48
Minn.	Duluth	29	49	54	55	54	56	58	66	61	52	48	34	40	54
	Minneapolis-St. Paul	41	51	58	54	56	59	63	71	67	61	57	39	40	58
Miss.	Jackson	15	47	55	59	62	60	69	61	62	58	67	54	48	59
Mo.	Kansas City	7	60	59	66	72	72	76	86	70	63	65	51	56	67
	St. Louis	20	53	52	54	56	61	68	71	65	64	62	48	44	59
Mont.	Great Falls	37	48	56	66	61	63	65	80	76	68	61	46	44	63
Nebr.	Omaha	43	55	54	54	57	62	68	74	71	67	66	52	49	62
Nev.	Reno	37	66	68	76	81	82	85	93	93	92	84	71	64	81
N.H.	Concord	38	51	55	52	53	54	58	63	60	55	54	42	47	55
N.J.	Atlantic City	19	49	51	53	55	54	58	58	63	59	56	48	44	55
N. Mex.	Albuquerque	40	72	73	73	77	79	83	76	76	80	80	77	72	77
N.Y.	Albany	41	45	51	52	53	55	59	63	60	56	52	36	38	53
	Buffalo	36	32	39	46	52	58	66	69	66	60	52	29	27	52
	New York City [2] [5]	100	50	55	56	59	61	64	65	64	63	61	52	49	59
N.C.	Charlotte	29	56	60	63	70	69	70	68	70	66	70	62	58	66
	Raleigh	25	55	60	63	64	59	61	61	61	60	62	61	56	60
N. Dak.	Bismarck	40	55	55	60	58	63	65	76	73	66	59	45	47	62
Ohio	Cincinnati	64	41	45	50	55	60	67	68	66	66	58	44	39	56
	Cleveland	36	31	37	44	52	58	65	67	64	60	53	31	27	51
	Columbus	28	36	42	44	51	57	60	62	62	62	57	37	31	52
Okla.	Oklahoma City	25	58	60	63	64	65	73	76	78	70	69	60	59	67
Oreg.	Portland	30	25	36	45	51	56	54	69	64	60	42	30	21	49
Pa.	Philadelphia	37	51	54	57	57	57	62	62	62	59	59	52	50	57
	Pittsburgh	27	34	38	45	48	51	57	58	56	58	53	39	30	49
R.I.	Providence	26	56	57	56	56	57	58	59	61	59	59	49	53	57
S.C.	Columbia	26	57	61	64	69	66	66	65	67	64	67	65	61	64
S. Dak.	Rapid City	37	55	60	61	59	57	61	71	73	68	66	55	54	62
Tenn.	Memphis	29	49	54	57	65	70	74	73	76	69	72	58	50	65
	Nashville	37	41	47	52	59	62	67	64	65	63	64	50	42	58
Tex.	Amarillo	38	69	69	71	73	72	77	77	77	74	75	72	68	73
	El Paso	37	78	82	85	88	89	89	79	81	82	84	83	78	83
	Houston	10	42	53	48	51	59	66	66	63	59	64	55	61	57
Utah	Salt Lake City [2]	41	48	55	64	67	73	79	84	83	84	73	54	45	70
Vt.	Burlington	36	41	48	51	50	56	59	65	61	54	49	31	33	50
Va.	Norfolk [1]	20	57	59	63	65	65	68	65	65	65	60	59	57	63
	Richmond	29	52	56	59	64	64	67	65	65	63	60	56	52	61
Wash.	Seattle-Tacoma	13	23	39	50	52	58	56	66	61	57	43	28	18	49
	Spokane	31	26	39	53	60	63	66	80	77	70	52	29	21	57
W. Va.	Parkersburg [2]	80	32	37	43	50	56	59	62	60	59	54	37	29	49
Wis.	Milwaukee	39	45	47	50	54	59	64	71	67	60	56	41	38	56
Wyo.	Cheyenne	44	62	65	65	61	59	65	68	67	69	69	60	59	64
P.R.	San Juan	24	66	69	73	66	60	59	66	65	60	60	58	59	64

[1] For period of record through 1978. [2] For period of record through 1977. [3] For period of record through 1975. [4] Data not available, figures are for a nearby station. [5] City office data.

Source: U.S. National Oceanic and Atmospheric Administration, *Comparative Climatic Data*, annual.

Table 2–2

NORMAL DAILY MEAN TEMPERATURE

[**In Fahrenheit degrees.** Airport data except as noted. Based on standard 30-year period, 1941 through 1970. See *Historical Statistics, Colonial Times to 1970,* series J 110–136 and J 164–267, for related data]

STATE	STATION	Jan.	Feb.	Mar.	Apr.	May	June	July	Aug.	Sept.	Oct.	Nov.	Dec.	Annual avg.
Ala	Mobile	51.2	54.0	59.4	67.9	74.8	80.3	81.6	81.5	77.5	68.9	58.5	52.9	67.4
Alaska	Juneau	23.5	28.0	31.9	38.9	46.8	53.2	55.7	54.3	49.2	41.8	32.5	27.3	40.3
→ Ariz	Phoenix	51.2	55.1	59.7	67.7	76.3	84.6	91.2	89.1	83.8	72.2	59.8	52.5	70.3 ←
Ark	Little Rock	39.5	42.9	50.3	61.7	69.8	78.1	81.4	80.6	73.3	62.4	50.3	41.6	61.0
Calif	Los Angeles	54.5	55.6	56.5	58.8	61.9	64.5	68.5	69.5	68.7	65.2	60.5	56.9	61.7
	Sacramento	45.1	49.8	53.0	58.3	64.3	70.5	75.2	74.1	71.5	63.3	53.0	45.8	60.3
	San Francisco	48.3	51.2	53.0	55.3	58.3	61.6	62.5	63.0	64.1	61.0	55.3	49.7	56.9
Colo	Denver	29.9	32.8	37.0	47.5	57.0	66.0	73.0	71.6	62.8	52.0	39.4	32.6	50.1
Conn	Hartford	24.8	26.8	35.6	47.7	58.3	67.8	72.7	70.4	62.8	52.6	41.3	28.2	49.1
Del	Wilmington	32.0	33.6	41.6	52.3	62.4	71.4	75.8	74.1	67.9	57.2	45.7	34.7	54.0
D.C	Washington	35.6	37.3	45.1	56.4	66.2	74.6	78.7	77.1	70.6	59.8	48.0	37.4	57.3
Fla	Jacksonville	54.6	56.3	61.2	68.1	74.3	79.2	81.0	81.0	78.2	70.5	61.2	55.4	68.4
	Miami	67.2	67.8	71.3	75.0	78.0	81.0	82.3	82.9	81.7	77.8	72.2	68.3	75.5
Ga	Atlanta	42.4	45.0	51.1	61.1	69.1	75.6	78.0	77.5	72.3	62.4	51.4	43.5	60.8
Hawaii	Honolulu	72.3	72.3	73.0	74.8	76.9	78.9	80.1	80.7	80.4	78.9	76.5	73.7	76.6
Idaho	Boise	29.0	35.5	41.1	49.0	57.4	64.8	74.5	72.2	63.1	52.1	39.8	32.1	50.9
→ Ill	Chicago	22.9	26.1	35.7	48.8	58.4	68.1	71.9	71.1	63.7	53.8	39.2	27.1	48.9 ←
	Peoria	23.8	27.7	37.3	51.3	61.5	71.3	75.1	73.5	65.5	55.0	39.9	28.0	50.8
Ind	Indianapolis	27.9	30.7	39.7	52.3	62.2	71.7	75.0	73.2	66.3	55.7	41.7	30.9	52.3
Iowa	Des Moines	19.4	24.2	33.9	49.5	60.9	70.5	75.1	73.3	64.3	54.3	37.8	25.0	49.0
Kans	Wichita	31.3	36.3	43.6	56.6	66.1	75.8	80.7	79.7	70.6	59.6	44.8	34.5	56.6
Ky	Louisville	33.3	35.8	44.0	55.9	64.8	73.3	76.9	75.9	69.1	58.1	45.0	35.6	55.6
La	New Orleans	52.9	55.6	60.7	68.6	75.1	80.4	81.9	81.9	78.2	69.8	60.1	54.8	68.3
Maine	Portland	21.5	22.9	31.8	42.7	52.7	62.2	68.0	66.4	58.7	49.1	38.6	25.7	45.0
Md	Baltimore	33.4	34.8	42.8	53.8	63.7	72.4	76.6	74.9	68.5	57.4	46.1	35.3	55.0
Mass	Boston	29.2	30.4	38.1	48.6	58.6	68.0	73.3	71.3	64.5	55.4	45.2	33.0	51.3
Mich	Detroit	25.5	26.9	35.4	48.1	58.4	69.1	73.3	71.9	64.5	54.3	41.1	29.6	49.9
	Sault Ste. Marie	14.2	15.2	24.0	38.2	49.0	58.7	63.8	63.2	55.3	46.2	32.8	20.1	40.0
Minn	Duluth	8.5	12.1	23.5	38.6	49.4	59.0	65.6	64.1	54.4	45.3	28.4	14.4	38.6
	Minneapolis-St. Paul	12.2	16.5	28.3	45.1	57.1	66.9	71.9	70.2	60.0	50.0	32.4	18.6	44.1
Miss	Jackson	47.1	49.8	56.1	65.7	72.7	79.4	81.7	81.2	76.0	65.8	55.3	48.9	65.0
Mo	Kansas City	27.1	32.3	40.7	54.2	64.1	73.0	77.5	76.5	68.0	57.6	42.3	31.3	53.7
	St. Louis	31.3	35.1	43.3	56.5	65.8	74.9	78.6	77.2	69.6	59.1	45.0	34.6	55.9
Mont	Great Falls	20.5	26.6	30.5	43.4	53.3	60.8	69.3	67.4	57.3	48.3	34.6	26.5	44.9
Nebr	Omaha	22.6	28.0	37.1	52.3	63.0	72.2	77.2	75.6	66.3	55.9	40.0	28.0	51.5
Nev	Reno	31.9	37.1	40.3	46.8	54.6	61.5	69.3	66.9	60.2	50.3	40.1	33.0	49.4
N.H	Concord	20.6	22.6	32.3	44.2	55.1	64.7	69.7	67.2	59.5	49.3	38.0	24.8	45.6
N.J	Atlantic City	32.7	33.9	41.1	51.7	61.6	70.3	75.1	73.4	67.1	56.7	46.0	35.1	53.7
N. Mex	Albuquerque	35.2	40.0	45.8	55.8	65.3	74.6	78.7	76.6	70.1	58.2	44.5	36.2	56.8
N.Y	Albany	21.5	23.5	33.4	46.9	57.7	67.5	72.0	69.6	61.9	51.4	39.6	25.9	47.6
	Buffalo	23.7	24.4	32.1	44.9	55.1	65.7	70.1	68.4	61.6	51.5	39.8	27.9	47.1
	New York[1]	32.2	33.4	41.1	52.1	62.3	71.6	76.6	74.9	68.4	58.7	47.4	35.5	54.5
N.C	Charlotte	42.1	44.0	50.6	60.8	68.8	75.9	78.5	77.7	72.0	61.7	51.0	42.5	60.5
	Raleigh	40.5	42.2	49.2	59.5	67.4	74.4	77.5	76.5	70.6	60.2	50.0	41.2	59.1
N. Dak	Bismarck	8.2	13.5	25.1	43.0	54.4	63.8	70.8	69.2	57.5	46.8	28.9	15.6	41.4
Ohio	Cincinnati	31.1	33.3	41.7	53.9	63.2	72.1	75.6	74.4	67.8	56.8	43.8	33.7	54.0
	Cleveland	26.9	27.9	36.1	48.3	58.3	67.9	71.4	70.0	63.9	53.8	41.6	30.3	49.7
	Columbus	28.4	30.3	39.2	51.2	61.1	70.4	73.6	71.9	65.2	54.2	41.7	30.7	51.5
Okla	Oklahoma City	36.8	41.3	48.2	60.4	68.3	76.8	81.5	81.1	73.0	62.4	49.2	40.0	59.9
Oreg	Portland	38.1	42.8	45.7	50.6	56.7	62.0	67.1	66.6	62.2	53.8	45.3	40.7	52.6
Pa	Philadelphia	32.3	33.9	41.9	52.9	63.2	72.3	76.8	74.8	68.1	57.4	46.2	35.2	54.6
	Pittsburgh	28.1	29.3	38.1	50.2	59.8	68.6	71.9	70.2	63.8	53.2	41.3	30.5	50.4
R.I	Providence	28.4	29.4	36.9	47.3	56.9	66.4	72.1	70.4	63.4	53.7	43.3	31.5	50.0
S.C	Columbia	45.4	47.6	54.2	64.1	72.1	78.8	81.2	80.2	74.5	64.2	53.8	46.0	63.5
S. Dak	Sioux Falls	14.2	19.4	30.0	46.1	57.7	67.6	73.3	71.8	60.9	50.2	33.1	20.0	45.4
Tenn	Memphis	40.5	43.8	51.0	62.5	70.9	78.6	81.6	80.4	73.6	63.0	50.9	42.7	61.6
	Nashville	38.3	41.0	48.7	60.1	68.5	76.6	79.6	78.5	72.0	60.9	48.4	40.4	59.4
Tex	Dallas-Fort Worth	44.8	48.7	55.0	65.2	72.5	80.6	84.8	84.9	77.7	67.6	55.8	47.9	65.5
	El Paso	43.6	[illegible]	54.0	[illegible]	[illegible]	[illegible]	[illegible]	80.5	74.2	64.0	51.6	44.4	63.4
	Houston	52.1	55.3	60.8	69.4	75.8	81.1	83.3	83.4	79.2	70.9	61.1	54.6	68.9
Utah	Salt Lake City	28.0	33.4	39.6	49.2	58.3	66.2	76.7	74.5	64.8	52.4	39.1	30.3	51.0
Vt	Burlington	16.8	18.6	29.1	43.0	54.8	65.2	69.8	67.4	59.3	48.8	37.0	22.6	44.4
Va	Norfolk	40.5	41.4	48.1	57.8	66.7	74.5	78.3	76.9	71.8	61.7	51.6	42.3	59.3
	Richmond	37.5	39.4	46.9	57.8	66.5	74.2	77.9	76.3	70.0	59.3	49.0	39.0	57.8
Wash	Seattle-Tacoma	38.2	42.3	44.1	48.7	54.9	59.8	64.5	63.8	59.6	52.2	44.6	40.5	51.1
	Spokane	25.4	32.2	37.5	46.1	54.7	61.5	69.7	68.0	59.6	47.8	35.5	29.0	47.3
W. Va	Charleston	34.5	36.5	44.5	55.9	64.5	72.0	75.0	73.6	67.5	57.0	45.4	36.2	55.2
Wis	Milwaukee	19.4	22.5	31.4	44.7	54.2	64.5	69.9	69.2	61.1	51.0	36.5	24.2	45.7
Wyo	Cheyenne	26.6	29.0	31.6	42.7	52.4	61.3	69.1	67.6	58.2	47.9	35.5	29.2	45.9
P.R	San Juan	75.4	75.3	76.3	77.5	79.2	80.5	80.9	81.3	81.1	80.6	78.7	76.8	78.6

[1] City office data.

Source: U.S. National Oceanic and Atmospheric Administration, *Climatography of the United States,* No. 81.

Table 2-3

NORMAL MONTHLY AND ANNUAL PRECIPITATION

[**In inches.** Airport data except as noted. Based on standard 30-year period, 1941 through 1970. See *Historical Statistics, Colonial Times to 1970*, series J 164-267, for related data]

STATE	STATION	Jan.	Feb.	Mar.	Apr.	May	June	July	Aug.	Sept.	Oct.	Nov.	Dec.	Annual
Ala.	Mobile	4.71	4.76	7.07	5.59	4.52	6.09	8.86	6.93	6.59	2.55	3.39	5.92	66.98
Alaska	Juneau	3.94	3.44	3.57	2.99	3.31	2.93	4.69	5.00	6.90	7.85	5.53	4.52	54.67
Ariz.	Phoenix	.71	.60	.76	.32	.14	.12	.75	1.22	.69	.46	.46	.82	7.05
Ark.	Little Rock	4.24	4.42	4.93	5.25	5.30	3.50	3.38	3.01	3.55	2.99	3.86	4.09	48.52
Calif.	Los Angeles	2.52	2.32	1.71	1.10	.08	.03	.01	.02	.07	.22	1.76	2.39	12.23
	Sacramento	3.73	2.68	2.17	1.54	.51	.10	.01	.05	.19	.99	2.13	3.12	17.22
	San Francisco	4.37	3.04	2.54	1.59	.41	.13	.01	.03	.16	.98	2.29	3.98	19.53
Colo.	Denver	.61	.67	1.21	1.93	2.64	1.93	1.78	1.29	1.13	1.13	.76	.43	15.51
Conn.	Hartford	3.28	3.17	3.82	3.75	3.50	3.53	3.41	3.94	3.55	3.03	4.33	4.06	43.37
Del.	Wilmington	2.85	2.75	3.74	3.20	3.35	3.24	4.31	3.98	3.42	2.60	3.49	3.32	40.25
D.C.	Washington	2.62	2.45	3.33	2.86	3.68	3.48	4.12	4.67	3.08	2.66	2.90	3.04	38.89
Fla.	Jacksonville	2.78	3.58	3.56	3.07	3.22	6.27	7.35	7.89	7.83	4.54	1.79	2.59	54.47
	Miami	2.15	1.95	2.07	3.60	6.12	9.00	6.91	6.72	8.74	8.18	2.72	1.64	59.80
Ga.	Atlanta	4.34	4.41	5.84	4.61	3.71	3.67	4.90	3.54	3.15	2.50	3.43	4.24	48.34
Hawaii	Honolulu	4.40	2.46	3.18	1.36	.96	.32	.60	.76	.67	1.51	2.99	3.69	22.90
Idaho	Boise	1.47	1.16	1.01	1.14	1.32	1.06	.15	.30	.41	.80	1.32	1.36	11.50
Ill.	Chicago	1.70	1.30	2.52	3.38	3.41	4.15	3.46	2.73	3.01	2.32	2.10	1.64	31.72
	Peoria	1.82	1.50	2.80	4.36	3.87	3.91	3.76	3.07	3.55	2.51	2.02	1.89	35.06
Ind.	Indianapolis	2.86	2.36	3.75	3.87	4.08	4.16	3.67	2.80	2.67	2.51	3.10	2.71	38.74
Iowa	Des Moines	1.14	1.05	2.31	2.94	4.21	4.90	3.28	3.30	3.07	2.14	1.42	1.09	30.85
Kans.	Wichita	.85	.98	1.78	2.95	3.60	4.49	4.35	3.10	3.69	2.50	1.17	1.12	30.58
Ky.	Louisville	3.53	3.47	5.05	4.10	4.20	4.05	3.76	2.99	2.94	2.35	3.33	3.34	43.11
La.	New Orleans	4.53	4.82	5.49	4.15	4.20	4.74	6.72	5.27	5.58	2.26	3.88	5.13	56.77
Maine	Portland	3.38	3.52	3.60	3.34	3.33	3.10	2.61	2.60	3.09	3.31	4.86	4.06	40.80
Md.	Baltimore	2.91	2.81	3.69	3.07	3.61	3.77	4.07	4.21	3.12	2.81	3.13	3.26	40.46
Mass.	Boston	3.69	3.54	4.01	3.49	3.47	3.19	2.74	3.46	3.16	3.02	4.51	4.24	42.52
Mich.	Detroit	1.93	1.80	2.33	3.08	3.43	3.04	2.99	3.04	2.30	2.52	2.31	2.19	30.96
	Sault Ste. Marie	1.92	1.48	1.74	2.22	3.01	3.31	2.60	3.10	3.85	2.85	3.26	2.36	31.70
Minn.	Duluth	1.16	.85	1.76	2.55	3.41	4.44	3.73	3.79	3.06	2.30	1.73	1.40	30.18
	Minneapolis-St. Paul	.73	.84	1.68	2.04	3.37	3.94	3.69	3.05	2.73	1.78	1.20	.89	25.94
Miss.	Jackson	4.53	4.62	5.63	4.65	4.38	3.40	4.27	3.59	2.99	2.22	3.87	5.04	49.19
Mo.	Kansas City	1.25	1.25	2.55	3.50	4.28	5.55	4.37	3.81	4.21	3.24	1.47	1.52	37.00
	St. Louis	1.85	2.06	3.03	3.92	3.86	4.42	3.69	2.87	2.89	2.79	2.47	2.04	35.89
Mont.	Great Falls	.88	.75	.97	1.18	2.37	3.11	1.27	1.09	1.17	.68	.81	.71	14.99
Nebr.	Omaha	.76	.98	1.59	2.97	4.11	4.94	3.71	3.97	3.27	1.93	1.11	.84	30.18
Nev.	Reno	1.21	.86	.70	.47	.66	.40	.26	.22	.23	.42	.68	1.09	7.20
N.H.	Concord	2.67	2.45	2.77	2.92	3.02	3.35	3.14	2.89	3.06	2.68	3.96	3.26	36.17
N.J.	Atlantic City	3.56	3.37	4.31	3.37	3.54	3.38	4.36	4.90	2.99	3.46	4.21	4.01	45.46
N. Mex.	Albuquerque	.30	.39	.47	.48	.53	.50	1.39	1.34	.77	.79	.29	.52	7.77
N.Y.	Albany	2.20	2.11	2.58	2.70	3.26	3.00	3.12	2.87	3.12	2.63	2.84	2.93	33.36
	Buffalo	2.90	2.55	2.85	3.15	2.97	2.23	2.93	3.53	3.25	3.01	3.74	3.00	36.11
	New York[1]	2.71	2.92	3.73	3.30	3.47	2.96	3.68	4.01	3.27	2.85	3.76	3.53	40.19
N.C.	Charlotte	3.51	3.83	4.52	3.40	2.90	3.70	4.57	3.96	3.46	2.69	2.74	3.44	42.72
	Raleigh	3.22	3.32	3.44	3.07	3.32	3.67	5.08	4.93	3.78	2.81	2.82	3.08	42.54
N. Dak.	Bismarck	.51	.44	.73	1.44	2.17	3.58	2.20	1.96	1.32	.80	.56	.45	16.16
Ohio	Cincinnati	3.34	3.04	4.09	3.64	3.74	3.81	4.12	2.62	2.55	2.15	3.08	2.86	39.04
	Cleveland	2.56	2.18	3.05	3.49	3.49	3.28	3.45	3.00	2.80	2.57	2.76	2.36	34.99
	Columbus	2.87	2.32	3.44	3.71	4.10	4.13	4.21	2.86	2.41	1.89	2.68	2.39	37.01
Okla.	Oklahoma City	1.11	1.32	2.05	3.47	5.20	4.22	2.66	2.56	3.55	2.57	1.40	1.26	31.37
Oreg.	Portland	5.88	4.06	3.64	2.22	2.09	1.59	.47	.82	1.60	3.59	5.61	6.04	37.61
Pa.	Philadelphia	2.81	2.62	3.69	3.29	3.35	3.70	4.09	4.11	3.03	2.53	3.39	3.32	39.93
	Pittsburgh	2.79	2.35	3.60	3.40	3.63	3.48	3.84	3.15	2.52	2.52	2.47	2.48	36.23
R.I.	Providence	3.52	3.45	3.99	3.72	3.49	2.65	2.85	3.90	3.26	3.27	4.52	4.13	42.75
S.C.	Columbia	3.44	3.67	4.67	3.51	3.35	3.82	5.65	5.63	4.32	2.58	2.34	3.38	46.36
S. Dak.	Sioux Falls	.57	1.04	1.40	2.30	3.37	4.32	2.94	2.84	2.85	1.50	.85	.74	24.72
Tenn.	Memphis	4.93	4.73	5.10	5.42	4.39	3.46	3.53	3.33	3.01	2.58	3.92	4.70	49.10
	Nashville	4.75	4.43	5.00	4.11	4.10	3.38	3.83	3.24	3.09	2.16	3.46	4.45	46.00
Tex.	Dallas-Fort Worth	1.80	2.36	2.54	4.30	4.47	3.05	1.84	2.26	3.15	2.68	2.03	1.82	32.30
	El Paso	.39	.42	.39	.24	.32	.60	1.53	1.12	1.16	.78	.32	.50	7.77
	Houston	3.57	3.54	2.68	3.54	5.10	4.52	4.12	4.35	4.65	4.05	4.03	4.04	48.19
Utah	Salt Lake City	1.27	1.19	1.63	2.12	1.49	1.30	.70	.93	.68	1.16	1.31	1.39	15.17
Vt.	Burlington	1.74	1.68	1.93	2.62	3.01	3.46	3.54	3.72	3.05	2.74	2.86	2.19	32.54
Va.	Norfolk	3.35	3.31	3.42	2.71	3.34	3.62	5.70	5.92	4.20	3.06	2.94	3.11	44.68
	Richmond	2.86	3.01	3.38	2.77	3.42	3.52	5.63	5.06	3.58	2.94	3.20	3.22	42.59
Wash.	Seattle-Tacoma	5.79	4.19	3.61	2.46	1.70	1.53	.71	1.08	1.99	3.91	5.88	5.94	38.79
	Spokane	2.47	1.68	1.53	1.12	1.46	1.36	.40	.58	.83	1.42	2.20	2.37	17.42
W. Va.	Charleston	3.39	3.11	4.03	3.33	3.48	3.31	5.04	3.68	2.94	2.45	2.81	3.18	40.75
Wis.	Milwaukee	1.63	1.13	2.24	2.76	2.88	3.58	3.41	2.68	3.02	1.98	2.01	1.75	29.07
Wyo.	Cheyenne	.46	.46	1.05	1.57	2.52	2.41	1.82	1.45	1.03	.95	.58	.35	14.65
P.R.	San Juan	3.73	2.50	2.04	3.40	6.54	5.64	6.41	6.98	6.07	5.64	5.49	4.71	59.15

[1] City office data.

Source: U.S. National Oceanic and Atmospheric Administration, *Climatography of the United States*, No. 81.

CHAPTER

3

Insurance

Insurance is one of the most important forms of risk management. Risk management is (1) the selection process involved in choosing from the alternative methods available for dealing with risk and (2) a means of transferring this risk. When you purchase insurance, you transfer the risk to a third party—in this case an insurance company. The insurance company accepts the risk in return for a payment (the premium). When you use a deductible plan, you agree to share the loss, and that reduces the cost of the insurance premium.

Dentists require many types of coverage. For example, there are several types of liability for which coverage is needed: professional, office, personal injury, medical, and employer's nonowned automobile coverage. The operatory and its contents, office records, money, patient charts, and radiographic equipment must be covered in case of natural disaster or fire. Insurance should also cover accounts receivable that are uncollectible as the result of lost or damaged records. Practice interruption coverage reimburses the practitioner for lost or reduced income resulting from damage or destruction of the dental office. Insurance should also be purchased that protects the practitioner from losses caused by a dishonest employee.

We dentists make several mistakes when acquiring insurance. Leading the list is our choice of agents. Frequently, dentists choose friends as insurance agents. These friends may see their companies as the complete answer to all our needs, but in reality no one insurance company can best meet all our needs. Like grocery stores, these companies may have one or two specials, but they seldom provide the best deals for every type of insurance needed. Many times other companies can provide better coverage for less money. For this reason, I recommend using an agent who evaluates similar insurance packages from more than one company.

When purchasing life insurance, study the alternatives. For example, in most cases term insurance is better than whole life universal insurance or any of the other hybrid policies currently available. A good agent will sift through what is available to locate the best packages for your individual needs. Insurance companies often have different claim experiences for different categories of coverage. Because the premiums they charge are related to their experiences, there may be significant variations in the cost to the prospective policyholder. For example, Company X and Company Z have similar packages, but Company Z can offer the person aged 40 to 45 a better rate because that company had a better experience with that age group. It pays to shop.

Not all insurance companies charge the same rates for the same or similar coverage. When purchasing insurance, spend time comparing prices and services. If you are new to the game, seek professional guidance. For those who want to do their own research, I recommend the *A.M. Best Flitcraft Compendium.* Most libraries have a copy of this. *Best* is to insurance what *Standard and Poor's* is to bonds. The book evaluates the different insurance contract costs; however, a reliable brokerage company will provide this same research. Because pure insurance is based on mortality alone, you could be paying too much for coverage if your policy is not based on the latest tables (1980).

Insurance is designed in packages, usually in amounts of $25,000, $50,000, or $100,000. Therefore, odd amounts such as $87,500 are not recommended. The most expensive insurance package is not necessarily the best. Inexpensive insurance from a company rated A or A+ by *Best* may provide excellent coverage. Check the ratings. Price differentials may run as high as 50%. Careful comparison shopping can provide additional funds for investments or additional insurance.

You should monitor your coverage regularly, at least yearly, because new policies and better packages may become available. Your insurance coverage should grow at the same rate as your practice or personal income. A good insurance broker or agent will make sure you know about changes in the industry so that you have the best coverage at all times.

Life Insurance

You know you need ample coverage, but you may not know what that means. I recommend what I call the Zero Approach. It's simple. Take your net income from the practice and add a zero. For example, if your current net income is $60,000 from your practice, then I recommend you start your calculations with $600,000 of insurance. Then add or subtract from there.

If you are age 45, have a wife and two teenage children, the usual number of investments and debts, and an average annual net income of $60,000, you probably need $600,000 to provide for your family, educate your children, and pay your debts. However, if you are age 60 and have an adequate retirement plan, other personal investments, and no dependent children, you may need only a small amount of life insurance—or none at all. Your lifetime financial plan should include being "self-insured" by the time you reach your early 60s.

Once you decide how much insurance you need, add $50,000 to $100,000 for good measure in case you become involved in a project that must be paid at your death. Again, a regular review of your policies will help you evaluate your needs and the protection provided by your insurance.

As the old adage admonishes, "Buy term and invest the rest." But this takes discipline. Many people will acquire a term policy only so they can buy a bigger car or boat. They are making the right decision for the wrong reason. Conversely, "Moneyholics" should buy whole life, universal life, or any of the hybrids because without them they may never save a dime!

In 1979, the Federal Trade Commission reported that the average rate of return paid to holders of whole life policies in 1977 was from 1.2% to 1.85%, the average being 1.3%. Although the policies issued since 1977 have higher rates, no one can afford to make an investment that is truly bad. Mutual "participating" companies claim to pay dividends. According to U.S. Treasury Decision Number 1743, "Dividends declared by participating companies are *not dividends* in a commercial sense of the word, but are simply *refunds* to the policy holder of a portion of the *overcharge* collected" (emphasis added). Investigate before you buy.

Life insurance policies should have the following features:

1. Waiver of premium (in case of an accident, you do not want to make payments)
2. A convertible clause
3. A grace period of 31 to 62 days
4. A guaranteed renewable clause
5. A choice of settlement options
6. A reasonable amount of time to receive your cash value if the policy is anything but term

Both spouses should be adequately insured. The old "breadwinner" theory has gone the way of the horse and buggy. Many professional families now have two salaries. However, even if one spouse stays home to care for the children, that spouse should be adequately covered. The annual cost of a housekeeper, cook, and chauffeur will greatly exceed the cost of an annual premium.

For tax reasons, the question of who owns a policy can be important to an estate. If you own the policy and your spouse is named as beneficiary, all benefits *should* pass to your spouse free of taxes at the time of your death. However, I think it is always wisest to let spouses own each others' policy; then there are no questions. If your estate, or anybody other than your spouse, is named as beneficiary, the proceeds will be valued as part of the estate for tax purposes.

Until 1981, it was common to make absolute assignment of life insurance policies to spouses to avoid estate tax on the proceeds. However, with the advent of the Economic Recovery Tax Act of 1981, the law made provisions for a 100% marital deduction. Under this law, the proceeds of life insurance policies payable to the surviving spouse are free of federal estate taxes. Therefore, the only time when absolute assignment should be considered is if the beneficiary of the policy is someone other than the dentist's spouse, for example a child or parent.

What to Buy

I recommend that you buy term insurance through group plans. The American Dental Association (ADA) has a fine policy.

If the ADA group were to leave its current insurer and start its own company, it would be the fifteenth largest insurance company in America. After purchasing ADA group coverage, add term insurance from assorted association policies such as the Academy of General Dentistry, a specialty society or organization, church groups, or other similar groups. The cost of term insurance has decreased in recent years. However, some individual policies may be less expensive than group policies.

For those who are older, term insurance could be more expensive (Fig. 3–1). A look at Fig. 3–2 will show you how your premium money is divided.

I recommend that you consider replacing current whole life insurance policies rather than just adding new ones. If you have

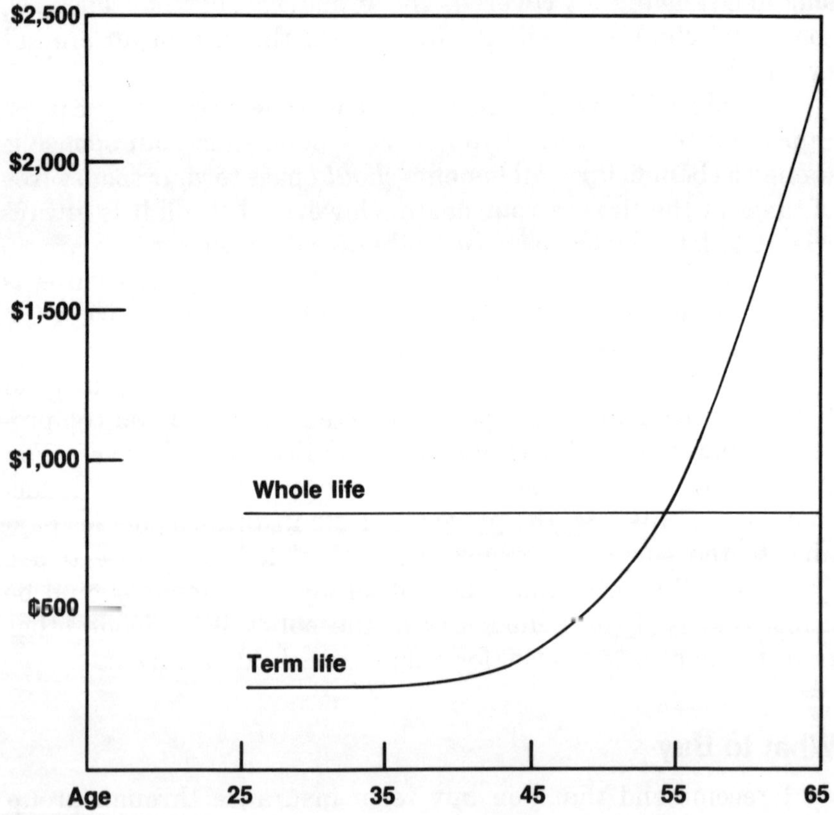

Figure 3–1 Individual policies, premium comparisons

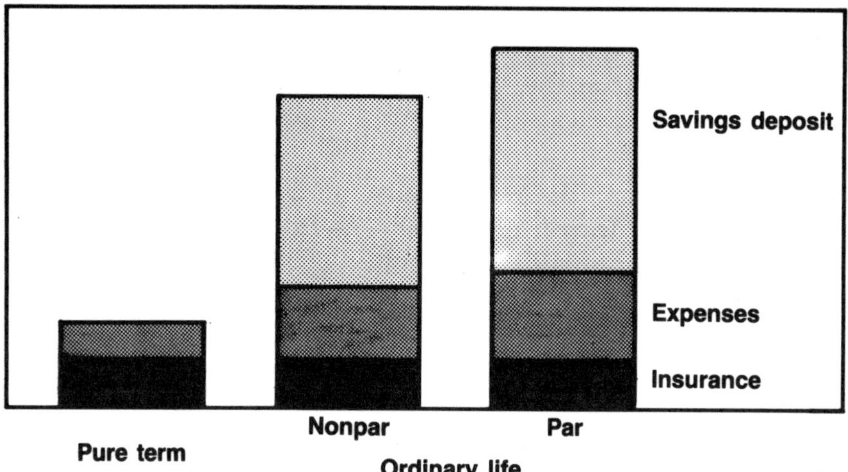

Figure 3–2 The life insurance dilemma

older life policies, it may be worth your while to re-examine the situation. The higher worth of cash value accumulations and dividends may make this an appealing strategy.

In its biweekly *Money Advisory,* the Research Institute of America provided the following case histories from one insurance company:

> 23% Saving: A male age 57, owned various cash value policies totaling $388,000, annual premium $11,013. He replaced these policies with a single $400,000 policy, premium $8,530; annual savings: $2,483.
>
> 34% Saving: A male age 53, with a $100,000 policy, premium $2,709, replaced it with another $100,000 policy, premium $1,773; annual savings: $936.

Some companies will analyze old policies, prepare a comparison, issue a new policy with a new premium, and handle the insurance department replacement forms (at least one company claims to do all this in 10 days). If you choose to have this done, you must check the following:

1. Be sure you can transfer the cash value on your old policies.
2. Some companies will issue a replacement policy for up to

$500,000 without requiring a medical examination.

3. A replacement policy should allow the old "incontestables" such as suicide to remain in force, rather than requiring a waiting period of two years before they become effective.
4. Be sure that the replacement policy contains the same coverages: waiver of premium, accidental death, etc.
5. Never relinquish an old policy until the new one is in effect.

Disability

Although we tend to think of life insurance first, statistically we are more likely to become disabled than die. Breaking it down by age, if you are in your mid-20s, you are seven times more likely to be disabled than you are to die; if you are in your early 40s, you are five times more likely to be disabled than die; at age 56, you are twice as likely to become disabled. Therefore, disability insurance should rank as high as life insurance. Unfortunately, many do not consider this until their practice begins to mature.

When purchasing disability insurance you should consider the following:

1. **Long-term benefits.** Some policies only insure you for seven years. Your policy should insure you until age 65.

2. **Waiting period.** If you choose a policy with a waiting period of 30 days, no benefits will be paid for the first 30 days you are disabled. Generally, the first benefit check is issued 61 days after the disability is reported; thus, you will receive a check on the 61st day for the second month (that is, 31 days) of the disability.

3. **Part-time benefits (residual benefits).** Be sure you know how the policy will pay if you are only able to work part time.

4. **Waiver of premium.** This inexpensive addition to any insurance is worthwhile.

5. **Definitions.** Make sure you understand the company's definition of "total disability," "own occupation," and "income."

The difference between "own occupation" and "income" is probably the most difficult concept to grasp. But it is important, as you will see by the following senario.

> Drs. Smith and Jones are both age 45. During the time they were in active practice, each earned $6,000 per month. Dr. Smith has purchased an income policy because it is less expensive than an own occupation policy. Dr. Jones has chosen an own occupation policy. Both policies will pay $4,000 if the dentists are disabled. Both dentists have heart attacks. Although they recover, they are advised by their physicians to sell their practices and discontinue the stressful life of dentistry. They both become automobile salesmen. After a short time, both former dentists are earning $3,000 per month.
>
> Dr. Smith has an income policy. Because he earns $3,000 per month as an automobile salesman (that is, 50% of his former income), the insurance company reduces his benefit to $2,000 per month (50% of his disability benefits). His monthly income is $5,000.
>
> Dr. Jones has an occupational policy. Although he earns $3,000 per month as an automobile salesman (that is, 50% of his former income), the insurance company continues to send him a benefit of $4,000 per month. His monthly income is $7,000. However, if Dr. Jones had earned the $3,000 per month by practicing dentistry part time, then the insurance company would have reduced its payment to $2,000 (50% of his disability benefits) per month. His monthly income would have been $5,000.

The best disability coverage is one payable when the covered illness or injury disables you from **performing the normal duties of your profession.**

When purchasing disability insurance, make sure that the amount will cover your income *after taxes*. To determine this figure, add all the perks that you get from your practice to what you take as a salary; then subtract the taxes you would pay. The remaining total should be insured. Usually, you can insure up to

70% of your total net income. I recommend that you purchase your coverage from a private company and from the American Dental Association. The private policy should be purchased first with as long a waiting period as possible. The ADA policy should be purchased with a much shorter waiting period. Here's an example using private and ADA coverage for a total of $7,000 per month: $4,000 from a private company and $3,000 from an ADA policy.

> Dr. Smith, age 49, purchases a private policy, the annual cost of which is $3,900. He will receive $4,000 per month with a 180-day waiting period (that is, some money will be received on the 211th day).
>
> He also purchases the ADA policy, the annual cost of which is $911. He will receive $3,000 a month with a 30-day waiting period (that is, some money will be received on the 61st day).

Private Policy ($4,000 per month): annual cost	=	$3,900
ADA Policy ($3,000 per month): annual cost	=	911
Total annual cost	=	$4,811

In this way, you can add an additional $1,000 to your ADA coverage when necessary. Currently, the maximum is $4,000, but this could increase in the future.

Office Overhead

Many dentists confuse office overhead with disability. Office overhead expense should not be covered by your disability insurance. You should have enough office overhead expense insurance to carry you for approximately one year. An office overhead expense plan will reimburse you for the fixed expenses that are normally incurred in the operation of a dental practice while you are totally disabled. These include:

1. **Office premise expenses.** Rent, mortgage interest, and real estate taxes
2. **Debt-servicing expenses.** Interest paid on loans made to you for the purchase of your practice or the furnishing of the office and operatory

3. **Employee expenses.** Salaries, payroll taxes, uniform and car allowances, and premiums paid by you for your employees' life, disability, and medical insurance coverage
4. **Depreciation expenses.** Depreciation on items detailed on Federal Income Tax Returns; for example, office equipment, instruments, and building (if owned)
5. **Professional liability insurance premiums.** Premiums paid for your personal coverage and that of your employees, except another dentist
6. **Utilities expenses.** Water, heat, air conditioning, laundry, telephone, janitorial services, and electricity
7. **Tax deductible and business-related insurance premiums.** Personal and office liability, operatory and office contents, workers' compensation, and practice interruption
8. **Membership dues and subscriptions.** Professional journals and magazines of the American Dental Association and its constituent and component societies, dental specialty groups, and other constituent and component societies
9. **Accounting fees and other fixed expenses** for which you were regularly liable at the time of the disability

Homeowner and Automobile Coverage

Today, the best coverage for both homeowners and automobiles is through a plan called the *Personal Comprehensive Protection Policy*. This plan places both home and automobile under one policy. The policy has been designed for those with above-average incomes, and the savings over other policies is considerable. Because the Continental Insurance Company has aggressively fostered this policy, it is probably the best. However, it is not available in Massachusetts, North Carolina, Mississippi, and Texas. Some of the other large companies are moving in to compete with Continental, so you might check St. Paul and comparable companies. Often, a regional company will have a similar policy, so it pays to do a little research.

Whatever policy you consider, it should contain the following:

1. Living expense endorsement
2. Protection of at least 10% of principal amount if located off main insured residence
3. Adequate coverage for personal property
4. Replacement value
5. Collision, liability, and comprehensive coverage for automobiles

Above all, check your exclusions. Omissions of coverage can be disastrous.

Health Insurance

Although group insurance is probably the most common and usually the best approach to buying health insurance, it is difficult to generalize because of the variety and number of tailored plans. Having said that, I will now generalize.

If we assume that healthcare professionals as a group tend to seek medical care more often than the general population and that they are (or should be) more aware of their physical health, then we can also assume that group rates for healthcare professionals will be higher than programs for the general population. Therefore, to receive the same coverage at a lower premium, I recommend obtaining group insurance through groups other than professional organizations, for example the Chamber of Commerce. Many of these programs are similar, if not identical, to the coverage offered through state and national professional organizations.

However, because of the ever-increasing cost of medical care and the new technologies to treat diseases once thought incurable, catastrophic coverage is imperative. As we age, we become more vulnerable to a variety of diseases, some of which may require extensive hospitalization and outpatient care. Therefore, in addition to your group medical plan, I recommend catastrophic coverage.

Three months before your sixty-fifth birthday, be sure to sign up for parts A and B of Medicare. Failure to do so will prove expensive. As it now stands, the deductible portion of Medicare increases each year. Therefore, you need supplemental insurance. An excellent supplemental program for retired dentists is available through the American Society of Retired Dentists.

Malpractice Insurance

Because we live in a litigious society, malpractice insurance is one of the most important coverages a practitioner needs. It is especially important for those who have amassed funds to be used during retirement. Today, adequate malpractice coverage has become an expensive but necessary concern for all healthcare professionals. Traditionally, physicians have been targeted by malpractice suits; however, the number of suits against dentists is growing. In my opinion, a successful dentist should have a $2 million malpractice policy. The ADA professional liability program, the Professional Protector Plan, is a comprehensive policy for dentists. Professional liability insurance defends against malpractice suits resulting from (1) professional services or failure to render professional services and (2) acts of omissions of employees for whom you are legally responsible. Currently, two types of coverage are available: **occurrence** and **claims made.**

I believe the occurrence policy offered by the ADA is one of the best plans available to dentists. With this policy, you are protected for all claims that arise from treatments rendered while the policy is in force, even if the claim is made after cancellation of the policy.

A claims-made policy requires that the malpractice claim occur and be reported while the policy is in force. The insurance company is not obligated if the claim is made after the policy has been cancelled, even if the incident occurred while the policy was in force.

> Drs. Smith and Jones retire from the practice of dentistry and move to Arizona. Dr. Smith purchased the claims-made policy. Dr. Jones purchased the occurrence policy.
>
> Dr. Smith becomes involved in litigation involving a patient he treated five years before he retired. If he loses, he will be required to pay all the costs and the jury award out of

his pocket unless he has purchased an extended reporting endorsement which protects him against claims reported after cancellation of the claims-made policy. In insurance jargon, this purchase is called "buying up the tail."

Dr. Jones also becomes involved in litigation involving a patient he treated five years before he retired. However, because he had an occurrence policy, Dr. Jones is automatically protected against any loss.

The customary cost for an extended reporting endorsement is 150% to 200% of the annual premium.

The Best Insurance

One of the best insurance plans you can have for your later years is good physical health. A lifetime of exercise, good nutrition, and a healthy lifestyle will slow the aging process. As Dr. Harold Wirth admonished, "The best thing you can save for your retirement is yourself!"

If you have been lax in getting this type of "insurance coverage," consult your physician before you begin any exercise program and use your common sense.

1. Excercise should be gradual and progressive.
2. Exercise for 20 to 30 minutes, excluding the warm-up and cool-down period.
3. Exercise at least three times a week.
4. Exercise should be ongoing, never start and stop. Make it a way of life.

Brisk walking, bicycle riding, and swimming are good forms of exercise that are also enjoyable. Swimming probably has the most to offer because the heart works best in a supine position; the water temperature will allow a longer workout, and the functional capacity of the lungs is increased. As you age, you can join the Master swimmers, a healthy way of staying involved with people—and life.

Summary

Good insurance coverage is essential, but the most expensive insurance does not necessarily provide the best coverage. Because comparison shopping is always wise, use an agent who is knowledgeable about more than one company. Too much coverage is as hard on the pocketbook as too little. Striking the right balance may not be easy, but in the long run it is essential for your financial well being.

Your insurance coverage should be reviewed regularly. Adequate malpractice insurance provides protection while you practice dentistry and will ensure that those funds you have earmarked for retirement will be used for your retirement. Again, wise decisions early in your career will help you meet your goals for the future.

Finally, the best insurance for a happy retirement is good health. Exercise, good nutrition, and moderate lifestyle will help you enjoy those years of well-earned relaxation.

CHAPTER

4

Estate Planning

Estate planning is the most difficult part of financial assessment. People do not like to think about dying, and certainly not about their money and dying at the same time. Estate planning is really a matter of making basic choices: spending, saving, and leaving possessions to your heirs. This chapter divides estate planning into two areas: (1) the nuts and bolts of preparing to meet with an attorney and (2) how to educate your children and perhaps help your parents or some other family members when they are beyond their active work years.

According to the American Bar Association, 80% of the Americans who die each year do so without leaving a will. Many of those who die without wills are professional people. Although I might understand this neglect in the general population, it is hard to comprehend why a professional person, who has worked so long and hard to accumulate an estate, would allow it to be subject to the laws of intestacy. Each state has a different set of laws of intestate succession that determine the distribution of an estate. When someone dies without a will, an administrator appointed either by the probate court or by your estate must post a bond. The cost of such bonds is usually well in excess of the cost of a simple will.

In some circumstances, dying without a will is not as bad as it may seem. Contrary to popular misconceptions, the state does not take all the property. You would have to die without any family at all, or at least no family as far back as your great-grandparents, before the state would take all the estate. If your property falls into any of the following categories, you need not worry:

1. Retirement plan proceeds and life insurance. These are

paid to the named beneficiary. Often a plan or insurance policy, but particularly a plan, will provide that the assets will go to the wife, or children; if no beneficiary is named, the estate is an alternate beneficiary. If you named your estate as beneficiary, it would be subject to the laws of intestacy with your other property.

2. Property jointly owned with another with right of survivorship. The two types of property are *Joint Tenancy with Right of Survivorship* and *Tenancy in Common*. A type of ownership known as *Tenants by the Entirety,* which is between a husband and a wife only, is a less common form of joint ownership. It is recognized in only a few states.
3. Property held in a living trust as the trust determines who will ultimately receive the property.
4. The spouse's half of community property in the nine states that have a community property law.

The worst-case scenario becomes a reality when none of your property, or at least a substantial part, is in the four categories listed above. Each state has its own way of solving the problem; some will give a spouse one-third, one-half, or a flat amount and divide the remainder among the children. In many cases when a spouse dies with no living relative, the surviving spouse will get everything. When this is not the case, though, it is very sad to see a spouse unable to live comfortably because the deceased spouse failed to make at least a simple "I love you" will which would have left everything to the surviving partner.

It seems almost incomprehensible that a professional person who has labored deligently to build an estate would let fate and the state laws decide who is to inherit what. With that in mind, let's turn to how you can begin to organize your affairs for your own and your family's best interest.

My attorney tells me that professional people tend to incur heavy legal fees because they are not good at compiling the information that the attorney needs. The worksheets in this book—the Estate Analysis Checklist in this chapter and the Net Worth Statement from Chapter 1—should be completed prior to your first meeting with the attorney. You may see some overlap in these two documents, but it is helpful for the attorney if he or she can look at some aspects of your affairs in two or more different ways. By so doing, the attorney can be more certain of understanding your estate and your desires.

To begin your estate planning, you will want to look at the twelve different areas that follow and see how they each affect the type of will you need and the trusts you should establish. This examination will help you better understand what you will be doing.

1. **Net worth and estate analysis checklist.** It is important to know who is the owner of a particular property or checking account, whether it be husband, wife, or jointly held. If owned jointly, what type of ownership is it and what is the property or account worth? Do not overinflate the value of anything on your net worth statement. If you are uncertain about the value within 10%, then err on the low side. It is important to include everything; your attorney may have some additional thoughts and ideas that are unknown to you. However, you should have a fairly good idea of the value of most of your assets.

2. **Data on debts.** Not only should you know what you owe, but also who owes you. The information on your practice accounts receivable will be easy to locate; it may not be needed until you begin valuing your practice. You should also know to whom you have lent any monies in excess of $500. Always have written proof of monies owed to you, even if it is only on one of those standard forms you can purchase at a stationery story. The last thing you want is to have a substantial amount owed you at your death with no means available for your heirs to retrieve it. The preceding includes notes signed by your children. You should never loan money in your family, whether immediate or extended, without a note—unless, of course, you are not concerned with its repayment.

3. **List and identify the location of important papers and insurance contracts.** Although most of us pretend to know where everything is located, few of us actually do. You should begin by having a "Finder's Day" and list every

important document that you and your spouse have. Stack everything on the dining room table. Both of you should understand what each document or contract is, what it does, and where it is stored. If you currently have a will, take it to the attorney who will be drawing your new one. Your attorney should also have life insurance beneficiary designations, deferred compensation including IRAs, and any other employer-provided benefits payable at death.

4. **Explanation of your deferred compensation.** IRA, Keogh, pension, and profit-sharing plans should have an explanation of payout procedures. If you have a state or federal retirement annuity, or any other type of deferred compensation, it should also be included. In addition to the explanation you give your spouse, attach an additional copy of the "layman's how-to" to the deferred compensation plan itself.

5. **Estate beneficiaries.** In the case of second marriages and unusual bequest, you should have a list of beneficiaries and their last known addresses. Some children of one marriage have never met the children of another. There are often things that have strong emotional rather than monetary value that need to be disposed of. A description of your family tree would help the attorney immeasurably; you may also want to list family members who have any unusual medical problem or other financial need. It is always wise to let the attorney know if any member of your family is designated to receive an inheritance from parents, grandparents, or anyone else.

6. **Power of attorney.** You and your spouse should discuss giving each other the power of attorney. If one spouse becomes mentally or physically incompetent, the other can handle the affairs without going through the normal legal proceedings for appointing a representative for the incompetent spouse.

7. **Disposition of practice and the "power of sale."** It is important that you discuss with your spouse the sale of your practice. A dental practice will begin to lose 2% to 4% of

its value per week after the practitioner dies. Because time is of the essence, the "power of sale" included in the will should allow the family to immediately sell the practice. It is also important that you have a plan to have your office staffed by friends or colleagues until the practice is sold. With knowledgeable help, a practice can be sold quickly. The value of practices has increased dramatically in the past 10 years; rarely will a dentist shut the doors of a fairly active practice. In the case of the dentist's death, the family should act promptly to sell the practice.

8. **Choice of executors and trustees.** Your spouse should, at the least, be co-trustee or co-executor with another member of the family. A list of successors can be named, and the bank or a similar institution should be at the end of the list. Although it is not necessary to have a bank, they are permanent, organized, and have record-keeping ability. However, I think banks are cold; many do not know the maker of the will or trust except superficially. In my opinion, banks are not known for having very good investment divisions in their trust departments. Although there are some that have done quite well, I think they are the exception and not the rule. If you have been a sharing spouse, your spouse will be able to find, hire, and fire financial advisors at will. These advisors could use a bank trust department, but your spouse would have the ability to move the funds at will. Do not hamper your loved ones by trying to call the shots from the grave.

9. **Layman's synopsis.** Any sharp attorney should give you a layman's synopsis. They do not understand our vocabulary and we sure don't understand all of the nuances in a legal document. Professionals who work with a limited vocabulary, as we do, have a limited grasp of other vocabularies and meanings. It is important to know that you have done what you thought you were doing. An example of a simple layman's synopsis follows:

Dr. James B. Jones
123 Western Street
Chicago, Illinois

Dear Dr. Jones:

Thank you for the opportunity of working with you and your wife. I wanted you to have a "layman's synopsis" so you would understand what is in your will.

You have left everything to your wife, Susan, with no strings attached, with these exceptions:

1. Your son James will receive your collection of guns, which has a current value of $4,800.00.
2. Your daughter Betsy will receive the equivalent amount in cash.
3. If the appraisal at your death is over $10,000, then James will have to buy the excess from the estate, as you feel that you only should have $10,000 in cash leave the estate.

I hope this will help you understand what you have done. It has been a pleasure caring for your legal needs as well as you have cared for my family's dental health over the years. Your wife's "layman's synopsis" is enclosed.

Sincerely,
Johnson Tisdale, Esq.

10. **The choice of an attorney.** I usually recommend a tax attorney for writing wills, trusts, and any other instrument used in your professional life. Tax law has changed so often in the past 10 years that it is difficult to remain current. Therefore, I want a specialist in that area to keep me abreast of changes. If you can not find a convenient tax attorney, then I strongly recommend that you have your family attorney draw up a rough draft of the instrument and let your CPA calculate the tax consequences for you. You should always know what the tax consequences are before you do anything—but not to the extreme. Ask questions such as "How can I?," not "Can I?." These questions let the attorney know you are interested in solving a problem and not just idly questioning.

11. **Research.** Do some reading so you will be able to convey to your attorney what you want. Do not let your attorney give you the old "just leave it to me" routine. Your attorney may have some good reasons to recommend one idea over another, but at least you will have some idea about what he or she is saying. The library has many books on estate planning; choose several that have recent publishing dates. The more you understand what you are trying to accomplish, the better the final result.

12. **Personal effects.** Some attorneys provide for personal effects going to your spouse or, if your spouse has predeceased you, to the children. Nevertheless, write a letter of instruction to your executor or trustee, stating to whom you would like to leave particular items. These are usually not lumped in with your estate per se; therefore, they tend to be lumped into the "I wonder who Joe wanted to have this" category. You can help by not forcing a close family member to choose for you.

Estate Plans to Consider

There are several basic estate plans that you should be aware of. Just as in dentistry we have a simple restorative procedure, for example a small occlusal amalgam on a six-year molar, so also does the legal profession have some basic estate plans that are worth discussion.

In the "I love you" or "Sweetheart" will, everything is left to the surviving spouse. This type of will is used when the combined assets do not greatly exceed the shelter of the current unified gift and estate tax credit or the exemption equivalent that determines how much we can leave to someone other than our spouse without creating a tax burden. In 1986, the amount is $500,000, and will be $600,000 in 1987 and thereafter. If the amount were to exceed the current exemption equivalent, perhaps a will with a trust should be considered.

Even with this simple will, a trust is sometimes considered necessary if young children are to be considered; if the remaining spouse would rather someone else manage the money; or if the first spouse to die would like to avoid giving a second husband or wife access to his or her hard-earned money. A trust is simply an agreement whereby a "grantor" transfers property to a "trustee" who holds it for the benefit of one or more persons called "beneficiaries."

The second type of will is one with a disclaimer trust. In many ways, this will is like the first in that it intends for outright ownership by the surviving spouse. This will and disclaimer trust is applicable for those whose estates are currently below the current exemption equivalent, but may well be above it by the time the survivor dies. The disclaimer trust is like betting on a football game after the game has been played—you know the score! In a will of this type, the surviving spouse can elect to "disclaim" part of the estate, allocating it to a trust. Although the surviving spouse receives income, the trust would not be subject to estate taxes when he or she dies. Thus, the surviving spouse could do a little estate planning.

The third basic type of will is geared for those couples whose combined assets will reach nearly $1 million. They might consider having a residual trust built into the will of the spouse with the largest assets. This type of will and trust is ideal when tax considerations are of the utmost importance. The exemption trust allows the spouse to use the income from the trust and invade it for support needs. An additional invasion of right, up to 5% per year, may be included for which no need must be shown. Perhaps the most important aspect of this trust is that surviving spouses have the power to rewrite the terms of the trust in their wills. A word of caution about this instrument: If your spouse chose to, he or she could conceivably leave your children out in the cold. It has happened!

The fourth type of plan uses a so-called "Q-Tip" trust (Qualified Terminable Interest Trust) that allows you to assure yourself that you will be able to know that your children will be receiving something at the death of your spouse. This is especially important if your children are the issue of a previous marriage. Of course, you want to take care of your spouse until his or her death, but by using a Q-Tip trust you will be able to allow the money to pass to your children or your designated beneficiary because your spouse will not have any power to specify a beneficiary. With the 1981 tax law changes, this will allow you to leave money to your children, with the income going to your spouse during his or her lifetime. You can leave the remainder that will not "fit" into the trust without taxation to your spouse, thereby eliminating estate taxes at your death.

Since 1981, there has been an ongoing discussion about tax law changes which simply state that sometimes it is not in the best interest of the eventual recipients (children) to set up a trust, pay taxes on it, and then allow the surviving parent to use the income until his or her death. If a surviving spouse lives five years, considering the time value of money, it may be better to allow the spouse to inherit the money without taxation and without a trust. In the end, it would allow the children to inherit, pay tax, and end up with more money. Of course, this assumes a reasonable rate of return.

In the final analysis, we each must do what we feel is best for our particular situation. After all, we understand our family better than any attorney.

The fifth type of estate plan is a "pour-over" will and a living trust (revocable). The pour-over will simply allows all tangible property left outside the trust to be poured over into the trust. Because this plan will essentially allow you to escape probate, it has received a black eye from some attorneys. I believe that anyone who has attained professional status can be shown how to use a living trust and pour-over will to his or her advantage. My tax attorney has suggested this to dentists who are interested in estate planning and want to be sure their families do not have to go through the trauma of probate. Putting a bank in charge of your funds at your death may assure them of experience, permanency, and record-keeping ability, but it does not assure them of investment intelligence.

In addition to the advantages of trusts already mentioned, a trust allows you to provide management of your funds, may put certain restrictions on property, and more importantly will allow you to name the time your beneficiary is to receive the property you are leaving. The reason a living trust avoids probate at your death is that there is no transfer of property. The trust already owns the property. A living trust has several other advantages in that it avoids the publicity, expense, and delays that probate of a testamentary (included in the will) trust would cause. If someone other than yourself is trustee, a living trust can enable you to see how well the trustee you have chosen is performing his or her duties. In addition, a living trust is less subject to attack by disgruntled family members. One of the most important advantages of a living trust is that it avoids the question of a legal representative for you if you become incompetent. If you are managing your own trust (which I recommend), a successor trustee could move in as prescribed in the trust agreement and pick up where you left off.

All in all, I think the advantages of a living trust for those of us older than age 50 is an ideal method of coping with estate planning. The trustee duties such as record-keeping and filing tax returns can be managed by your accountant. You should be the trustee or at least the co-trustee of this living trust. Put your successors in line as trustees, and only as a last resort use the bank trust department—that is, unless the bank trust officer is your best friend and understands your wishes.

Educating the Children

There is more than one good method to educate your children; you will have to decide which fits best into your plans. The five methods I will discuss are particularly relevant to private dental practitioners.

1. **The short-term or "Clifford" trust.** The trust can be combined with a so-called gift leaseback of equipment. This is a particularly good method because it will allow you to give your depreciated equipment to a trust into which you can pay a monthly amount for leasing the equipment for at least 10 years and a day. Conservatively invested, this money provides a painless way to save for the education of your children.*

Have your equipment appraised by your dental supply company representative. Once the appraisal is complete, ask how

---

*By the time the current tax law is replaced, this trust may be obsolete. However, do not despair! There is always a mouse, i.e., tax attorney, who can figure out how to get to the cheese.

much the company would charge if you rented the equipment from them. Ask the representative to put the cost of the rental in writing. Have your attorney establish a short-term trust for 10 years and a day. The lease agreement between the trust and you will stipulate the monthly payment. This arrangement, coupled with a conservative investment, will make a sizeable amount available for your children when they begin college. Eventually the equipment returns to you, however old it may be at that time. The advantages of the trust are that unlike custodianships with only one beneficiary, the trust can have multiple beneficiaries, including children born after the trust is established. All things considered, it is an excellent way to educate children. Because federal courts frown on the gift-leaseback technique, it is important to discuss any of these measures with your attorney.

Parents can be supported in the same way. Although the trust is established in the same way, it terminates when the parent dies, and the equipment or other property will immediately revert to you.

2. **Interest-free loans.** These can still be used as long as they do not exceed $10,000. The lower-bracket borrower (your child or parent) invests the money to produce income, not exceeding $1,000. The borrower pays taxes in their bracket. Many people think the interest-free loan has been totally eliminated; however, to some extent it is still viable. I do not believe the interest-free loan should be used with any other method other than a trust agreement. It is foolish to give anyone monies that you may need in the future without attaching some strings.

3. **The spousal remainder trust.** This trust has been around for a long time but was given no attention because the interest-free loan was the preferred method. Now, with the interest-free loan impaired, the spousal remainder is ideal.

One spouse establishes a trust to revert to the other spouse upon termination. The money *must* come from the spouse who establishes the trust and not from a joint checking account. The trust is established for any period desired, the child or parent designated as the beneficiary. The beneficiary receives the income from the trust during the trust period. At the end of the trust period, the remainder reverts to the spouse.

Unlike the short-term or Clifford trust, this type of trust does not have to be held 10 years and a day and monies can be added to it. Finally, in one year you can put more money into one of these trusts without incurring gift taxes than you can with a Clifford trust.

The disadvantages are that you may have to establish the trust more than once because your child may choose to attend graduate school or pursue some type of professional education. In the event of a divorce, money given from one spouse to another might not be considered when property is divided.

4. **Compensation.** Compensation for work performed is an ideal way to actively involve your children in saving for their education. A 1981 court decision known as the Eller case decided that a child's age was important only inasmuch as the case of reasonableness was concerned. Certainly a 7-year-old cannot perform periodontal surgery or assist a dentist chairside, but he or she could empty the trash, lick stamps, or help with copying. As the child grows, he or she could work some afternoons and summers in the office to fill in at different tasks and be paid accordingly. The Eller case allowed a deduction of $1,200 a year for a 7-year-old child for maintenance, cleaning, and office work. If you are not incorporated, services performed by a child younger than age 21 in the employ of a parent are not included in the definition of wages for employment tax purposes. The main disadvantage is that the money becomes the sole possession of the child at majority—the child could choose a Corvette instead of college. (Just because they are your children doesn't make them perfect!)

Your parents could be hired to copy and send statements, call delinquent accounts, or a myriad of jobs that would not thrust them before the public eye—and allow you to support them in other ways.

In offices where a considerable amount of laboratory work is done, the children or your parents could own and profit from the laboratory. This is sometimes done in orthodontic and prosthetic dentistry, two areas requiring considerable laboratory work.

5. **Corporations.** In some states, anyone can be an officer of a corporation. You might have your college-age child become an officer and pay him or her a salary while they are attending school. Several thousand dollars a year would not be out of line to serve as secretary, provided services to the corporation are well documented. This is not available in all states, so you should check with the attorney who incorporated your practice.

There are other popular ways, such as gifts to a custodian under a gifts-to-minors statute, but again it gives the child unfettered control of the asset plus the accumulations upon reaching majority. Seeing a college education spent on a flashy car may make parents deeply regret their original decision. Numerous other ways exist, such as family partnerships, Subchapter S corporations, and certain uses of regular corporations; however, those specifically discussed seem to be the best with the least number of disadvantages.

The Estate Analysis Checklist, Table 4–1, coupled with your Net Worth Statement (Table 1–1) will provide an attorney with the necessary information for will preparation and estate planning.

Table 4–1
ESTATE ANALYSIS CHECKLIST

PERSONAL DATA

CLIENT:
Full Name______________________________
Address______________________________
Domicile_______________Vote Where_______________
Auto Tags Where__________State Income Tax Paid Where__________
Date of Birth_______________Place of Birth_______________
Location of Birth Certificate______________________________
Occupation_______________Annual Income_______________
Previous Marriages______________________________
____
State of Health_______________Insurable?_______________

CLIENT'S SPOUSE:
Full Name_______________Known by Any Other Names_______________
Date of Birth_______________Place of Birth_______________
Location of Birth Certificate______________________________

Date of Marriage________________Place of Marriage____________________
Occupation______________________Annual Income______________________
Previous Marriages____

____

State of Health___________________________Insurable?______________

CLIENT'S CHILDREN:
Is there a physical possibility of more children?______________________
Are any children adopted?____
Are any children handicapped or in poor health?______________________

1. Child's Name_________________________Date of Birth______________
   Education Completed______________if not, Educational Goal___________
   ________________________________Business Ability__________________
   Occupation____________Net Worth____________Annual Income__________
   Child's Spouse's Name____
   Occupation__________________________Annual Income________________
   Child's Children______________________________________Age________
   ____Age________
   ____Age________
   Comments:____
   ____

2. Child's Name_________________________Date of Birth______________
   Education Completed______________if not, Educational Goal___________
   ________________________________Business Ability__________________
   Occupation____________Net Worth____________Annual Income__________
   Child's Spouse's Name____
   Occupation__________________________Annual Income________________
   Child's Children______________________________________Age________
   ____Age________
   ____Age________
   Comments:____
   ____

3. Child's Name_________________________Date of Birth______________
   Education Completed______________if not, Educational Goal___________
   ________________________________Business Ability__________________
   Occupation____________Net Worth____________Annual Income__________
   Child's Spouse's Name____
   Occupation__________________________Annual Income________________
   Child's Children______________________________________Age________
   ____Age________
   ____Age________
   Comments:____
   ____

Table 4–1 (continued)

CLIENT'S PARENTS: Father Mother

Name________________________ ________________________

Address________________________ ________________________

Age________________________ ________________________

State of Health________________________ ________________________

Financially Dependent?________________________ ________________________

CLIENT'S WIFE'S PARENTS:

Name________________________ ________________________

Address________________________ ________________________

Age________________________ ________________________

State of Health________________________ ________________________

Financially Dependent?________________________ ________________________

EXPECTED INHERITANCES:

Client Client's Wife

From Whom?________________________ ________________________

Approximate Value________________________ ________________________

From Whom?________________________ ________________________

Approximate Value________________________ ________________________

CLIENT'S BROTHERS AND SISTERS:

Name____Living__________

Age______________Married______________Children______________

Comments:____

Name____Living__________

Age______________Married______________Children______________

Comments:____

Name____Living__________

Age______________Married______________Children______________

Comments:____

Name____Living__________

Age______________Married______________Children______________

Comments:____

Name____Living__________

Age______________Married______________Children______________

Comments:____

CLIENT'S SPOUSE'S BROTHERS AND SISTERS:

Name____Living__________

Age______________Married______________Children______________

Comments:____

Name______________________________Living________
Age______________Married______________Children______________
Comments:______________________________
Name______________________________Living________
Age______________Married______________Children______________
Comments:______________________________
Name______________________________Living________
Age______________Married______________Children______________
Comments:______________________________
Name______________________________Living________
Age______________Married______________Children______________
Comments:______________________________

Other relatives or friends of client and spouse who would be immediate beneficiaries or ultimate beneficiaries if client, spouse, all issue, and parents are dead:

Name______________ ______________ ______________
Residence______________ ______________ ______________
Age______________ ______________ ______________
Relation______________ ______________ ______________

Charities as immediate beneficiaries or ultimate beneficiaries if all individual beneficiaries are dead:

Name______________ ______________ ______________
Address______________ ______________ ______________
Special Purpose if Any______ ______________ ______________

Client's Social Security No.______________Covered Since________
Client's Spouse's Social Security No.______________Covered Since________
Armed Forces Service:
Serial No.______________Branch of Service______________
Dates of Service______________________________
Pension or Profit-Sharing Plans:
Description of Benefits:______________________________
____
____

Location of Lock Box______________In Whose Name?______________
Any Property of Others in Box?__________Identifiable as Such?__________
Where are Other Valuable Papers Kept?______________________________
Name of Broker______________________________
Name of Accountant______________________________
Name of Life Insurance Agent______________________________
Name of Casualty Insurance Agent______________________________
Bank Preference______________________________

Table 4–1 (continued)

LIABILITIES

Amount	Owed to Whom	Due Date	Secured by What Asset
________	________________	________	________________
________	________________	________	________________
________	________________	________	________________
________	________________	________	________________

Have you made any substantial gifts in the past or placed property in joint names? ________________________ Details: ________________________
____

Do you or your spouse have any powers of appointment? ________________
Details: ____
____

Are you or your spouse the beneficiaries under any trust? ________________
Details: ____
____

BANK ACCOUNTS AND SAVINGS ACCOUNTS

1. Name of Bank, Savings and Loan, or Credit Union ________________
   Average Balance ________________ Type of Account ________________
   (checking-savings)
   In Whose Name ____

2. Name of Bank, Savings and Loan, or Credit Union ________________
   Average Balance ________________ Type of Account ________________
   (checking-savings)
   In Whose Name ____

3. Name of Bank, Savings and Loan, or Credit Union ________________
   Average Balance ________________ Type of Account ________________
   (checking-savings)
   In Whose Name ____

4. Name of Bank, Savings and Loan, or Credit Union ________________
   Average Balance ________________ Type of Account ________________
   (checking-savings)
   In Whose Name ____

5. Name of Bank, Savings and Loan, or Credit Union ________________
   Average Balance ________________ Type of Account ________________
   (checking-savings)
   In Whose Name ____

STOCKS AND BONDS*

Number of Shares or Amount	Name of Company	Description of Security	In Whose Name	Fair Market Value

REAL ESTATE

1. Residence Address__________
   Brief Description__________
   __________Fair Market Value__________Assessed Value__________
   Legal Title in Whose Name__________
   Mortgage: Account__________Mortgagee__________
   If property was a gift or is in joint names–details__________
   ____

2. Address__________
   Brief Description__________
   __________Fair Market Value__________Assessed Value__________
   Legal Title in Whose Name__________
   Mortgage: Amount__________Mortgagee__________
   If property was a gift or is in joint names—details__________
   ____

3. Address__________
   Brief Description__________
   __________Fair Market Value__________Assessed Value__________
   Legal Title in Whose Name__________
   Mortgage: Amount__________Mortgagee__________
   If property was a gift or is in joint names—details__________
   ____

---

*For all marketable stocks and bonds acquired before 1–1–77, 12–31–76 fair market value. For all others acquired before 1–1–77 (for the time being), cost. All acquired after 12–31–76, cost.

Table 4–1 (continued)

LIFE AND ACCIDENTAL DEATH INSURANCE

Face Amount	Type	Policy No.	Name of Company	Beneficiaries	Amount of Loan on Policy	Cash Value

Comments on Life Insurance:______________________________

Is the insured the owner of the policies?________________________

BUSINESS INTEREST

(If the client has an interest in partnership, joint venture, closely held corporation, proprietorship, or other similar entity, the lawyer must obtain complete information about its assets and liabilities, buy-sell agreements, and all other related information, including carryover basis.)

COMMUNITY PROPERTY

OTHER ASSETS

Automobile (State: Model, Make, Fair Market Value, in Whose Name, and Mortgage)______________________________

Boats, Trailers, etc.____

____

Mortgages Owned or Other Receivables________________________________

____

____

Coin Collections, Guns, Family Heirlooms______________________________

____

____

Other Assets____

____

____

Summary

Granted that it's a less-than-gleeful subject, estate planning is essential to protect our heirs and attain our wishes. This chapter has emphasized the importance of wills and has offered discussion of several types.

As with any subject that relates to assets and liabilities, it is necessary to assemble data when engaged in estate planning activities. By doing so in advance of a meeting with an attorney, the transactions can be facilitated and the legal fees minimized. Completing the forms offered in this chapter will help serve that end.

SECTION II

VALUING A DENTAL PRACTICE AND BRINGING IN AN ASSOCIATE

The valuation of a practice and the act of bringing in an associate has as many solutions as there are practice management consultants, accountants, and dentists who attempt to negotiate these treacherous waters on their own.

With increasing competition in the marketplace, an ongoing, healthy dental practice is a valuable asset in today's economy. As a potential asset for retirement, the financial implications can be significant. The key is to plan ahead, obtaining the necessary knowledge and expertise to structure the sale in an advantageous manner.

For simplicity of reading, the host or owner-dentist is written as "you" and the associate as the "candidate" or "associate." The sample contracts that appear in this section should not be used without thorough consultation with your attorney. The sale of any practice is unique to a point, and contracts usually need to be customized.

CHAPTER

5

Valuation of a Practice

Practices should be valued for a number of reasons such as retirement, estate planning, and bringing in a partner or associate. There are more values than just tangible assets; the unique character of a practice should also be included in the valuation. Valuation is both subjective and objective, both tangible and intangible. Many consultants try to ignore the subjective and intangible parts of the valuation and use, instead, a cookbook formula for all the practices they value. Be wary of this approach. I believe it is impossible.

For most practitioners, buying or selling a dental practice is an infrequent transaction that occurs only once or twice during a professional career. Therefore, this process is often confusing to the novice and, if not handled properly, potentially hazardous to your financial health.

The Internal Revenue Service defines fair market value as "... the price at which the property would change hands between a willing buyer and a willing seller, neither being under any compulsion to buy or sell and both having reasonable knowledge or relevant facts." In most cases, the tangible and intangible assets of an ongoing practice are determined by a combination of approaches: (1) expert appraisal using standard methods such as capitalization of net cash flow, (2) summation of market values, and/or (3) a formula valuation based on gross or net. These are only three of many methods and should be coupled with an arm's-length negotiation between the parties. A word of caution: do not confuse *value* with *price*. From the buyer's perspective, *value* is what the practice should realistically be worth based on an objective analysis. *Price* is what the buyer agrees to pay to assume ownership of the practice.

The concept of value has many dimensions. For insurance purposes, replacement value is the primary objective. In disposing of estate assets, liquidation value implies the salvage value of the equipment and furnishings. For purposes of this section, the practice will be valued at "fair market value" as a going concern. The presumption is that the dental office will continue to operate without any significant interruptions.

It is certainly true that the valuation process involves an element of subjectivity. Depending on circumstances, it is likely that a particular dental practice will have different economic values to different parties. It's like two parties wanting to buy the same house. In reality, each dental practice must be valued independently based on buyer and seller needs at the time of negotiations. A formula valuation approach, of and by itself, is therefore inherently arbitrary and simplistic.

One of the major difficulties in valuing dental practices is the lack of readily available information and statistics regarding recent sales. Records of sales are not shared by a central clearinghouse, thereby making comparison impractical or impossible. Although regionally you may be able to gather some information to compare sales, often there are unusual circumstances in the transaction influencing the sales price which further complicates the issue.

Selling a practice has become more important as a result of the hardships of starting a practice in the 1980s. The younger dentist should understand that goodwill is real and has an expected life of three to five years. Most people place great importance on their dental records and will go back to the old office at least once to meet a new dentist. Because growth is usually accelerated when purchasing a practice as opposed to establishing a new one, the financial strain is not as great as it would be if the young person were starting out on his own.

A discussion of some of the components of a practice will help you understand why there are so many variations in a valuation. Generally, a practice should be appraised for sale by a disinterested third party who can also help mediate the sale if necessary. Banks generally require more today than "I think the practice is worth X" while the guessor scratches his head. But before you go to a third party, be aware of the following areas.

1. **The office location, building, and land.** The office location should be in an area that is not stagnant or becoming the "wrong side of town." Even though the building and land should always be in a separate contract of sale, if they are to be offered for sale, they should be appraised, preferably by a certified real estate appraiser, so there is more than a price placed by a friendly realtor. If the office location is convenient and the socioeconomic level of the patients is good, the practice would be worth more than one grossing the same amount, but on the "wrong" side of town.

If the office is leased, be sure you understand whether the lease can be assumed or if you can or cannot sublease or bring in an associate. If your lease is unexpired and transferable, it may be worth a premium. For example, your rental contract has 5 years remaining. Assuming your monthly rent is $1,000 and the current market value for identical space is $1,200, the potential value of this lease would be $200 × 12 × 5, or $12,000. This amount should be discounted and the present value calculated using present interest rates. Leasehold improvements are generally calculated at up to 50% of original cost, depending on condition and estimated remaining life.

2. **Equipment, supplies, and furniture.** These items can be evaluated by a dental supply house. The equipment should be valued as fair market value in use. The "in use" will add some value to a unit that is in place, plumbed, and electrified. A typewriter does not have the same value because it can be moved and plugged in without much effort. To understand a little about equipment value, let's use a 5- to 7-year-old Panorex machine as an example. It may have a fair market value in use of 60% to 70% of its original cost as a result of the escalation in cost of the new machines. Generally, current items that have not changed in several years, such as an Executive Unit from Pelton and Crane, will retain greater value than if design alterations had been made. Obsolete items may be relatively new, but if the manufacturer has gone out of business and another supplier has not purchased the equipment line, the value is depressed. You may have new equipment that has almost no resale value.

The average dental practice generally maintains a two-month inventory of consumables and drugs. An estimate is usually made by using the average monthly expense figures for the past year.

3. **The patient profile.** A profile will tell you a lot about your practice. How many active patients do you have? An active patient may be defined as one who has been seen for care within the past 18 to 24 months. The average general practice has approximately 1,500 to 2,000 active patients. Their ages, income levels, and needs will also have a lot to do with value. If most of your patients are old and wearing dentures, the demand for your services will not be as great as if the average patient age is 32 and the majority of your practice were considered "upwardly mobile."

4. **Evaluate the last three to five years' income statements.** Remember, despite what you hear, there is no direct relationship between gross and net income. There are many "perks" which are paid through the office that have to be added to your income, and an examination of these is necessary to determine the exact percentage of your overhead to income. This will be discussed in more detail in Chapter 6 on bringing in an associate.

5. **Accounts receivable.** These can be handled in many ways. Sometimes the younger dentist purchases ARs to have an immediate cash flow, or the seller will contract with a member of the office staff to collect them. If the accounts receivable are not purchased, the collection process should be fully discussed and agreed on. In practices for which there is "work in progress" such as orthodontics, the two dentists must come to some agreement as to how much work has been done and what is left to do.

6. **Records.** Records are the property of the selling dentist. The American Dental Association's *Principles of Ethics and Code of Professional Conduct* takes the position that it is unethical to sell a record of a patient. The value is actually in the continuity of the patient. The distinction between selling patient

records and placing a monetary value on records for tax purposes should be clearly understood. This economic value from the buyer's perspective is simply the expectation that patients will return to the practice for future treatment. To determine a fair price, records should be catalogued to realistically project treatment expectations, for example, active, maintenance, or inactive. A value can be placed on the record, and it can be depreciated over the years by the purchaser and claimed as capital gain by the seller.

The seller may choose to put a section in the contract for sale that would state that the buyer is the legal custodian of the records. The selling dentist should have access to those records during routine office hours as needed, for example, for litigation. If the buyer decided to destroy the records, the seller must be notified 60 days before the destruction by certified mail so that the seller can make plans to store the records.

7. **Specialty practice referrals.** Specialty practices should be concerned about the ability to continue to draw referrals from the previous referrors. The age of the referrors should also be considered. A buyer would like to have a wide range of referrors, not just the ones in the latter stages of their dental careers. If your practice receives many referrals from the older segment, then, all things being equal, it would not be worth as much as a practice with a wide age range of referring dentist.

8. **Goodwill.** This area is neither depreciable nor deductible. But goodwill does exist, and in most instances 5% to 10% of the selling price is considered a sufficent amount to apply toward this aspect of the sale. Generally, the Internal Revenue Service will set an amount higher than that if it has to determine an amount. The seller tends to value goodwill based on past financial performance. The buyer thinks in terms of future potential from assuming an existing patient base. In the final analysis, this calculation involves a myriad of factors, including the attractiveness of the office location, retention of phone numbers

and staff, reputation of the practice, influx of new patients, and economic and demographic trends.

9. **The restrictive covenant or noncompetition convenant.** These covenants are generally enforced in most states if is reasonable. For them to be reasonable in the eyes of the law, the following questions should be answered negatively.

a. Is the restraint on the seller greater than is necessary to protect the legitimate interest of the buyer?
b. Is the restraint on the seller unduly harsh or oppressive?
c. Is the restraint harmful to the public interest?
d. Is the restraint unreasonable in terms of geographic area?
e. Is the restraint unreasonable in terms of the length of time during which it is effective?

A restrictive convenant should not last more than two years at most and should define a specific geographic radius. The contract should also include a financial value for breaking the covenant (liquidating damages). I believe a dentist leaving a practice can not harm an ongoing practice after 12 to 18 months. If it is intended that this relationship lead to a partnership, I believe a restrictive covenant should continue in effect for perhaps five years.

In some instances, younger dentists refuse to sign a restrictive covenant. This might be when the younger dentist is planning to return to his hometown. In other instances, it is better for the younger dentist not to sign the agreement and limit his options, and for the more established dentist not to establish a practice for the younger dentist who may leave and take part of the practice with him. This area is discussed further in Chapter 6.

10. **Maximizing patient retention.** Generally, it is best that the selling dentist remain in the practice for six months to formally introduce the buyer to the patients. If desirable by both parties, the length of time involved and the duties and responsibilities of

the seller should be clearly stated in the contract. If the seller is treating patients during this period, a compensation scale should be established. Most practices will lose 15% to 20% of the old patient load during the first year; however, the flow of new patients generally offsets this loss. With a going concern, the new dentist can see his practice accelerate in growth.

11. **Understand the tax ramifications of the sale.** Table 5–8 shown should only be used as a guide. Carefully review the tax ramifications with your tax advisor. The provisions of the Internal Revenue Code and related regulations are complex and changing.

12. **Understand the economics of the sale.** Sometimes, less is more. Using your financial calculator, try to decide on several methods of payment that would be acceptable to you. But remain flexible. Many practices are left wanting because the owner will not be flexible or was unable to decide what he wanted. Time is of the essence in many cases.

How do you begin?

First, fill out the Dental Practice Profile that follows (Tables 5–1 to 5–7). It will tell you a lot about your practice that an interested purchaser will want to know. Being ready with information will help the negotiations.

Table 5–1
DENTAL PRACTICE PROFILE
AS OF ______________, 19__

1. Name of practice:____
2. Office address:__________________________________

   ____

   ____
3. Office telephone number: (___) ____________________
4. Type of practice (general/specialty):______________________________
5. Practice legal status (solo, partnership, group, incorporated):____________

   ____

Table 5–1 (continued)

OFFICE SETTING

6. Office square footage: ______________
7. Is ample parking available at the office? ______________
8. Number of years at present location: ______________
9. Number of fully equipped operatories: ______________
10. Is the office owned or rented? ______________
11. If the office is rented, what is the remaining number of years on the lease? ______. Is there a renewal option? ______. Is there provision in the lease for your bringing in an associate? ______
    For subletting? ______
12. How many hours is office currently in use per week?
    Monday ____________ a.m. to ____________ p.m.
    Tuesday ____________ a.m. to ____________ p.m.
    Wednesday ____________ a.m. to ____________ p.m.
    Thursday ____________ a.m. to ____________ p.m.
    Friday ____________ a.m. to ____________ p.m.
    Saturday ____________ a.m. to ____________ p.m.
    Sunday ____________ a.m. to ____________ p.m.

STAFF AND PROCEDURAL INFORMATION

13. Including yourself, please indicate the total number of full- and part-time dentist positions in each of the following practice areas (full-time is considered 32 hours or more per week):

	Dentist Positions	
	Full Time	Part Time
General dentistry	________	________
Oral and maxillofacial surgery	________	________
Endodontics	________	________
Orthodontics	________	________
Pedodontics	________	________
Periodontics	________	________
Prosthodontics	________	________
Oral pathology	________	________

14. Please indicate the total number of full- and part-time employee positions:

	Employees	
	Full Time	Part Time
Dental hygienist	________	________
Chairside assistant	________	________
Secretary/receptionist	________	________
Dental lab. technician	________	________
Bookkeeper or business personnel	________	________

Other (please specify)________________ ________ ________

____

15. Please list any staff benefits (insurance, retirement, vacation):__________

____

16. What percentage of your *weekly* practice time is devoted to the following procedures?

	Percent of Time
Diagnostic (exam, X-ray, etc.)	________%
Preventive (fluoride treatments, prophylaxis, patient education, etc.)	________%
Operative (restorations, amalgams, inlays, etc.)	________%
Prosthodontic	________%
Endodontic	________%
Periodontic	________%
Orthodontic	________%
Oral and maxillofacial surgery	________%
General services (anesthesia, patient management, counseling, miscellaneous)	________%
Total	100%

17. What procedures do you normally refer out of your practice?__________

____

____

PATIENT PROFILE

18. Number of active patients:____________
19. Number of recall patients:____________
20. How many new patients did you see last year?____________________
21. Average number of patients per week:
    Dentist:____________
    Hygienist:____________
22. Average number of emergency patients per week:______________
23. How many broken appointments per month?____________________
    How many cancellations?____________
    How many appointments without rescheduling per month?__________
    How many cancellations?____________
    How many appointments which rescheduled per month?____________
24. How many days in advance is your appointment book scheduled?________
25. In the past year, approximately what percentage of patients were:

4 years of age or younger	________%
4 to 15 years of age	________%
15 to 35 years of age	________%
35 to 65 years of age	________%
65 years of age or older	________%
Total	100%

Table 5–1 (continued)

Note: You may elect to pull the first 200 charts in your active files and use an average patient age if you are not relatively sure of the above. Average patient age:__________

26. What was the driving distances for your patients?

1–10-minute drive or mass transportation	________%
11–40-minute drive or mass transportation	________%
Over 40-minute drive or mass transportation	________%
Total	100%

27. Estimate the average family income per active patient:

under $10,000	________%
$10,000 to $29,999	________%
$30,000 or $74,000	________%
$75,000 or more	________%
Total	100%

28. In the past year, approximately what percentage of gross receipts were received:

	Gross Receipts
As direct patient payment	________%
As payment from government program, (e.g., Medicare, Medicaid, or other public insurance)	________%
As direct payment from private insurance carriers	________%
Other sources (specify)________________	________%
Total	100%

29. What is your average monthly laboratory bill?__________
20. What is your collection ratio?__________
31. When was your fee schedule last revised?__________
32. What is your average monthly accounts receivable *not* over 90 days old?__________

GROWTH AND COMPETITION CONSIDERATIONS

33. Number of active dentists in city or area:__________

    example: The greater Charleston, South Carolina, area has a population of 400,000 and has 250 dentist. Patients will go from one area to another for medical and dental care.
34. Dentist-to-population ratio:__________
35. If this is a specialty practice, give the ages of your major referring dentists and the number of patients they referred last year. (Major referrors would be responsible for 80% of your dental referrals.)__________

TRANSITIONAL PERIOD

36. Will you stay to introduce patients?__________How long?__________
37. Will you encourage your staff to remain with the practice?__________
    Are there any exceptions to this?__________
38. Will you write an introductory letter to your patients?__________

Table 5–2
STATEMENT OF INCOME AND EXPENSES FOR THE FISCAL YEARS ENDING __________

	19__	19__	19__	19__	19__
Professional fees					
Other income-interest earned					
Total income					
Expenses					
Dentist salary					
Other salaries					
Repairs					
Rent					
Taxes					
Depreciation					
Laboratory fees					
Professional supplies					
Office expenses					
Telephone					
Office insurance					
Automobile					
Travel/entertainment					
Professional fees					
Equipment rental					
Medical insurance					
Pension/profit sharing					
Other					
Total expenses					
Net Income					

Table 5–3
ADJUSTED PRACTICE NET INCOME

	19__	19__	19__	19__	19__
Professional fees					
Dentist salary					
Automobile					
Depreciation					
Insurance					
Interest					
Pension/profit sharing					
Travel/entertainment					
Spouse salary					
Retained earnings (if incorporated)					
Adjusted net practice income					
Overhead percentage					
Profit percentage					

Table 5–4
EMPLOYEE SALARIES AND BENEFITS
AS OF ____________, 19__

Name	Position	Length of Service	Annual Salary	Benefits	Total
1.					
2.					
3.					
4.					
5.					
6.					
7.					
8.					
9.					

Table 5–5
INVENTORY OF DENTAL AND OFFICE EQUIPMENT, FURNITURE AND FIXTURES

Operatory #1	Acquisition Date	Cost Basis	Book Value	Fair Market Value*
		Total fair market value		
Operatory #2				
		Total fair market value		
Operatory #3				
		Total fair market value		
Operatory #4				
		Total fair market value		

*Should be valued as in place and functional immediately.

Table 5–6 cont'd

Laboratory

Total fair market value

Support Equipment

Total fair market value

Reception Area

Total fair market value

Business Office

Total fair market value

Table 5–6
SUMMARY OF LEASEHOLD IMPROVEMENTS
AS OF ________________ , 19__

Acquisition Date	Description	Cost Basis	Depreciation Life	Book Value

Table 5–7
BUILDING AND LAND

Acquisition Date	Description	Cost Basis	Fair Market Value

Endeavor to make your practice as physically appealing as possible. Sit alone in your reception area for five minutes and look at the furniture, paint, pictures, and so on. The same advice holds for the remainder of your office. Selling a practice is like selling any business. It would be to your advantage to show it at its best.

Be sure to have ready answers to the following questions. By so doing, you will demonstrate to the buyer that you have given a good deal of thought to the sale and that you are not just on a fishing expedition.

1. Why is the practice being sold?
2. What specific assets are to be sold?
3. What is the asking price and the terms? Is seller financing possible?
4. What are the seller's future plans?
5. Anticipated date to close?
6. Any other thoughts which might clear up a concern of any purchaser.

Tax returns, leases, and other pertinent documents ought to be made available to the purchaser's accountant or attorney. They should not, however, be casually given to the prospective purchaser. Such material should be treated confidentially. This may not be the right purchaser.

Example of Capitalization of Net Cash Flow Method

This pro forma (assumption) example shows that the new dentist will be able to maintain a gross income that is the average of the last three years. Even though the practice grew at 11% during those years, we are not considering that the new dentist will keep all the patients or that he or she will be able to work as rapidly.

> All expenses were projected the same as the last year with the exception of salaries, payroll taxes, and fringe benefits; these were raised 8%. Advertising and promotion, which had been minimal, were raised to $2,000. The equipment and furnishings are being depreciated over 5 years and the patient records are being amortized over 5 years. The qualified retirement plan was reduced in this example.

Third year in past	$174,000
Second year in past	195,510
Last year	219,674
Average professional fees of last three years =	$196,395

Expense breakdown for average professional fees:

Dentist salary	53,000
Employee salaries	34,575
Repairs	900
Retirement plan	10,255
Depreciation	6,900
Amortization	15,600
Advertising and promotion	2,000
Other employment benefits	4,345
Business licenses and taxes	2,000
Employee taxes	4,345
Dental supplies	13,000
Laboratory fees	17,000
Utilities	4,500
Professional development	3,000
Office supplies and expense	2,525
Insurance	2,650
Legal and accounting	6,000
Laundry and uniforms	1,000
Dues and subscriptions	1,700
Travel and entertainment	1,000
Rent	9,600
Miscellaneous	500
	$196,395

Based on the projections of the pro forma financial statement above:

Net earnings from practice	$ 0
Add depreciation and amortization	22,500
Total cash flow	$ 22,500
Cash flow capitalized at	15%*
Practice equity value	$150,000

This example is only one of many methods of valuing a practice. No one method should be used exclusively. Most competent

*The capitalization rate of 15% is based on a safe return on investment of 10% and a 5% factor for business risk and management skill and talent.

people who value practices will use three methods and weigh them according to the particular circumstances. The other methods used to value this particular practice were:

Summation of assets at market value	$156,750
Formula valuation	142,440

We decided to weigh the results in the following manner:

Summation of assets at market value	40%
Capitalization of net cash flow	40%
Formula valuation	20%

The practice value was $151,188, as determined by these three methods, so we round the figure to $150,000 as reasonable to all.

How will the practice be paid for? This particular practice was paid for in the following manner:

Down payment (obtained through family loan)	$40,000
Payment for 7 years (calculated at 9%)	$21,855

The money set aside for depreciation and amortization, plus the growth of the practice, made this an easy way for this young dentist to take on an established practice. I'd say it was about the most "painless" way to success currently available.

Computer Valuation

Computer valuation is a new and acceptable method for determining the approximate value of a practice. I do not believe it should be used with the immediate sale of a practice because the importance of subjective areas cannot be computed. It can, however, be a low-cost second appraisal that may complement a more detailed practice valuation. It is an excellent cost-effective method to use for estate planning purposes or when business insurance needs require a periodic update. The best of the computerized methods now available is from Snyder and Felmeister, 383 North Kings Highway, Cherry Hill, New Jersey 08034, a division of Patterson Dental company. Their data are collected through from a 65-item date sheet and then fed into a computer.

Table 5–8
TAX TREATMENT FOR PRACTICE ASSETS

Assets	Seller	Buyer
Equipment and furniture	Gain over basis (part ordinary, part capital)	Depreciable over 5 years; possible 10% tax credit
Supplies	Ordinary income (if previously deducted)	Deductible
Leasehold improvements	Gain over basis (part ordinary, part capital)	Depreciable over the life of the lease or useful life
Office lease (premium paid to assume lease)	Capital gain	Depreciable over remaining lease term
Buildings	Gain over basis (may be partly ordinary)	Depreciable over 18 years
Accounts receivable	Ordinary income	If purchased, deduction against actual collections
Goodwill	Capital gain	Not deductible
Restrictive covenant	Ordinary income	Depreciable over covenant period
Chart value	Capital gains	Depreciable over 3–5 years

Contracts

One of the most important considerations of the sale will be the tax implications that should be taken care of when writing the contract. The allocation of segments of the practice in the contract of sale will govern the way your money is taxed. Table 5–8 will help you make decisions on this important aspect.

Examples of a contract of purchase and sale (Table 5–9), bill of sale (Table 5–10), promissory note (Table 5–11), and security agreement (Table 5–12) illustrate the legal instruments that are required in a practice sale. These examples are only a guide and should not be utilized without the counsel of competent legal assistance.

Table 5–9

STATE OF ________________ X
COUNTY OF ______________ X

CONTRACT OF PURCHASE AND SALE

THIS CONTRACT, MADE AND ENTERED INTO THIS _____ DAY OF __________, 19__, BETWEEN ________________ (herinafter called "SELLER"), and ________________, (herinafter called "PURCHASER").

WITNESSETH:

Section 1. Contract of Purchase and Sale. At closing, SELLER agrees to sell and PURCHASER agrees to buy, upon the terms and conditions hereinafter stated the personal property located at _____ Street, __________ (City), __________ (County), __________ (State) __________ (Zip), including but not limited to, the items described in the attached Exhibit A, and all goodwill, patient records, and telephone number(s) connected with the practice, a Covenant Not to Compete, and the cooperation of the SELLER in helping the PURCHASER during the period of transfer.

Section 2. Purchase Price The purchase price shall be the sum of TWO HUNDRED AND TEN THOUSAND DOLLARS ($210,000.00) payable by PURCHASER to SELLER in the following manner: ONE HUNDRED AND FIVE THOUSAND DOLLARS ($105,000.00) in cash or cashier's check at closing and a PROMISSORY NOTE in the amount of ONE HUNDRED AND FIVE THOUSAND DOLLARS ($105,000.00), bearing interest at the rate of ten percent (10%), payable over forty-eight (48) months with equal payments of TWO THOUSAND, SIX HUNDRED AND SIXTY-THREE DOLLARS AND SEVEN CENTS ($2,663.07). Payments to begin thirty (30) days after closing.

Section 3. Accounts Receivable. It is specifically understood and agreed between SELLER and PURCHASER that the patient accounts attributable to the professional services of SELLER for work done through __________, 19__, shall be owned by retained and belong solely to the SELLER. Collection of these accounts shall become the responsibility of the SELLER, and PURCHASER incurs no responsibility or liability, but does agree not to interfere with the collection of these accounts and will remit any payments made on these accounts to SELLER no less frequently than monthly within the first (1st) ten (10) working days following the end of each month. SELLER and PURCHASER further agree that in the event that any credit balances exist on patient accounts at the time of closing, SELLER agrees to compensate patients for those credit balances such that they are not the responsibility of PURCHASER.

Section 4. Allocation of Purchase Price. SELLER and PURCHASER agree that the purchase price, as defined in Section 2 of the CONTRACT, will be allocated as follows:

Physical Assets	$ 45,000.00
Covenant Not to Compete	20,000.00
Goodwill	20,000.00
Patient Records	125,000.00
	$210,000.00

Section 5. Debts. SELLER agrees that all debts, claims, or liabilities whatsoever attributable to SELLER'S practice up to the day of closing shall be the sole responsibility of SELLER, and SELLER agrees to indemnify and hold PURCHASER harmless from all debts claims or liabilites attributable to SELLER'S practice through said date.

PURCHASER agrees that PURCHASER will be responsible for all debts, claims, or liabilities attributable to PURCHASER'S practice on or after the date of closing, and PURCHASER agrees to indemnify and hold SELLER harmless from any and all debts, claims, or liabilities attributable to PURCHASER'S practice after said date.

Section 6. Warranties. SELLER warrants that SELLER is the owner of and has the right to convey good and marketable title to the personal property described in Section 1 of this Contract and that such property is free and clear of all liens and encumbrances. SELLER expressly excludes all other warranties expressed or implied. SELLER agrees that equipment has been maintained as is ordinary to closing and agrees to transfer all equipment to PURCHASER on closing in good working condition.

SELLER agrees to transfer and assign title to the property described in Section 1 of this Contract by a BILL OF SALE transferring and assigning to PURCHASER good and marketable title to such property subject to the conditions and warranties contained in this paragraph.

Section 7. Covenant Not to Compete. For the sum of TWENTY THOUSAND DOLLARS ($20,000.00) and other good and valuable consideration, SELLER agrees that he will not, for a period of five (5) years from date of closing, engage in the practice of general dentistry within a ten (10) mile radius of the office located at ______ Street, ____________ (City), ____________ (County), ____________ (State) ____________ (Zip). SELLER agrees to honor the spirit of this covenant and specifically agrees not to solicit patients treated at said location in the event said SELLER practices elsewhere in the future.

PURCHASER agrees that, in the even of a default by him on any PROMISSORY NOTE(S) to SELLER, he will not engage in the practice of general dentistry within a radius of ten (10) miles from the above referenced location for a period of five (5) years from the date of default in accordance of the Section of this CONTRACT concerning "Notices."

PURCHASER further agrees that, in the event of such default, as herein defined, any Covenant Not to Compete that had been provided him by SELLER will be of no further force and effect.

SELLER AND PURCHASER both agree that a breach of the Covenant Not to Compete may materially damage the ability of the PURCHASER to practice successfully in the future subsequent to such a breach. Accordingly, SELLER and PURCHASER both agree to a Schedule of Liquidated Damages which would be paid by SELLER to PURCHASER in the event of a breach of the Covenant.

The amount of liquidated damages specified below will vary with the length of time such a breach of the Covenant occurred subsequent to the closing date.

First Year after Closing	$100,000.00
Second Year after Closing	$ 80,000.00
Third Year after Closing	$ 60,000.00
Fourth Year after Closing	$ 40,000.00
Fifth Year after Closing	$ 20,000.00

After the fifth (5th) year subsequent to closing, the Covenant Not to Compete will expire and no liquidated damages would be paid.

Section 8. Broker's Fee. SELLER acknowledges that he has incurred liability to a Broker in connection with the sale of his practice. SELLER agrees that such Broker's fee shall be SELLER'S sole obligation, and SELLER agrees to indemnify and hold PURCHASER harmless from any and all claims or liabilities whatsoever for Broker's fees or commissions arising in connection with the sale of SELLER'S practice.

Section 9. Transfer Period. SELLER agrees to provide his assistance and advice, as BUYER deems necesary, to assure an orderly transfer of the practice of dentistry to PURCHASER. Further, SELLER agrees to rémain in the practice as an INDEPENDENT CONTRACTOR subsequent to the date of sale. For the first (1st) and second (2nd) months subsequent to the date of sale, SELLER agrees to work up to four (4) days per week, Monday through Thursday. PURCHASER reserves the right to alter the working arrangement with SELLER at any time at his discretion.

Section 10. Independent Contractor. During such a transfer peiod, as defined in Section 9 above, SELLER will become an INDEPENDENT CONTRACTOR to PURCHASER. Compensation for production of SELLER during this period will be at the rate of THREE THOUSAND DOLLARS ($3,000.00) per month.

Section 11. Records. PURCHASER agrees to become custodian, as will as owner, of the patient records. In the event that SELLER requires a record for reason of suit against SELLER subsequent to the date of sale, or for any other necessity, PURCHASER further agrees that upon consideration of disposal of any or all patient charts, as hereunder transferred, PURCHASER will make available such records to SELLER before such disposal.

Section 12. Hold Harmless. SELLER shall indemnify and hold PURCHASER harmless from any and all liabilities that may arise as a result of acts performed or not performed by SELLER or SELLER'S employees prior to the closing date relating to said practice. PURCHASER shall indemnify and hold SELLER harmless from any and all liabilities that may arise as a result of acts performed or not performed by PURCHASER and/or PURCHASER'S employees on or subsequent to the date of closing.

SELLER further agrees to indemnify and hold PURCHASER harmless from any and all liabilities that may arise as a result of acts performed and/or not performed by SELLER during the period of transfer, as defined in Section 9 of this CONTRACT.

Sectin 13. Risk of Loss It is understood by both parties that the risk of loss, injury, or destruction of any or all of the assets sold hereunder, by any cause whatsoever, at all times subsequent to the date of sale, is assumed by the PURCHASER and such loss, injury, or destruction shall not in any manner release the PURCHASER from the obligation to make the payment agreed to herein, nor shall any renewal or extension in this payment granted by SELLER release PURCHASER from any of the terms of this CONTRACT.

Section 14. Telephone Number(s). SELLER agrees that PURCHASER has the exclusive right to the use of the telephone number [000/000-000] of said practice and will assist PURCHASER in securing this number for his use.

Section 15. Use of Name. SELLER agrees that PURCHASER has the right to the use of SELLER'S name to be associated with the practice for a period of six (6) months subsequent to the date of sale. This would include listings in the telephone directory, maintenance of the SELLER'S name on the exterior of the building and in other places where SELLER'S name has generally appeared in the past.

Section 16. Contract Binding. This CONTRACT contains all the terms and conditons agreed on by the parties and no other contracts, oral or otherwise, regarding the subject matter of this CONTRACT shall be deemed to exist or bind any of the parties hereto. This CONTRACT shall be binding upon and inure to the benefit of the respective heirs, personal representatives, successors, and assigns of the parties hereto.

Section 17. Fees and Costs. In the event either party hereto shall commence action against the other for the enforcement or breach of any of the terms and conditions of this CONTRACT, the party in whose favor final judgment shall be obtained shall be entitled to recover from the other their costs and reasonable attorney's fees.

Section 18. Separability of Provisions. Each provision of this agreement shall be considered separable if, and to the extent that, any provisions of this CONTRACT are determined by a court of competent jurisdiction to be invalid and, after deleting such invalid or contrary provisons, the mutual considerations among the parites to this CONTRACT shall not be deemed materially altered and the disregarding of such provisions shall not significantly impair the operation, or effect, of the portions of this agreement which are valid.

Section 19. Life Insurance. PURCHASER agrees to purchase and assign a life insurance policy in the amount of the unpaid balance of the NOTE borne by SELLER, naming SELLER as the primary beneficiary on the policy. In the event that such proceeds are in excess of the unpaid balance of the NOTE, the excess will be paid to the secondary beneficiary after the retirement of such NOTE.

Section 20. Notice. Any notice required to be given pursuant to the terms of this CONTRACT will be in writing. The notice will be deemed given on the date sent postage prepaid, by registered or certified mail. Notice will be sent as follows:

To SELLER: ____________________
____
____

To PURCHASER: ____________________
____
____

Or as directed by each party.

Section 21. Enforcement of Contract. This CONTRACT shall be interpreted and enforced in accordance with the laws of the State of ___________ . If any profision(s) of this CONTRACT are determined to be unenforceable by a court of competent jurisdiction, such provision(s) shall be deemed severable and this CONTRACT may be enforced with such provision(s) severed, or as modified by such court.

IN WITNESS WHEREOF, the undersigned have set their signatures on the day and year first above written.

SELLER PURCHASER:

_____________________________ _____________________________

____

STATE OF _______________
COUNTY OF ______________

On this _____ day of ___________ , 19_____, before me, a Notary Public, personally appeared ________________ to me known to be the person described in and who executed the foregoing CONTRACT OF PURCHASE AND SALE and acknowledged that he executed the same as his free act and deed.

In Testimony Whereof, I have herunto set my hand and affixed by official seal in the County and State aforesaid, the day and year first above written.

____

NOTARY PUBLIC in and for ___________ County, ___________ (State)

My commission expires:

____

STATE OF _______________
COUNTY OF ______________

On this _____ day of ___________ , 19_____, before me, a Notary Public, personally appeared ________________ , Individually, to me known to be the person described in and who executed the foregoing CONTRACT OF PURCHASE AND SALE and acknowledged that he executed the same as his free act and deed.

In Testimony Whereof, I have hereunto set my hand and affixed my official seal in the County and State aforesaid, the day and year first above written.

____

NOTARY PUBLIC in and for ___________ County, ___________ (State)

My commission expires:

____

STATE OF _______________
COUNTY OF ______________

On this _____ day of ___________ , 19__, before me, a Notary Public, personally appeared ________________ to me known to be the person described in and who executed the foregoing CONTRACT OF PURCHASE AND SALE and acknowledged that he executed the same as his free act and deed.

In Testimony Whereof, I have hereunto set my hand and affixed my official seal in the County and State aforesaid, the day and year first above written.

____

NOTARY PUBLIC in and for __________ County, __________ (State)

My commission expires:

____

EXHIBIT A

Reception Room

4 chrome-based/cane-backed chairs
1 brown loveseat
1 wicker étagère
2 wicker side tables
1 brass coat rack
2 doormats
2 original oil paints of animals
Assorted decorations

Business Office

1 swivel/secretarial chair
1 IBM memory typewriter
2 white lateral file cabinets
1 stereo cassete/AM-FM player wired to office speakers
1 Texas Instruments electric calculator
All office and statistical forms, ledger files, etc.

Records/Exam Room

1 Americana Ceph/Pandrex machine
1 chrome-based/cane-backed chair
1 Dexta orthodontic chair (blue naugahyde)
1 bubbler with set of hoses for vacuum, handpiece, saliva ejector, 3-way syringe
1 cabinet and sink (white formica)
1 Dexta stool to match chair

Private Office

(Doctor's personal office)

1 Dome circular consultation table with built-in X-ray viewer
3 tobacco-colored padded chairs
1 executive desk chair
2 sets miniblinds

Treatment Bay

3 Dexta chairs (yellow naugahyde)
3 Dexta stools to match
1 long cabinet behind chairs with 3 sinks and multiple drawers (white formica)
1 toothbrush area with "frog fountain"
3 sets miniblinds
3 sets of: hoses for handpieces, 3-way syringes, evacuator hoses, saliva ejectors
Archwires and supplies

Lab

1 Great Lakes model trimmer with accessories
1 Whipmix vacuum spatulator
1 Dexta yellow stool just like in treatment bay
1 small refrigerator
1 ultrasonic cleaner
1 air compressor
1 vacuum pump
1 Hoover vacuum cleaner
1 Phillips 810 automatic processor

Table 5–10

STATE OF ________________

COUNTY OF ______________

BILL OF SALE

THAT I, ________________ Inc. and ________________, Individually, of the County of __________ and the State aforesaid, for and in consideration of the sum of TWC HUNDRED AND TEN THOUSAND DOLLARS ($210,000.00), consisting of ONE HUNDRED AND FIVE THOUSAND DOLLARS ($105,000.00), to me in hand paid by ________________, plus a PROMISSORY NOTE in the amount of ONE HUNDRED AND FIVE THOUSAND DOLLARS ($105,000.00) all in hand delivered by ________________, the receipt of which is hereby acknowledged, and the further consideration of all the terms and conditions contained in that certain CONTRACT OF PURCHASE AND SALE dated __________, 19__, between ________________ Inc. and ________________, Individually, SELLER, and ________________, PURCHASER, all of the following personal property in __________ County, __________ (State), to wit:

1. General dental practice owned and operated by ________________, D.D.S., located at __________ (Street Address), __________ (City), __________ (County), __________ (State) __________ (Zip Code).
2. All office and dental equipment, instruments, furnishings, and supplies, a Covenant Not to Compete, and the cooperation of the SELLER, as further defined in the CONTRACT OF PURCHASE AND SALE referenced above and more particularly described on the Exhibit A attached thereto.
3. The patient records of those patients seen and treated by ________________, Individually.

AND I DO hereby bind myself, my heirs, executors, and administrators to forever Warrant and Defend the title to the aforesaid property unto the said ________________, against lawful claim or claims of any and all persons whosoever.

EXECUTED this _____ day of __________, 19__.

________________, GRANTOR

____________________, D.D.S, Inc.

____________________, D.D.S., Individually

State of ________________

County of ________________

On this _____ day of __________, 19__, before me, a Notary Public, personally appeared ________________, Inc., to me known to be the person described in and who executed the foregoing instrument and acknowledged that he executed the same as his free act and deed.

In Testimony Whereof, I have hereunto set my hand and affixed my official seal in the County and State aforesaid, the day and year first above written.

____

NOTARY PUBLIC in and for __________ County, __________ (State)

My commission expires:

____

STATE OF ________________

COUNTY OF ______________

On this _____ day of __________, 19__, before me, a Notary Public, personally appeared ________________, Individually, to me known to be the person described in an who executed the foregoing instrument and acknowledged that he executed the same as his free act and deed.

In Testimony Whereof, I have hereunto set my hand and affixed my official seal in the County and State aforesaid, the day and year first above written.

____

NOTARY PUBLIC in and for __________ County, __________ (State)

My commission expires:

____

Table 5–11
PROMISSORY NOTE

$105,000.00 __________, 19__

________________ (MAKER), Individually for value received, promises to pay to the order of ________________ (BEARER) the sum of ONE HUNDRED AND FIVE THOUSAND DOLLARS ($105,000.00) in legal and lawful tender of the United States of America bearing interest at the rate of ten percent (10%) from date hereof until maturity.

This NOTE is payable as follows:

This NOTE shall be due and payable in forty-eight (48) equal and consecutive installments of TWO THOUSAND, SIX HUNDRED AND SIXTY-THREE DOLLARS ($2,663.00), to begin thirty (30) days subsequent to closing, as provided in that certain CONTRACT OF PURCHASE AND SALE between ________________ Inc. and ________________ Individually (SELLER), and ________________ (PURCHASER). Provided, however, upon the death of the MAKER hereof, all of the then outstanding principal and interest shall be immediately due and become payable (90) days thereafter. To secure payment, MAKER agrees to purchase and/or assign a life insurance policy to BEARER equal to the principal balance of the NOTE. Any benefit provided under such policy in the excess of the then remaining principal balance, plus any accrued unpaid interest, will be distributed to the secondary beneficiary on the subject policy.

It is expressly provided that upon default in the punctual payment of this NOTE, or any part thereof, as the same shall become due and payable, MAKER agrees that the NOTE will accrue interest, retroactive to the date of default, such interest to be ten percent (10%) per annum on the unpaid balance of the NOTE.

If the same shall remain uncured twenty (20) days after mailing of written notice of such default by BEARER to MAKER, the entire indebtedness due, principal and interest, under this NOTE shall be matured at the option of the BEARER thereof and in the event default is made in the prompt payment of this NOTE when due, or declared due, and the same is placed in the hands of an attorney for collection; or suit is brought on the same, or the same is collected through Probate, Bankruptcy, or other judicial proceedings, then the MAKER agrees and promises to pay a reasonable attorney's fee, to be not more than ten percent (10%) of the principal amount then outstanding for collection.

MAKER further agrees that in addition to all other provisions of this NOTE, that in the event of a default, as provided herein, he will abide by the provisions of the Covenant Not to Compete, contained in that certain CONTRACT OF PURCHASER AND SALE dated ___________, 19__, and executed by the MAKER and BEARER hereof.

In the event that MAKER of the NOTE should sell the practice during the term of the NOTE, BEARER may at his option call for the full payment of the balance, to be paid at the time of closing. In the event that this NOTE is retired prior to the forty-eight (48th) month after closing, BEARER agrees not to charge any prepayment penalty to MAKER.

To secure the payment of this NOTE and the indebtedness evidenced hereby, BEARER shall have a valid second lien on the physical assets, accounts receivable, and supplies transferred from BEARER to MAKER on ___________, 19__, and described more fully in that certain CONTRACT OF PURCHASE AND SALE between _______________, Individually (SELLER), and _______________ (PURCHASER).

BEARER may, at his option, file customary documents indicating the above described liens.

MAKER:

____

STATE OF _______________

COUNTY OF _____________

On this _____ day of ___________, 19__, before me, a Notary Public, personally appeared _______________, Individually, to me known to be the person described in and who executed the foregoing Promissory Note and acknowledged that he executed the same as his free act and deed.

In Testimony Whereof, I have hereunto set my hand and affixed my official seal in the County and State aforesaid, the day and year first above written.

____

NOTARY PUBLIC in and for ___________ County, ___________ (State)

My commission expires:

____

Table 5–12

STATE OF____________

COUNTY OF__________

SECURITY AGREEMENT

THIS SECURITY AGREEMENT is made and entered into by _______________ (DEBTOR) and _______________ (SECURED PARTY). This AGREEMENT is supported by a good and valuable consideration and is entered into for the purposes of securing a loan by SECURED PARTY to DEBTOR. This AGREEMENT creates a "security interest" in property. The rights of the parties are governed by the __________ (State) Uniform Commercial Code.

DEBTOR does now Pledge and Mortgage all assets of the DEBTOR including, but not limited to, those assets described on the attached Exhibit A and all replacements thereto and proceeds therefrom.

I. This AGREEMENT, as described above, is security for a Promissory Note of even date herewith in the amount of ONE HUNDRED AND FIVE THOUSAND DOLLARS ($105,000.00), executed by _______________ (DEBTOR), in favor of SECURED PARTY until the Note is paid in full.

II. DEBTOR makes the following express warranties:

(a) DEBTOR has full and complete authority to pledge the above described collateral and, upon execution and delivery of this SECURITY AGREEMENT, SECURED PARTY will have a second lien on the collateral described above. It is agreed that this lien is second and inferior to a first lien held by _______________ Bank, __________ (City), __________ (State).

(b) DEBTOR shall keep the mortgaged property free from all taxes and notify SECURED PARTY in writing immediately of any seizure, levy, or attachment of the property and indemnify SECURED PARTY against loss for these reasons.

III. Subject to the cure provisions contained in the Promissory Note executed by _______________ (DEBTOR), if the indebtedness of _______________ (DEBTOR) owed SECURED PARTY is not paid as provided, or in the event a warranty or agreement or condition set forth in this AGREEMENT is not true or is breached by DEBTOR, or if a receiver is appointed over any substantial part of the property of DEBTOR or _______________, under any provision of the bankruptcy act, or DEBTOR or _______________ is insolvent or makes an assignment for the benefit of creditors, then SECURED PARTY may, at his option, declare all of the indebtedness immediately due and payable and SECURED PARTY may, in addition to other rights and remedies which he may have, immediately exercise the rights and remedies granted to a SECURED PARTY upon default under the __________ (State) Uniform Commercial Code. No remedy of the SECURED PARTY is exclusive of any other remedy, including the remedy of a Note or other evidence of indebtedness held by SECURED PARTY, and each and every remedy is cumulative and is in addition to every other remedy given by agreement, statute, and rule of law.

Should the SECURED PARTY exercise the rights and remedies granted a SECURED PARTY upon default under the __________ (State) Uniform Commercial Code, the SECURED PARTY is expressly authorized to sell the collateral at private or public sale as deemed best in the sole discretion of the SECURED PARTY. In addition, the collateral may be sold to one (1) or more bidders, separately or collectively, and at different times and location. The SECURED PARTY is empowered to foreclose upon a portion of the collateral without being required to foreclose upon all of the collateral.

IV. This SECURITY AGREEMENT shall continue to give the SECURED PARTY the same secured position in the mortgaged collateral if and when any indebtedness for which this AGREEMENT is given as security is renewed and extended.

V. This AGREEMENT is binding on the successors and assigns of DEBTOR, where applicable, and inures to the benefit of SECURED PARTY, his heirs and assigns.

DEBTOR HEREBY ACKNOWLEDGES THAT THIS AGREEMENT WAS COMPLETED AS TO ALL ESSENTIAL PROVISIONS BEFORE IT WAS SIGNED BY DEBTOR IN MULTIPLE COPIES AND ONE (1) EXECUTED COPY THEREOF WAS DELIVERED TO DEBTOR AT THE TIME THIS AGREEMENT WAS SIGNED.

The parties hereto have caused this AGREEMENT to be executed this ______ day of ____________, 19__.

By: ________________
DEBTOR

By: ________________
SECURED PARTY

EXHIBIT A

Reception Room

4 chrome-based/cane-backed chairs
1 brown loveseat
1 wicker étagère
2 wicker side tables
1 brass coat rack
2 doormats
2 original oil paintings of animals
Assorted decorations

Business Office

1 swivel/secretarial chair
1 IBM memory typewriter
2 white lateral file cabinets
1 stereo cassete/AM-FM player wired to office speakers
1 Texas Instruments electric calculator
All office and statistical forms, ledger files, etc.

Private Office
(Doctor's personal office)

1 Dome circular consultation table with built-in X-ray viewer
3 tobacco colored padded chairs
1 executive desk chair
2 sets miniblinds

Lab

1 Great Lakes model trimmer with accessories
1 Whipmix vacuum spatulator
1 Dexta yellow stool just like in treatment bay
1 small refrigerator
1 ultrasonic cleaner
1 air compressor
1 vacuum pump
1 Hoover vacuum cleaner
1 Phillips 810 automatic processor

Table 5–12 continued

Records/Exam Room

1 Americana Ceph/Pandrex machine
1 chrome-based/cane-backed chair
1 Dexta orthodontic chair (blue naugahyde)
1 bubbler with set of hoses for vacuum, handpiece, saliva ejector, 3-way syringe
1 cabinet and sink (white formica)
1 Dexta stool to match chair

Treatment Bay

3 Dexta chairs (yellow naugahyde)
3 Dexta stools to match
1 long cabinet behind chairs with 3 sinks and multiple drawers (white formica)
1 toothbrush area with "frog fountain"
3 sets miniblinds
3 sets of: hoses for handpieces, 3-way syringes, evacuator hoses, saliva ejectors
Archwires and supplies

Summary

Knowing the value of a practice is vitally important to retirement and estate planning. It is also essential information when forming a partnership or corporation. Have your practice valued on a regular basis in advance of a particular need.

Every dental practice is unique and, therefore, no standard formula for determining value can be totally accurate. Among others, some of the factors involved in practice valuation include location, equipment and supplies, patient profile, gross and net incomes, and restrictive covenents.

Goodwill, which is neither depreciable nor deductible, has very real value which must be determined in the negotiations of the sale.

Assembling data is the first step in arriving at a meaningful practice valuation. This chapter has provided sample forms for such needs.

The sales contract in this chapter is for illustrative purposes only. With the assistance of attorneys and other advisors, the parties to a practice sale must always develop their own contract.

CHAPTER

6

Bringing in an Associate

Adding an associate is an important step both in the growth of your practice and in your plans for retirement. The decision to hire an associate could be one of the most difficult of your career because it has personal and financial ramifications. Most practitioners consider the financial aspects to be the most relevant; the actuality, however, is that the personal, or qualitative, questions are the most important and the ones that should be addressed first.

If your plan includes selling a part or all of your practice to the associate with the option of becoming his associate, then the order of the questions addressed and their thorough exploration is critical to your success.

You must have a clear understanding of why you need an associate and how that associate will fulfill that need. When interviewing prospective associates, you should clearly communicate your needs and plans for the future.

Perhaps the best way to illustrate the importance of communication between associates is to show what happens when people misunderstand what to expect and what is expected of them. This misunderstanding is based on those famous words "But I thought you meant . . ." The true example that follows shows what can really happen.

> The scenario begins when the associate is told that he will be paid 40% of the gross collections, less 50% of the attributable laboratory charges. Sounds simple. But the associate saw it this way:

$10,000	Collections
(500)	Laboratory charges
$ 9,500	
× 0.40	Associate's percentage
$ 3,800	Net to associate

The owner-dentist, on the other hand, saw it this way:

$10,000	Collections
× 0.40	Associate's percentage
$ 4,000	
(500)	Laboratory charges
$ 3,500	Net to associate

> The associate assumed that he would receive $3,800 per month; the owner-dentist assumed the associate would receive $3,500 per month. This monthly difference of $300 becomes a source of contention because, when multiplied by twelve months, the associate believes he is losing $3,600 per year!

This failure to communicate can result in a strained business relationship that will affect your practice.

The problem can be avoided if you carefully evaluate your need for an associate, determine if adding an associate is philosophically and economically reasonable for your practice, and then establish guidelines to help you interview, choose, and communicate accurately with the associate.

Frequently, the contemplation of an associate brings on a myriad of problems, the total effect of which is to provide enough inertia for you to easily postpone the decision. If the answer concerning the choice of an associateship was easily understood, none of the accompanying problems would arise.

Although you may be interested in an associateship, the decision-making process may be unclear. On the other hand, if the parts of the decision could be identified separately and the mechanics of each of the parts of the process explored, such a question could then be resolved.

Before any attempt is made to determine the financial feasibility of an associateship, you must first identify some basic reasons for considering an associate. An associateship will not work without satisfying two important preconditions: (1) identifying your exact reasons for offering an associateship and then (2) determining if those reasons will achieve the goals you were seeking by offering the position in the first place. The importance of determining the reasons for offering the position cannot be overemphasized. As the section on "Quantifying the Decision" will illustrate, your projection must satisfy the "need" issue first.

With this in mind, it would be best to first discuss the basic reasons why such an opportunity might be offered to an associate.

Economic Reasons

Income Generation. Within the bounds of reasonable effort, it is probably the goal of nearly all professional practices to maximize practice income. This can often be accomplished more easily through the use of a second practitioner. It does not necessarily follow that an associate will merely divide the patient volume between two doctors. In fact, experience has shown the reverse to almost always be true. Practices that include an associate usually experience a growth rate that was not previously possible. Although this may decrease the net income available to the established practitioner for a short period, the increased production as a result of the new associate will correct this problem. Therefore, a practitioner considering an associate must be aware of the potential to temporarily lower net income and be prepared to manage during this period. However, the chance of recovering from this deflection and surpassing it within a reasonable time is excellent.

Utilization of the Office or Capital Base. For a moment, consider yourself a management consultant. You will notice that the money invested in the capital base—that is, equipment, furnishings, leasehold improvements, instruments, and supplies—is usually substantial; it is not unusual for this capital base to cost $100,000 or more. In your role as management consultant, it will also be obvious to you that this investment is sometimes used as few as 32 or 36 hours per week, based on a 4- or 4½-day work schedule. Several problems come with this underutilization of the office. First, for you to realize a reasonable return on this investment, fees must be frequently adjusted. Second, any additional hours added to the work week will have to come from the established practitioner. For example, assuming a 36-hour work week, a 12-hour increase (33%) in hours of operation may be more than you are willing to do. No doubt, as a management consultant you would seriously consider advising the established practitioner to consider an associateship. Almost certainly, the return on investment will be more easily realized and the income to the practice will increase.

Overhead Reduction. It has often been said that what you keep is more important than what you make. The major item standing between your present net income and an increase is the overhead. Worse yet, 60% to 70% of the overhead spent by your practice is fixed. That is, no matter what your present level of production, those fixed expenses must be met each month. This is true even when you go on a vacation or become ill. Bringing in an associate in your practice is an excellent way to "spread out" the fixed expenses. For example, even if the addition of an associate may require an extra salary (for a dental assistant), most of the rest of the fixed expenses such as telephone, utilities, insurance, and office supplies should remain relatively the same. Unless you make a conscious decision to add office space, bringing in an associate will not increase the lease or rent payment. Therefore, if you have not increased these cost items, you have reduced them by the simple fact that more than one person will be contributing to their payment. There may be a temporary deflection in the net income through a reduction, or spreading out, of the fixed expense base.

Expanded Hours and/or Service. In some ways, we have already discussed the expansion of the practice. All too frequently, practitioners send some patients away from the practice—not so much because of the difficulty of the cases presented, but because of a simple preferential selection process. This drain need not continue. Although it may not be attractive to you to expand the hours that the practice is available to the public, an associate is almost always willing to provide the manpower for this practice expansion effort. If the practice is operated less than 36 hours per week, or if a check of the appointment book indicates that appointments at the end of the day are booked further ahead than appointments during the middle of the day, your patients are probably telling you something. In short, the market may be asking for one thing while you are providing another.

Relief of Excessive Patient Load. Although this is not true of many practices, it does sometimes happen that a practice can become the victim of its own success. In these instances, there are more patients than a dentist can adequately see without being booked ahead for an unusually long period or working inordinately long hours. Bringing an associate into the practice will help reduce the length of time patients must wait to be seen or cut down the number of hours that the established practitioner must work, all the while improving the cash flow of the practice in several ways. First, patients who are unwilling to wait long enough for an appointment will not be lost. Second, the cash flow to the practice can be substantially improved because more patients are seen in a shorter time.

Noneconomic Reasons

Ready Buyer for the Practice. There is a considerable amount of security and prudence in providing a place for an associate who may purchase the practice. Naturally, this purchase can take place at any point in the future, but it may also provide the ability to sell the practice to the associate. Subsequently, the established practitioner can become the associate of the new owner.

There are several advantages to this sale and hire-back concept. You receive the value of the practice yet retain the ability to practice. If you become the purchaser's associate, you will both be working with someone you know and feel comfortable with—not someone new and unknown. Finally, an additional benefit that should never be underestimated is that in the event of your permanent disability or death, the estate clearly has a purchaser in place who has the most to gain from this transaction. The associate may want to carry a life insurance policy on you to fund such a transaction without borrowing the money. This is an added advantage to the estate, which will not be required to take a promissory note from the associate/purchaser.

Reduced Involvement in the Practice. Frequently, dentists want to reduce the amount of time they are involved in the practice. This may be a preretirement slowdown, or it may be that other endeavors are becoming increasingly attractive. In either case, this generally produces several undesired results. First, the practice income will begin to deteriorate because the work week can only be compressed so far; when this happens, the market value of the practice will simultaneously decline.

Over and above these financial considerations, there are patients you will not be able to see as a result of your reduction in time. Finally, the reduction in time may ultimately mean reduction in the size of the staff that, in no small way, has contributed to your success. An associate can be a potential remedy for these undesired effects. In fact, the associate may be able to undertake some of the management responsibilities previously borne entirely by you. The same sort of scenario can be repeated when you wish to concentrate on a narrow scope of procedures such as implants or crown and bridge prosthetics. No doubt, someone would still need to maintain the production of the practice of the other, less demanding procedures.

Assist New Graduates. Some practices have found considerable value in providing associateships for new graduates with little or no intention of the positions becoming permanent. For example, the position may be available to the associate for the first year following graduation with the understanding that at the end of this time, the associate must find a new position or plan to acquire his or her own practice. Alternatively, some practices do have more patients than the practitioner can adequately treat within a reasonable time. Such practices are ideal for a program that is established to assist new graduates. As many established dentists know, the new graduates emerge from dental school with a reasonably complete set of technical skills but are almost always lacking in the ability to provide these services in an expeditious (and therefore profitable) manner. In short, new graduates rarely have the ability to understand and operate the business side of the practice; exposure to this experience is valuable in assisting graduates in their career course.

Although most of the reasons listed above for providing an associate position may seem obvious, their consideration cannot be overemphasized. As the calculations that are to follow demonstrate, it will be necessary to make certain assumptions about projected income and expenses. The assumptions vary, depending on the reason the position is being offered.

Before any discussion of where an associate might be found, how to interview candidates, narrow the field of choice, and ultimately secure and define the position, it is prudent to "look at the numbers" to make certain that the decision to hire an associate is feasible financially. This presumes that by this point in the planning process, you have determined the need or needs that you are trying to meet in bringing in an associate.

Determining Accurate Compensation for Associates

To determine if adding an associate is a financially viable alternative, two basic questions must be answered: "What percentage (or salary) can the practice afford to pay an associate?" and "With an accurate determination of what the practice can afford to pay, can the financial impact on net income be determined in advance?"

The answers to both these questions are easily determined with a little homework using some of the financial information that is usually found in your income tax returns. Let's assume the following:

1. All income received by the practice will ultimately either become overhead (expenses) or profit in one form or another, such as salary, pension and profit-sharing contributions, business promotion, travel and entertainment, and similar discretionary items.
2. Stated mathematically:

   $$\text{Income} = \text{Profit} + \text{Overhead}\ (I = P + O)$$

   Stated another way, we could also agree to the following equation by simply moving some of the variables:

   $$\text{Profit} = \text{Income} - \text{Overhead}\ (P = I - O)$$

3. If you can isolate the true profit of the practice and subtract this dollar figure from the income, you will derive the overhead of the practice, or its operating costs.
4. There are two reasons why profit and overhead must be accurately determined: (1) it is from the profit that you and the associate will be paid and (2) any projection of revenue and expenses (pro forma) requires isolating the operating costs and overhead expenses. With this done, you can move into an actual example for determining an accurate compensation level for an associate and the projection of its impact on the net income into the future.

Table 6–1 BASE PLUS 1

Form **1120** Department of the Treasury Internal Revenue Service

U.S. Corporation Income Tax Return

For calendar 19 or tax year beginning ________, 19 , ending ________, 19 ____

▶ For Paperwork Reduction Act Notice, see page 1 of the instructions.

OMB No. 1545-0123 19

Check if a—	Use IRS label. Other-wise please print or type.		
A. Consolidated return ☐	Name: Dr. Thomas P. Tooth	D. Employer identification number	
B. Personal Holding Co. ☐	Number and street: 1000 Pleasant Drive	E. Date incorporated	
C. Business Code No. (See the list in the Instructions)	City or town, State, and ZIP code: Sunnyland, FL 10000	F. Total assets (see Specific Instructions) $	

G. Check box if there has been a change in address from the previous year ▶ ☐

Section	Line	Description			Line No.	Amount
Gross Income	1	(a) Gross receipts or sales 191,354.02 (b) Less returns and allowances ________ Balance ▶			1(c)	191,354.02
	2	Cost of goods sold and/or operations (Schedule A)			2	
	3	Gross profit (line 1(c) less line 2)			3	
	4	Dividends (Schedule C)			4	
	5	Interest			5	
	6	Gross rents			6	
	7	Gross royalties			7	
	8	Capital gain net income (attach separate Schedule D)			8	
	9	Net gain or (loss) from Form 4797, line 14(a), Part II (attach Form 4797)			9	
	10	Other income (see instructions—attach schedule)			10	
	11	TOTAL income—Add lines 3 through 10 and enter here ▶			11	191,354.02
Deductions	12	Compensation of officers (Schedule E)			12	63,365.00
	13	(a) Salaries and wages 22,773.51 (b) Less jobs credit ________ Balance ▶			13(c)	22,773.51
	14	Repairs			14	3,422.38
	15	Bad debts (Schedule F if reserve method is used)			15	
	16	Rents			16	7,945.98
	17	Taxes			17	4,474.52
	18	Interest			18	
	19	Contributions (**see instructions for 10% limitation**)			19	35.26
	20	Depreciation (attach Form 4562)	20	959.51		
	21	Less depreciation claimed in Schedule A and elsewhere on return	21(a)		21(b)	959.51
	22	Depletion			22	
	23	Advertising			23	
	24	Pension, profit-sharing, etc. plans			24	20,803.08
	25	Employee benefit programs			25	
	26	Other deductions (attach schedule)			26	66,905.02
	27	TOTAL deductions—Add lines 12 through 26 and enter here ▶			27	190,684.26
	28	Taxable income before net operating loss deduction and special deductions (line 11 less line 27)			28	669.76
	29	**Less:** (a) Net operating loss deduction (see instructions)	29(a)			
		(b) Special deductions (Schedule C)	29(b)		29(c)	
	30	Taxable income (line 28 less line 29(c))			30	669.76
Tax	31	TOTAL TAX (Schedule J)			31	83.38
	32	**Payments:**				
		(a) 1983 overpayment allowed as a credit				
		(b) 1984 estimated tax payments				
		(c) Less 1984 refund applied for on Form 4466 ( )				
		(d) Tax deposited with Form 7004				
		(e) Credit from regulated investment companies (attach Form 2439)				
		(f) Credit for Federal tax on gasoline and special fuels (attach Form 4136)			32	
	33	Enter any **PENALTY** for underpayment of estimated tax—check ▶ ☐ if Form 2220 is attached			33	83.38
	34	**TAX DUE**—If the total of lines 31 and 33 is larger than line 32, enter AMOUNT OWED			34	
	35	**OVERPAYMENT**—If line 32 is larger than the total of lines 31 and 33, enter AMOUNT OVERPAID			35	
	36	Enter amount of line 35 you want: **Credited to 1985 estimated tax** ▶	**Refunded** ▶		36	

Please Sign Here — Under penalties of perjury, I declare that I have examined this return, including accompanying schedules and statements, and to the best of my knowledge and belief, it is true, correct, and complete. Declaration of preparer (other than taxpayer) is based on all information of which preparer has any knowledge.

▶ Signature of officer | Date | ▶ Title

Paid Preparer's Use Only — Preparer's signature ▶ | Date | Check if self-employed ▶ ☐ | Preparer's social security number

Firm's name (or yours, if self-employed) and address ▶ | E.I. No. ▶ | ZIP code ▶

You can work through the following steps to find an answer:

1. Determine adjusted profit
2. Determine actual overhead rate
3. Determine past growth
4. Determine a realistic return on investment (ROI)
5. Determine the past variable cost ratio(s)
6. Determine the amount (%) available for compensation to an associate
7. Determine the impact on net income (pro forma)

To provide an example by which you may calculate your own levels of compensation and net income, a background has been provided on three years' tax returns (Tables 6–1, 6–2, and 6–3).

Table 6–1 (continued)

OTHER DEDUCTIONS — LINE 26 (BASE PLUS 1)

Bank Service Charge	$ .01
Collection Fees	17.34
Dental Supplies	11,150.28
Dues and Subscriptions	1,677.98
Equipment Rental	8,004.00
Floral Remembrances	224.43
Gas, Oil and Tires	1,651.54
Insurance	4,492.90
Laboratory Charges	22,333.76
Linens and Uniforms	675.38
Legal and Accounting	3,450.54
Licenses	10.01
Medical Reimbursement Plan	1,781.61
Office Supplies	2,043.77
Outside Services	284.81
Professional Goodwill	6,683.95
Postage	391.08
Professional Seminars	26.68
Professional Promotion	29.55
Secretarial Service	56.70
Telephone	1,898.73
Travel	19.97
TOTAL OTHER DEDUCTIONS	$66,905.02

Table 6–2 BASE PLUS 2

Form **1120** — Department of the Treasury, Internal Revenue Service

U.S. Corporation Income Tax Return

For calendar 19 or tax year beginning ________, 19 , ending ________, 19 ____

▶ For Paperwork Reduction Act Notice, see page 1 of the instructions.

OMB No. 1545-0123 — 19

Check if a—
A. Consolidated return ☐
B. Personal Holding Co. ☐
C. Business Code No. (See the list in the Instructions)

Use IRS label. Otherwise please print or type.

Name: Dr. Thomas P. Tooth
Number and street: 1000 Pleasant Drive
City or town, State, and ZIP code: Sunnyland, FL 10000

D. Employer identification number
E. Date incorporated
F. Total assets (see Specific Instructions) $

G. Check box if there has been a change in address from the previous year ▶ ☐

Section	Line	Description		Amount
Gross Income	1	(a) Gross receipts or sales 205,134.55 (b) Less returns and allowances ____ Balance ▶	1(c)	205,134.55
	2	Cost of goods sold and/or operations (Schedule A)	2	
	3	Gross profit (line 1(c) less line 2)	3	
	4	Dividends (Schedule C)	4	
	5	Interest	5	
	6	Gross rents	6	
	7	Gross royalties	7	
	8	Capital gain net income (attach separate Schedule D)	8	
	9	Net gain or (loss) from Form 4797, line 14(a), Part II (attach Form 4797)	9	
	10	Other income (see instructions—attach schedule)	10	
	11	TOTAL income—Add lines 3 through 10 and enter here ▶	11	205,134.55
Deductions	12	Compensation of officers (Schedule E)	12	61,635.11
	13	(a) Salaries and wages 11,402.23 (b) Less jobs credit ____ Balance ▶	13(c)	11,402.23
	14	Repairs	14	1,147.67
	15	Bad debts (Schedule F if reserve method is used)	15	
	16	Rents	16	7,429.52
	17	Taxes	17	2,475.64
	18	Interest	18	427.08
	19	Contributions (**see instructions for 10% limitation**)	19	667.07
	20	Depreciation (attach Form 4562) — 20: 2,565.54		
	21	Less depreciation claimed in Schedule A and elsewhere on return — 21(a)	21(b)	2,565.54
	22	Depletion	22	
	23	Advertising	23	
	24	Pension, profit-sharing, etc. plans	24	21,137.94
	25	Employee benefit programs	25	
	26	Other deductions (attach schedule)	26	80,136.21
	27	TOTAL deductions—Add lines 12 through 26 and enter here ▶	27	189,023.99
	28	Taxable income before net operating loss deduction and special deductions (line 11 less line 27)	28	16,110.58
	29	Less: (a) Net operating loss deduction (see instructions) 29(a); (b) Special deductions (Schedule C) 29(b)	29(c)	
	30	Taxable income (line 28 less line 29(c))	30	16,110.58
Tax	31	TOTAL TAX (Schedule J)	31	2,528.57
	32	**Payments:** (a) 1983 overpayment allowed as a credit; (b) 1984 estimated tax payments; (c) Less 1984 refund applied for on Form 4466 ( ); (d) Tax deposited with Form 7004; (e) Credit from regulated investment companies (attach Form 2439); (f) Credit for Federal tax on gasoline and special fuels (attach Form 4136)	32	
	33	Enter any **PENALTY** for underpayment of estimated tax—check ▶☐ if Form 2220 is attached	33	2,528.57
	34	**TAX DUE**—If the total of lines 31 and 33 is larger than line 32, enter AMOUNT OWED	34	
	35	**OVERPAYMENT**—If line 32 is larger than the total of lines 31 and 33, enter AMOUNT OVERPAID	35	
	36	Enter amount of line 35 you want: **Credited to 1985 estimated tax** ▶ **Refunded** ▶	36	

Please Sign Here — Under penalties of perjury, I declare that I have examined this return, including accompanying schedules and statements, and to the best of my knowledge and belief, it is true, correct, and complete. Declaration of preparer (other than taxpayer) is based on all information of which preparer has any knowledge.

▶ Signature of officer — Date — ▶ Title

Paid Preparer's Use Only — Preparer's signature ▶ — Date — Check if self-employed ▶ ☐ — Preparer's social security number

Firm's name (or yours, if self-employed) and address ▶ — E.I. No. ▶ — ZIP code ▶

Table 6–2 (continued)

OTHER DEDUCTIONS—LINE 26 (BASE PLUS 2)

Automobile	$ 1,717.16
Bank Service Charge	52.49
Collection Fees	18.57
Dental Supplies	17,729.85
Dues and Subscriptions	1,132.83
Equipment Rental	6,622.79
Insurance	2,074.64
Laboratory Charges	35,513.59
Linens and Uniforms	925.46
Legal and Accounting	1,705.39
Licenses	12.01
Medical Reimbursement Plan	2,786.21
Office Supplies	1,202.43
Outside Services	216.78
Professional Goodwill	6,707.09
Postage	190.10
Professional Seminars	3.34
Telephone	1,525.48
TOTAL OTHER DEDUCTIONS	$80,136.21

As you can see, these are for a practice that was incorporated. In the event your practice is not incorporated, the source of information will be the Schedule C portion of your personal tax return. The only substantial changes will be that on a Schedule C there is no officer's salary, and you will substitute the figure labeled "Net Profit" (usually the last line of a Schedule C) for Corporate Profit (loss).

For the sake of convenience, the years are labeled Base plus 1, Base plus 2, and Base plus 3. One point in the calculations will require knowing the gross income of the year labeled Base; accordingly, that gross income for Base Year is $178,415. Other than this one figure, it is not necessary to display the tax return for the year labeled Base. This information will be repeated again at the point that it becomes necessary to use this figure.

Table 6–3 BASE PLUS 3

Form **1120** — Department of the Treasury, Internal Revenue Service

U.S. Corporation Income Tax Return

For calendar 19 or tax year beginning ________, 19 , ending ________, 19 ____

► For Paperwork Reduction Act Notice, see page 1 of the Instructions.

OMB No. 1545-0123 — 19

Check if a—
A. Consolidated return ☐
B. Personal Holding Co. ☐
C. Business Code No. (See the list in the Instructions)

Use IRS label. Otherwise please print or type.

Name: Dr. Thomas P. Tooth
Number and street: 1000 Pleasant Drive
City or town, State, and ZIP code: Sunnyland, FL 10000

D. Employer identification number
E. Date incorporated
F. Total assets (see Specific Instructions) $

G. Check box if there has been a change in address from the previous year ► ☐

Section	Line	Description	Line no.	Amount
Gross Income	1	(a) Gross receipts or sales 225,283.93 (b) Less returns and allowances ______ Balance ►	1(c)	225,283.93
	2	Cost of goods sold and/or operations (Schedule A)	2	
	3	Gross profit (line 1(c) less line 2)	3	
	4	Dividends (Schedule C)	4	
	5	Interest	5	
	6	Gross rents	6	
	7	Gross royalties	7	
	8	Capital gain net income (attach separate Schedule D)	8	
	9	Net gain or (loss) from Form 4797, line 14(a), Part II (attach Form 4797)	9	
	10	Other income (see instructions—attach schedule)	10	
	11	TOTAL income—Add lines 3 through 10 and enter here ►	11	225,283.93
Deductions	12	Compensation of officers (Schedule E)	12	75,540.06
	13	(a) Salaries and wages 20,400.51 (b) Less jobs credit ______ Balance ►	13(c)	20,400.51
	14	Repairs	14	3,681.07
	15	Bad debts (Schedule F if reserve method is used)	15	
	16	Rents	16	7,796.96
	17	Taxes	17	3,999.83
	18	Interest	18	396.10
	19	Contributions (**see instructions for 10% limitation**)	19	42.33
	20	Depreciation (attach Form 4562) — 20: 1,635.67		
	21	Less depreciation claimed in Schedule A and elsewhere on return — 21(a)	21(b)	1,635.67
	22	Depletion	22	
	23	Advertising	23	69.47
	24	Pension, profit-sharing, etc. plans	24	21,682.77
	25	Employee benefit programs	25	
	26	Other deductions (attach schedule)	26	89,234.90
	27	TOTAL deductions—Add lines 12 through 26 and enter here ►	27	224,479.67
	28	Taxable income before net operating loss deduction and special deductions (line 11 less line 27)	28	804.26
	29	**Less:** (a) Net operating loss deduction (see instructions) — 29(a); (b) Special deductions (Schedule C) — 29(b)	29(c)	
	30	Taxable income (line 28 less line 29(c))	30	804.26
Tax	31	TOTAL TAX (Schedule J)	31	17.27
	32	**Payments:** (a) 1983 overpayment allowed as a credit; (b) 1984 estimated tax payments; (c) Less 1984 refund applied for on Form 4466 ( ); (d) Tax deposited with Form 7004; (e) Credit from regulated investment companies (attach Form 2439); (f) Credit for Federal tax on gasoline and special fuels (attach Form 4136)	32	
	33	Enter any **PENALTY** for underpayment of estimated tax—check ► ☐ if Form 2220 is attached	33	17.27
	34	**TAX DUE**—If the total of lines 31 and 33 is larger than line 32, enter AMOUNT OWED	34	
	35	**OVERPAYMENT**—If line 32 is larger than the total of lines 31 and 33, enter AMOUNT OVERPAID	35	
	36	Enter amount of line 35 you want: **Credited to 1985 estimated tax** ► **Refunded** ►	36	

Please Sign Here — Under penalties of perjury, I declare that I have examined this return, including accompanying schedules and statements, and to the best of my knowledge and belief, it is true, correct, and complete. Declaration of preparer (other than taxpayer) is based on all information of which preparer has any knowledge.

► Signature of officer — Date — ► Title

Paid Preparer's Use Only — Preparer's signature ► — Date — Check if self-employed ► ☐ — Preparer's social security number

Firm's name (or yours, if self-employed) and address ► — E.I. No. ► — ZIP code ►

Table 6–3 (continued)
OTHER DEDUCTIONS — LINE 26 (BASE PLUS 3)

Dental Supplies	$18,744.05
Dues and Subscriptions	1,820.26
Equipment Rental	8,004.00
Total Reimbursement	22.54
Gas, Oil & Tires	1,046.62
Insurance	5,928.00
Laboratory Charges	37,544.40
Linen & Uniforms	840.42
Legal & Accounting	1,846.26
Licenses	125.07
Medical Reimbursement Plan	4,357.37
Office Supplies	1,794.96
Outside Services	479.73
Professional Goodwill	3,830.85
Postage	836.86
Professional Seminars	256.96
Secretarial Service	26.68
Telephone	1,729.87
TOTAL OTHER DEDUCTIONS	$89,234.90

1. Adjusted Profit. Table 6–4 uses information from the three tax returns presented.

Table 6–4
DATA FROM TAX RETURNS

Adjusted Profit	Year B+1	Year B+2	Year B+3
Officer's Salary	$ 63,365	$ 61,635	$ 75,540
Corporate Profit (Loss)	670	16,110	804
Pension/Profit Sharing	20,803	21,138	21,682
Depreciation	959	2,565	1,635
Interest Paid	0	427	396
Travel/Entertainment	6,683	6,707	3,831
Automobile	1,651	1,717	1,047
Equipment Rent/Lease	8,004	6,623	8,004
Medical Expense Reimbursement	1,782	2,786	4,357
	$103,917	$119,708	$117,296

As you can see, I have chosen to add back most items that could be construed as either direct profit to the practitioner or items that are discretionary. There may be some question about the figure labeled "Equipment Rent/Lease." It was included because this particular dentist owned his equipment and leased it to the corporation. This may or may not be applicable in your particular case. Also provided are several blank lines should you have other discretionary overhead items that should be added back as adjusted profit.

2. **Determine Profit and Overhead (percentages).** The next steps are to determine the percentage of the income represented by the profit as derived and to isolate the operating costs, or overhead, of the practice. You will be dividing each year's adjusted profit by the gross income for that year to determine the percentage of the adjusted profit. Once this percentage has been computed, that number subtracted from 100% will represent the overhead cost.

Profit & Overhead Determination (%)

Year B + 1	Adjusted profit	$103,917	= 54%	100.0%	
	Gross income	$191,354		(54.0)	Profit %
				46.0	Overhead %
Year B + 2	Adjusted profit	$119,708	= 58%	100.0%	
	Gross income	$205,134		(58.0)	Profit %
				42.0	Overhead %
Year B + 3	Adjusted profit	$117,296	= 52%	100.0%	
	Gross income	$225,284		(52.0)	Profit %
				48.0	Overhead %

(Gross income was taken from the tax returns above.)

For the three years sampled, we have determined that the overhead has run as little as 42% to as much as 48% on an *adjusted* basis. If you are used to thinking of your overhead as considerably higher than this, bear in mind that this is on an adjusted basis. Whether your numbers match these exactly is not important. What is important is that you determine what your practice can afford to pay an associate based on your real operating costs rather than establish a compensation plan for an associate based on what other dentists in the area are paying or what you estimate may be available for compensation.

3. **Past Growth Experience.** To complete any projection for the future, it will be necessary to base some of our estimates of growth based on past experience. The table below will illustrate how to determine the rate of change in your practice. This is the one place referred to earlier for which it will be necessary to use the income for the base year. As the table shows, this figure is $178,415.

Historic Rate of Growth

B + 1	\$191,354	= 1.07%
Base year	\$178,415	

Calculated % is 107.0 less 100.0 = 0.07%

B + 2	\$205,134	= 1.07%
Plus B + 1	\$191,354	

Calculated % is 107.0 less 100.0 = 0.07%

B + 3	\$225,284	= 1.10%
Plus B + 2	\$205,134	

Calculated % is 1.10 less 100.0 = 0.10%

In this particular practice, the rate of change has been 7% for the two prior years and 10% for the most recent year. There is a good possibility that the 10% increase in the most recent year is the result of a fee increase in addition to natural growth of the practice.

4. **Return on Investment (ROI).** It is necessary to compute a return on investment because you may have a $100,000 investment in your capital base (equipment, leasehold improvements, furnishings, and other depreciable items). You have a right to expect a return on your investment. When determining compensation for the associate, you must make sure you do not distribute income to him or her that should be retained by the practice as a return. Although the following example has been simplified,

it will still require careful attention to each step to be successfully completed. This is an important step in your decision to add an associate. Although this might be the most difficult part of the calcualtion, once it is behind you, the remaining work will probably seem easier. To calculate this, you should understand the following:

1. The economic life of the tangible assets that you use in your practice is almost always longer than the useful life used for taxable depreciation. These are simply different points of view; one is tax consideration, the other economic. For example, your accountant may have set up a piece of equipment to be depreciated in five years. This equipment will almost certainly last five years and may well last more than ten years. Thus, it is not correct to imply that after five years this equipment has no value to the practice. Nor is this meant to imply that there is anything wrong with taxable depreciation.

2. Assuming that the same piece of equipment had an estimated economic life of ten years, it would still be necessary to impute some residual value if that piece of equipment lasts longer than ten years and is still instrumental in producing income.

3. Most of the assets in your practice can be grouped into three or four basic categories: equipment, furnishings, leasehold improvements, and (sometimes) automobile(s).

With these assumptions in mind, it is now possible to calculate the return on investment. For example, assume the following groupings of assets, estimated useful life (economic basis) and residual value at the end of the economic life.

Type of asset	Estimated Economic Life, years	Residual Value, %
Equipment	10	20
Furnishings	5	15
Leasehold improvements	7	35

For the purposes of this example, let's assume that each category of assets listed above was purchased at the same time. (In reality, this is not likely to be true, but this assumption will simplify the example.)

Type of Asset	Cost Basis, $	Remaining Useful Life
Equipment	27,800	5 years or 60 months
Furnishings	9,750	2 years or 24 months
Leasehold improvements	24,500	3 years or 36 months

To calculate the return on investment, first determine its fair market value using the concept of economic life as discussed above. The formula for determining this follows:

$$\frac{\text{Cost basis (residual)}}{\text{Adjusted basis}} \times \frac{\text{Adjusted basis}}{\text{Useful life (mos.)}} = \begin{array}{c}\text{Economic}\\ \text{Depreciation}\\ \text{per Month (ED/M)}\end{array}$$

$$\text{ED/M} \times \text{Remaining life (mos.)} + \text{Residual} = \text{Fair market value}$$

Substituting in the formula for the equipment costs brought to its present fair market value, you would have:

Cost basis	$27,800	
Residual @ 20% of cost	(5,560)	
Adjusted basis	$22,240	
Adjusted basis	$22,240	
Useful life (months)	120	= $185.33 ED/M
ED/M	$185.33	
Life remaining (months)	× 60	
	$11,120	
Residual value	5,560	
Fair market value (FMV)	$16,680	

In this example, the equipment has a fair market value (in place) of $16,680, about 60% of its original cost. Using taxable depreciation, this equipment would probably have been classified as 5-year equipment; because 5 years have elapsed, its book value (balance sheet) would be zero. This demonstrates the need for this type of adjusting process.

The other two classes of assets—furnishing and leasehold improvements—would be similarly calculated.

The following computations illustrate the return on investment, in dollars, necessary for each of the classes of assets whose fair market value was derived as above. The expected return is directly related to the estimated useful life. For example, furnishings and fixtures have an estimated useful life of 5 years. Therefore, we need a 20% recovery each year to recover the total amount in 5 years. Likewise, equipment will have a 10% expected return and leasehold improvements, 14%. You may alter the estimated useful lives and residual values to reflect your situation, but the parameters provided are reasonably typical and generally applicable to most situations.

	Calculated Fair Market Value	×	Expected Rate of Return	=	Return on Investment (ROI)
Machinery/equipment	$16,680	×	0.10%	=	$1,668
Furnishings/fixtures	$ 4,778	×	0.20%	=	$ 956
Leasehold improvements	$15,400	×	0.14%	=	$2,156
			Total ROI	=	$4,780

This figure divided by the most recent year's gross income will determine the necessary return. Thus:

$$\frac{\text{Total ROI of \$4,780}}{\text{Gross Income of \$225,281}} = 0.021\%\ \text{ROI}$$

What this means is that for each dollar collected by the practice, it will be necessary to assume that 2.1¢ is to be "set aside" as a reasonable return on investment. This figure seems insignificant until you realize that his is 2.1¢ on *each* dollar collected. Furthermore, in this example a practice with a relatively smaller capital base was used. Add the cost basis for each of the three classes of assets and you will see that the cost basis is just over $62,000 ($27,800 + $9,750 + $24,500 = $62,050). Had this been a practice for which the capital base was closer to $100,000, the necessary ROI would have been approximately 3.4¢ of each dollar, or an increase of more than 60% from the example used. If the same cost basis was used in the illustration but the gross income lowered, it would have correspondingly increased the necessary return.

Therefore, no practice should distribute income to an associate until the return on the investment has been realized.

5. **Variable Costs (VC) Calculation.** Certain costs in a professional practice vary with production; others are more fixed. An example of a fixed cost is rent or lease on the office space; an example of a variable cost is laboratory charges. In a dental practice most of the variable costs are in two categories: laboratory charges and dental supplies. Because you will soon be projecting income into the future and subtracting operating costs, and these costs will vary with production, it will be necessary to determine the historic percentages that these have represented. This is a relatively easy process. The basic formula for determining this follows:

$$\text{Laboratory Charges (LC)} + \text{Dental Supplies (DS)} = \text{Variable Costs (VC)}$$

$$\frac{\text{Variable Costs (VC)}}{\text{Gross Income (GI)}} = \text{Variable Costs (VC), \%}$$

You are simply adding the two categories of variable charges and dividing them by each year's gross income to determine a percentage that the variable costs represent of each dollar of gross income. With this in mind, refer back to the tax returns presented earlier and calculate this for each year. The following computations illustrate this process.

LC + DS = VC
VC / GI = VC, %

Year B + 1: $22,334 + $ 11,150 = $33,484
$33,484 / $191,354 = 17%

Year B + 2: $35,514 + $ 17,730 = $53,244
$53,244 / $205,134 = 26%

Year B + 3: $37,544 + $ 18,744 = $56,288
$56,288 / $225,284 = 25%

6. **Determine Amount (%) Available for Compensation to Associate.** You can now calculate, by percentage, the amount available for distribution to an associate in this particular example. As an established practitioner, you have invested a great deal of time and effort in building your practice to its present level.

Therefore, you should include an amount for starting and successfully running the practice, commonly known as entrepreneurial profit. In effect, this is a reward for your investment of time and effort. As a general guideline, this should run between 5% and 10%. For the example cited, a 10% entrepreneurial profit was used.

The formula for calculating the amount available for an associate is:

Income collected
(Calculated overhead)
(Return on investment)
(Entrepreneurial profit)
Amount available for associate

Substituting the calculated values, this would look as follows:

$ 1.00	Income collected
(0.48)	Calculated overhead (see 2)
(0.02)	Return on investment (see 4)
(0.10)	Entrepreneurial profit (see above)
$ 0.40	Amount available for associate

For this example practice, we have determined that 40% of each dollar is available for distribution to an associate. That is not to say that this could not be varied slightly if the associate were to pay some of his or her own expenses. For example, if the associate were to pay half of the laboratory costs, the 40% could be raised to 45%. Any other variations can be done on this basis. The point is that 40% will cover all of the costs of the practice and will provide for an entrepreneurial profit and a return on the investment. Depending on the reason that you have decided to use the services of an associate, you may wish to make an adjustment in the amount to be paid to the associate. If you decided to employ an associate to sell him or her half or all of the practice at some future point, it may be best to pay the associate less than the 40%, thereby making it more attractive to become an owner rather than to remain an associate. Again, you must decide early on what need(s) the associate satisfies by his or her employment.

If there is no possibility of this person ever obtaining an ownership status, then you may want to make it as attractive as possible for him to remain an associate.

At this point, the first of the two questions posed earlier has been answered: "What is the amount that my practice can afford to pay an associate?" With this in mind, we can now calculate the answer the second question: "What will the likely impact be on the net income available to me over the next several years?"

7. **Pro Forma (Projection) with an Associate.** The best way to determine the total impact of having an associate in the practice for several years is a pro forma, or projection. Three items are necessary for you to complete this process:

a. Depending on the reason that you are going to employ an associate, decide what percentages you will offer. In the example cited, which runs for five years, the associate will begin at a lower percentage than the practice could actually afford; this percentage will increase in the five years to 40%. If you are considering selling a portion or all of your practice to an associate after one or more years, you need only project for that time period.

b. Some estimate of the annual production by the associate will be necessary to determine compensation. Clearly, this will be determined by factors relating to the need that the associate will satisfy. For example, factors such as you hope to reduce your amount of time in the practice, you are attempting to spread out the fixed overhead, or there is a lack of or an excess of patients available will bear on your estimates of the associate's annual production.

c. You will need to estimate the percentage growth that the practice will enjoy for the number of years that you intend to project. This is why it was necessary earlier to calculate the previous growth rates of the practice. Although these growth rates should provide some guidance for the future, they should be increased somewhat because the number of dentists has increased in your office, unless you intend to reduce your time in the office to correspond with the time the associate adds to the hours of operation.

The formula for growth rate mentioned in item *c* is:

	19XX
Income	
(Variable costs)	VC% × This year's income
(Fixed overhead)	Including ordinary increases
(Associate costs)	Must assume production levels
Net profit before taxes	

By way of explanation, because the percentage of total overhead (see 2) and the variable costs as a percent (see 5) have been determined, you can easily determine the percentage of fixed overhead simply by subtracting variable costs as a percentage from fixed overhead as a percentage. For example, you determined that the total overhead is approximately 48% and the variable costs are approximately 20%; then the fixed overhead is approximately 28%.

For this example, it is assumed the following percentages will be paid to the associate, by year:

Year 1 30% of income attributable to associate
Year 2 32% of income attributable to associate
Year 3 35% of income attributable to associate
Year 4 38% of income attributable to associate
Year 5 40% of income attributable to associate

Furthermore, the following production levels will be assumed for the associate. The production level is multiplied by your collection ratio of 95% to determine the amount that the associate will be paid each year.

Year	Production Level (000's)	Collection %	% Compensation	Actual Compensation, $
1	$ 72.0	0.95	0.30	20.5
2	$ 84.0	0.95	0.32	25.5
3	$ 96.0	0.95	0.35	31.9
4	$110.0	0.95	0.38	39.7
5	$120.0	0.95	0.40	45.6

With all of these facts and percentages identified, the projection is a matter of completing Table 6–5.

Table 6–5
PROJECTION WITH ASSOCIATE (000'S)

Year	**1**	**2**	**3**	**4**	**5**
Projected growth	N/A	12%*	10%	10%*	8%
Income	$225.3	$252.3	$277.6	$305.3	$329.8
Variable expenses (@ 20%)	(45.1)	(50.5)	(55.5)	(61.1)	(66.0)
Gross profit	$180.2	$201.8	$222.1	$244.2	$263.8
Fixed costs (@ 28%)	(63.1)	(70.6)	(77.7)	(85.5)	(92.3)
Cash flow projection	$117.1	$131.2	$144.4	$158.7	$171.5
Associate (from above)	(20.5)	(25.5)	(31.9)	(39.7)	(45.6)
Net profit	$ 96.6	$105.7	$112.5	$119.0	$125.9
			Cumulative net profit:		$559.7

* Assumes fee increases in these years.

To make this as accurate as possible, you may wish to break out the fixed costs into separate line items to study each more thoroughly. For the example above, these were collectively labeled fixed costs for ease of computation. A partial listing of the items that would be included in fixed costs include salaries, rent, telephone, utilities, insurance, dues and subscriptions, legal and accounting fees, office supplies, payroll taxes, miscellaneous, and other items that are operationally necessary and nondiscretionary.

Although in the past variable costs have been more than 20%, for purposes of projection 20% was selected. This decision is based on the fact that an associate will usually increase income in the areas for which there are few laboratory charges. As a result, this percentage will almost always drop; it is unlikely that the associate first entering a practice will immediately take over the crown and bridge sector of the practice. More likely, the associate will be doing amalgams and endodontia for some time.

This pro forma can be varied. The projected growth percentages in the example are conservative when extended hours or services (or both) are taken into account. More than likely, the percentages of growth will be higher than those used in the example.

At this point, the second question, "What is the likely impact on the net income of my practice from hiring an associate?" has been answered. Using your own information, a similar projection may be accomplished.

Locating an Associate

Once you settle the issue of your need for and the ability of your practice to support an associate, it is time to begin locating an appropriate candidate for the position. The sources of candidates for associate positions will generally fall into several broad categories.

Individual contacts are probably one of the best sources of available candidates. This simply means that the dentist who has decided to hire an associate should inform as many people as possible who have daily contact with other dentists or senior dental students. For example, many of the professors at the dental schools will know a number of people looking for positions. This is not necessarily restricted to just those individuals who are still in school because students tend to retain some contact with the school for some time after graduation.

National and state dental organizations frequently have programs to assist individuals who are looking for a position or are trying to fill a position. These matching services are an excellent potential source.

Bulletin boards and placement services that are part of the dental schools are frequently a rich source of referrals. The only disadvantage is that the individuals who might contact you are not screened.

Dental supply representatives are excellent referral sources. They have contact with individuals who are already practicing and who may be looking for a position; they are also in contact with senior dental students. Obviously, it also is to their advantage to be able to place candidates because eventually this will create a need for some of the products they sell.

The classified advertising sections of various dental publications are usually effective. As a matter of interest, any advertisement placed should be detailed and specific with respect to the position. Generally, these ads are not expensive. Ordinarily, advertisements placed in the state dental publication are the most effective, although national or local society publications should not be overlooked.

Commercial matching services are beginning to appear in the marketplace. This is a natural development of the market because more candidates are and will be looking for positions. Ordinarily, these services do provide some initial screening and are able to send resumes on the candidates before you interview the candidates. Although there is a fee with these services, this can sometimes be amortized over a number of months.

You should try to interview a number of candidates. Attempt to schedule the interviews within a reasonably close period so impressions gathered from each candidate do not become stale before interviewing the next one.

The Interview

Like dentistry, interviewing is part science, part art. In order to maximize the benefit from the interview process, you should establish a list of questions to be explored with each candidate. The answers should be recorded so an objective comparison of the candidates can be made. Although no list of questions and considerations to be explored during an interview is complete, the following guideline could help you devise questions.

1. Determine the **type of person** you are interviewing. Although you are not looking for an exact duplicate of yourself, it is important that your patients accept the associate. Therefore, someone with a personality similar to yours will probably be the most successful. You may want to have the final candidates interviewed by an objective third party to assess personality match; for example, a consulting service specialist in testing or a psychologist.

2. The **community** in which your practice is located is another important consideration. For example, if the candidate prefers a rural setting and the practice is in a large city, the associate-

ship may not have long-term potential. On the other hand, if you practice in a relatively small community and the associate is only familiar with big cities, there is a significant likelihood that he may eventually return to the big-city atmosphere.

3. Although **practice philosophy** is difficult to detect during an interview, most especially with candidates who have limited experience, it is important to try to explore this subject with the candidate. If the candidate has some work experience, check with the dentist for whom he worked. If the candidate is a new graduate, a conversation with several of the instructors at the dental school would be appropriate.

4. **Administrative and management duties** can sometimes be tiresome and onerous to the owner-dentist. If you are hoping to shift some of these responsibilities to the associate, discuss this during the interview to determine the candidate's willingness to accept these responsibilities.

5. The **type of work** conducted in the practice should be discussed thoroughly with the candidate; particular emphasis should be placed on the kind of work you envision the associate performing. For example, if you envision the associate doing most of the amalgams and endodontia but few crown and bridge services, this should be made clear in the interview to assess the candidates' willingness to accept these clinical guidelines.

6. **Physical conditions** are going to be important to the associate. Make certain that a tour of the office is conducted, indicating the area in which the candidate will do most of his or her work.

7. **Patient and treatment distribution** are points related to an earlier discussion. Discuss with the candidate how existing patients and new patients will be assigned and what he or she might expect.

8. **Office coverage** will cover what days and hours you expect the associate to work. Additionally, you should discuss coverage for any emergencies or extended hours of operation you may be considering.

9. Discuss what **obligations** you expect the candidate to fulfill, such as payment of his or her malpractice insurance, dues and subscriptions to professional societies, state and federal taxes, and any memberships that you expect the candidate to maintain.

10. **Compensation** is probably the subject of most interest to the candidate. Thoroughly discuss how compensation will be determined and how often the associate will be paid. The associate should know if he or she is to pay all respective laboratory bills, part or all of a chairside assistant's salary, and whether he or she will receive any income from the hygienist's production. Additionally, the candidate will want to know what insurance programs, such as medical insurance, will be available. Associates who are classified as an independent contractor ordinarily do not receive any fringe benefits (such as medical insurance); however, those who are classified as an employee are eligible for such benefits.

11. The **office staff** should be introduced to the candidate, possibly on a second round of interviews. This is important because the office staff's support and cooperation is critical to your success and that of your associate.

12. **Possibility of purchasing the practice** is probably second only to compensation as an area of interest to the candidate. Depending on the reason you are seeking an associate, you may indicate what possibility exists. Discuss the length of time before such an option might be offered and whether the option would be for part or all of the practice. If the option is for the entire practice, your status as a potential associate after the sale and other related issues should be understood.

Once you have interviewed all the candidates and have recorded their responses, set the information aside for a few days before you review each candidate's responses. Ideally, you should narrow the field to no more than three possibilities, who should be interviewed a second time. During the second interview, introduce the candidates to your staff and invite them to spend some time in the office during operational hours to assess their reaction to the operating environment. Discussing a case or two during the day while the patient is in the chair may provide meaningful insight into the clinical skill levels of the candidate and his or her ability to relate to people. Finally, from the second round of interviews, select one or two individuals to whom you would like to offer the position. These finalists could be interviewed by a third party. Rank these finalists and offer the position to them in that order.

Contract Agreement

Once the candidate has accepted the position, a contract should be drawn so as many hidden or gray areas as possible can be defined. The following list of items should serve as a minimal guideline and should be included in your associateship agreement. No doubt your attorney can suggest others.

1. **Association.** The length of time that the agreement will be effective should be defined. Also, this provision should state whether the term is automatically renewable.

2. **Termination.** The termination procedure, including when notice of termination should be submitted, should be stated.

3. **Exclusivity.** The contract should state whether the associate is obliged to provide services to the established practitioner. This option is not available if you are hiring the associate as an independent contractor.

4. **Status.** The contract should state whether the associate is classified as an employee or independent contractor.

5. **Compensation.** The contract should articulate the basis for compensation, frequency of pay, and an example of computation. If there is a base salary, it should also indicate whether this is a salary or a draw against a selected percentage. This section should indicate how long accounts receivable attributable to the associate will continue to be paid in the event of termination. This would not apply if the associate is paid on the basis of production.

6. **Your obligations.** The contract should state what services, facilities, supplies, equipment, and expenses will be provided or borne by you.

7. **Associate obligations.** The contract should identify all the obligations or expenses the associate is expected to provide.

8. **Vacations and sick pay.** The contract should state how many, if any, days will be paid for vacation, sick leave, continuing education, meetings, and similar absences.

9. **Operations and management responsibilities.** The contract must detail how patients will be assigned to the associate and what, if any, management responsibilities will be charged to the associate.

10. **Patient records.** Whether the associate is an independent contractor or employee, the contract must make it clear that patient records will remain with the practice in the event of disassociation, unless there is some specific reason and agreement to the contrary.

11. **Business records.** Generally, the business records of the practice should not be available to the associate unless access to the business records is necessary to verify compensation or when the associate is to acquire part or all of the practice.

12. **Covenant not to compete.** Most associateship agreements will require that an associate agree not to compete with you subsequent to any termination, whether voluntary or otherwise. This agreement must be realistic in the length of time or the range of the covenant. The enforceability of a covenant is almost always directly judged by the reasonableness of the covenant and the area from which patients are drawn. Generally, it is prudent to increase the length of time and the range of the covenant with the number of years that the associate may be with the practice. Frequently, it is a good idea for the covenant to detail liquidated damages if the convenant is breached, although this would not normally be seen in a contract of one year or less. Obviously, the liquidated damages would increase with the length of time the associate remains in the practice.

13. **Insurance.** The contract will ordinarily state that the general office liability is to be provided by the owner-dentist. If the associate is to provide his or her own malpractice insurance, this should be included. Many contracts are based on a stated minimum coverage level (usually a dollar amount per occurrence) and may require that you be named as an additional insured on the associate's policy.

14. **Death or disability option.** Most contracts provide that if you are permanently disabled or die, the associate will have the right of first refusal of the purchase of the practice.

15. **Purchase option.** If it is your intention to consider offering an option to purchase part or all of the practice after an appropriate trial period, this option should be stated in the contract. The contract should detail when the option may first be available; how long such an option would be open to the associate; how the fair market value, or sales price, would be determined; and some general recitation of how income to the practice might be divided subsequent to such a sale if less than 100% of the practice were to be optioned to the associate.

16. **Entire agreement.** The contract must indicate that this is the entire agreement and that any amendment would require the mutual written consent of both parties.

17. **Notice.** The contract should state that any notices would be sent to an appropriate address listed in the contract as required, especially for termination.

18. **Separability of provisions.** The contract must indicate that if any part of the contract is held to be invalid, that ruling does not materially alter any of the other provisions.

19. **Enforcement of agreement.** The contract should indicate that it will be interpreted and enforced in accordance with the laws of the state in which the practice is located.

20. **Fees and costs.** The contract should indicate that if action is brought by one individual against the other, that prevailing party may recover the associated fees and costs.

21. **Signature.** The contract must be signed by both parties and notarized.

Contractor or Employee?

A subject of considerable interest to you is classifying the associate as an employee or an independent contractor. Generally, it is less expensive to have an associate who is classified as an independent contractor, but there are certain tests by which this is judged. Basically, whether an associate is labeled an independent contractor or an employee depends on who is in control of the service to be provided by the associate. If associates have the right to control their work, to decide how and when the work will be done, they would most likely be qualified as independent contractors. Obviously, an independent contractor may contract to work in other situations. Alternatively, an employee is controlled from the standpoint of how the work is done and the flow of the work that is provided. Because this person will generally not have other sources of income, his or her practice income would be entirely dependent on you, the employer.

When an associateship is consummated, check with your attorney or CPA to verify that the parties are on firm ground with respect to this question.

The following list can serve as a guideline for these determinations.

Employee

1. Employer assumes responsibility for the employee's work.
2. Employer may direct the working habits and conditions of the employee.
3. Employer can determine when the employee will work.
4. Employer determines the plan of work for the employee.
5. Employee lacks any significant control over environmental conditions.
6. Employer will furnish the employee with equipment and instrumentation.
7. The employer will furnish all materials necessary to accomplish the work.

Independent Contractor

1. Independent contractor is generally paid on the basis of work accomplished and not time spent in the office.
2. State and federal taxes are not deducted from the independent contractor's compensation; this is his or her responsibility.
3. Independent contractor will control the area in which he or she works to the extent that it affects his or her work.
4. Independent contractor is not directly supervised.
5. Independent contractor controls the performance and method of his or her own work.
6. Independent contractor provides his or her own liability insurance.
7. Independent contractor may be able to delegate his or her work to a subordinate, such as a dental hygienist.
8. Independent contractor may be obligated to pay for any loss or damages as a result of his or her work.
9. Independent contractor may furnish his or her own instruments.

Purchase Option

If you have offered the associate the option to acquire part or all of the practice, several issues should be considered. This option must be discussed with the associate and mentioned in any contract provisions. Additionally, as the contract provisions indicate, some method of valuing the professional practice to determine its fair market value should be mentioned. How this value is established should be mutually agreeable to both parties. A professional valuation firm can be used for this purpose, or you and the associate can agree on the value of the practice. It is important that the date of valuation also be established. I recommend valuing the practice at or near the time when the associate joins the practice, assuming that the option is not too far in the future. If this is the case, the valuation process should take this time into account.

Summary

The process of considering and hiring an associate should not be undertaken lightly. In many ways, this is one of the most difficult decisions of your professional career. You will spend as much time with this individual as you do your own family. In addition, some of your professional reputation will rise and fall with the abilities of the associate. Clearly, the decision involves financial and qualitative considerations which must be thoroughly addressed.

Specifically, there is little point in attempting to decide whether an associate is a financially viable alternative until you have first established that the candidate will satisfy the needs of your practice. Once this has been decided, the questions of finances should be undertaken. Then and only then should the search for a candidate be undertaken in a thorough and objective manner. Finally, once a candidate has accepted the position, the position must be defined in writing through a contract agreement. If any acquisition possibilities exist, the effects of these should be thoroughly explored with the candidate when the position begins. Done correctly, this can be exactly the right move for you and your professional career.

SECTION III

INVESTING

Success in investing is not as glamorous as it is depicted on television. While we always want to catch the brass ring on the first try, you know from your experiences in becoming an excellent dentist that most worthwhile things take long years of hard work. The best way to grow rich is s-l-o-w-l-y, with consistent saving and investing, plodding along. Successful investing cannot be a once-a-year effort. You have to stick with it. It's no mystery either. Find a few techniques that work for you and stick with them.

CHAPTER

7

Understanding Investing

Before we get into investing per se, I want you to consider where the money comes from for investment. Most comes from our professional abilities. But where will the money come for retirement? The sources for most professionals are individual retirement plans, personal savings, perhaps a small inheritance, and Social Security.

For those of you reaching the age to draw Social Security, consider yourself lucky. Today 100 workers pay into the system to support 31 retirees. By the year 2025, the number of retirees supported by that 100 will be between 50 and 60. Congress keeps saying it's safe, but I would recommend that you consider Social Security only the icing on the cake—and the icing is getting thinner every day. If you are considering working between ages 62 and 65 to receive larger payments, don't. Your financial calculator will show you that if you begin drawing at age 62 as opposed to age 65, you will be years ahead. It actually will take until age 67 before it begins to favor waiting for the age 65 retirement date.

Not only might it be less than you had one day hoped for, but you should also keep in mind that all retirement funds over $25,000 for a single person and $32,000 for a married couple currently trigger a tax. It is paid on 50% of the money received over those sums or 50% of your Social Security payments, whichever is less. Taxation has a way of increasing, so you may be paying on more than that as a successful retiree one day.

Regardless of when you decide to retire, you should keep up with what the Social Security computers show you have paid into the system. If you would like to know either how many quarters you have worked toward eligibility or how much you would receive in benefits if you retired today, get a "statement of earnings" postcard (#7004) and fill it out. You can find out how many quarters you have worked anytime, but the estimate of benefits is done from age 55 onward. The answer usually takes 90 days to receive.

I recommend that, if you are nearing retirement, you set up an appointment at the Social Security office nearest you and go in to learn what to do ahead of time. If you will be eligible for Social Security, apply approximately three months before you intend to start receiving a check. It takes that long to get the ball rolling.

There is more to investing than just putting your money on the line. Unfortunately, most investors are so eager to see their money grow that they readily throw good money after bad. This section on investing will shed some light on what you should know to help you more clearly see your way to successful retirement investing.

Successful investors set goals before they invest. As you read through this chapter, ask yourself five basic questions (the answers in the parentheses are mine):

1. Why are you investing? (capital accumulation)
2. What are your objectives? (to retire comfortably)
3. What rate of return do you expect? (at least 3% above inflation)
4. How much risk are you willing to take? (moderate amount)
5. How much time will you commit to investing? (three hours per week)

Obviously, your answers may be different from mine; none of us are exactly alike. But the answers to these questions will help satisfy your investment goals.

Human nature being what it is, most of us will have to eliminate some bad habits before we really move forward. Things such as procrastination, accepting the erroneous advice of a neighbor or friend, not having a basic emergency or opportunity fund before investing, and hearing only what you want to hear about an investment are habits that we can overcome through conscious effort.

Understand Inflation

Most of us are familiar with the classic inflation of the German Weimar Republic in the early '30s, when it took a wheelbarrow full of money to buy a loaf of bread. The final ratio of the German mark was 1,422,900,000 : 1. In today's economic climate, there are two types of inflation we should be concerned with: *demand-pull,* too many dollars chasing too few goods, and *cost-push,* when you think the price will escalate and you rush out to buy at the old lower price. Cost-push is what happened in the late 1970s. Many financial historians believe our latest bout with inflation is the result of the protracted Viet Nam War and the federally supported Great Society of the Johnson administration years that preceded it.

Monetarists believe inflation can be controlled by controlling the money supply. Their theory is that money growth should equal the Gross National Product (GNP). On the other hand, fiscalists believe that controlling government spending and taxation will control inflation. You should be aware that every time the money supply is increased by $4.00, approximately $100.00 of the new money enters circulation. This happens through the "reuse" of the money through a variety of means, for example, bank loans.

Each family's inflation rate is different due to things such as variable-rate mortgages and lifestyle. Understanding your family's inflation rate will make it easier for you to prepare for your own retirement. Because there are so many variables, inflation cannot be predicted on an exact basis; however, the worksheet in Table 7–1 will allow you to figure yours for the year. You'll be surprised that your inflation rate is not the same as for the whole country.

Table 7–1
YOUR YEARLY INFLATION RATE

Inflation-Affected Expenses	
Food	__________
Clothing	__________
Auto expenses	__________
Utilities	__________
Real estate taxes	__________
House maintenance	__________
Vacation	__________
Medical/dental	__________
Entertainment	__________
Charitable contributions	__________
Insurance	__________
Taxes: federal and state	__________
Miscellaneous	__________
Total Inflation Expenses	$__________
Noninflation Expenses	
Mortgage (fixed)	__________
Auto payment	__________
Life insurance premiums	__________
Social Security	__________
Savings	__________
Total Noninflation Expenses	$__________
Grand Total	$__________

How to Figure the Problem

$$\frac{\text{Inflation-Affected Expenses}}{\text{Total Expenses}} = \text{Inflation Quotient}$$

$$\text{Your Inflation Rate} = \text{Quotient} \times \text{National Inflation Rate}$$

Understand Interest Rates

The "cost" of money is simply supply and demand. When economists forecast higher deficits, it usually causes a higher short-term rate and fuels the fear of cost-push inflation. Think of the money supply as a swimming pool. If the pool is big enough for all the people who want to swim, there is no problem. But if the pool can only hold one giant (the U.S. government) and a few people, then when the giant is in the pool there will be competition for the remaining space. You can see by this little story that the government is able to take what it wants. Because our deficit continues to rise as a result of all the COLAs (Cost of Living Adjustments) the government built-in during the Great Society years, the government will have to continue to borrow large sums to meet its own debt service. When there is not enough money to go around, the government will force the interest rate up, pushing us out of the pool.

Understand Timing

Timing is a chief object of the *technical analysis followers,* also known as the "elves" of Wall Street. However, remember the old adage to "Buy into fear and sell into greed." In other words, buy when no one else wants it, when it appears that a depression is around the corner, and when small investors are taking a blood bath. Sell when everybody wants to own it. It's hard to sell stock when times are booming and record profits and dividends are announced, but nothing lasts forever. Buy and sell when your profit objectives have been met. Never be afraid to sell. Do not invite stock to "join the family circle."

Fig. 7–1 will show you, for example, that a $100 investment that loses 20% will have to move back 25% to break even.

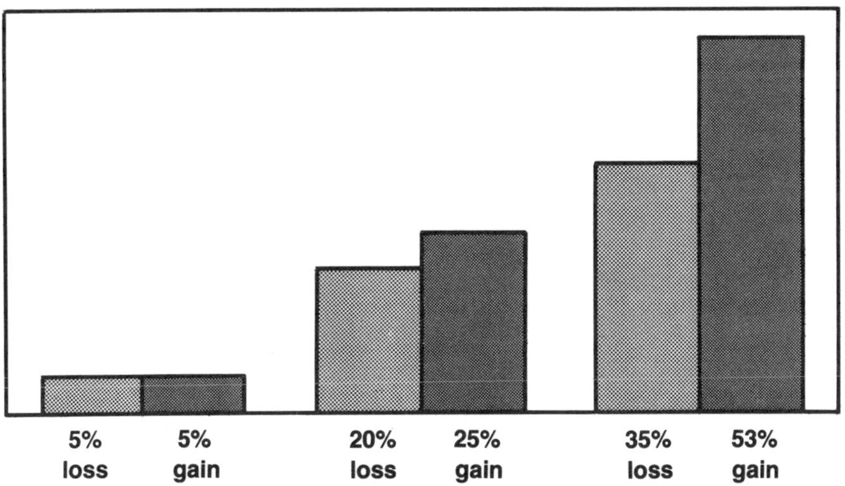

Figure 7–1 The difficult task of regaining losses

Understand Economic Cycles

Since the Old Testament book of Ecclesiastes brought our attention to the fact that there was a time for everything under the sun, we have been aware of cycles. However, sometimes we do not understand cyclical information because the cycle is simply too long and we forget—for example, the real estate cycle of 18⅓ years. How many people thought the incredible rises in the real estate values of the late '70s would last forever? The business and presidential cycles are short enough for us to remember.

If we use the presidential cycle starting in 1936 and invested $10,000 in the first 15 to 18 months after that election, withdrawing our money after that period and waiting for another election, we would end up with less than $3,000 today. On the other hand, if we invested in the last 30 to 33 months of a presidential term, we would have in excess of $500,000 today. What does this mean to an investor, you ask. Presidents start all their unpopular programs immediately; think about it as taking your medicine early. They spend the remaining two-thirds of their term trying to win you back so you'll vote for them again. The lesson: wait until the euphoria of a new administration has died down before you invest.

If you understand how to invest with that type of cyclical information in mind, you will limit your losses. After all, Will Rogers was reputed to have said that he was "interested in the return *of* his money as well as the return *on* his money."

Understand Liquidity and Marketability

Although the terms "liquidity" and "marketability" are used interchangeably, they have totally different meanings. *Liquidity* is the ease of converting an asset into cash without a loss. *Marketability,* on the other hand, only relates to the ease with which an item may be bought or sold. If your stock is liquid, it will at least return your initial investment. However, if its value has decreased, it is no longer liquid, even though it is marketable. Often, dentists tell me they are liquid, but what they really mean is they have marketable stocks or other investments. Be sure that when you are discussing this point with an advisor, you both have the same point of reference. It's too late when you are telling the advisor "But I thought you meant . . . ."

Understanding Risk and Reward

There is a certain fallacy about equating risk with reward in today's investing. Those who thought Certificates of Deposit (CDs) were safe in the 1970s found they were really "certificates of depreciation" because of the high inflation rate. In fact, minimum returns should go to the most passive investors. All you have to do is look at the widows of the early '70s who safely put their money in bonds and CDs, thinking they were set for life—they took the most risk. Today, it is important to realize that the reward is commensurate with the amount of intelligent effort, not necessarily with the particular form of investment.

Risk is measured most often as the *beta* of a stock. A stock's beta shows its volatility relative to the market. A beta of one means that it will match the swings in the market, up and down. A beta higher than one reflects above-average volatility; a beta below one indicates less-than-average volatility. Only stock that runs contrary to the market, such as gold stocks, will have a negative beta. For example, a stock with a beta of 1.70 will move up like a rocket—but down like a bomb.

Another method of judging risk is the square root volatility, which proves the point that low-priced stocks are more volatile than high-priced stock. Square root volatility is a better measure than beta when you have a large portfolio, but both are good and valuable tools to use when choosing stock for your portfolio. (Beta and square root volatility are defined in the glossary at the back of the book.)

Understand Yourself

Perhaps the hardest thing to do is for you to understand what *you* want. For years writers have suggested that success comes to those who understand their goals, temperament, and circumstances. But that sounds mundane, so we immediately skip that part and go on to throwing our money toward the brass ring. We have a basic choice when it comes to money: we can try to understand it and let it work for us, or we can work for it. Too many of us work for money when, with a little training, it can be the other way around.

Spend just half the time learning to manage your money as you did going through dental school, and you will see how much more money accumulates—and how easily. A few weekend courses or seminars will not do it! These courses may give you the impetus you need to begin, which is the reason they were probably designed. Be wary of courses or seminars given by brokerage houses or financial planners. Generally, they are looking for customers, so a little cynicism will serve you well when you attend a meeting of this sort. Do not be gullible.

Here are a few ideas I think will be helpful as you begin to understand yourself and your investment goals.

1. Decide what return you should have on a particular investment before you invest. When your goal is reached, do not be greedy; get out. After you have had that experience, you can begin to let your profits roll and concentrate on cutting your losses.
2. Be courageous; do not be afraid to take a loss. Your goal in investing should be to take away more money from your total investments than you put in. Even if your losses are in a ratio of 3:2, you win. In the end, profit is what counts.
3. Try to achieve *your* goals, not goals set by someone else. Most investors fail because they are investing using someone else's frame of reference. I have talked to some of the wealthiest dentists in the country who did not have the "$500,000" practice. They grew rich s-l-o-w-l-y, with a simple plan to which they painstakingly adhered.
4. You do not have to be smart to be wealthy. Most successful people tend to follow a plodding and predictable course. There is no correlation between brains and wealth.
5. Be responsible and independent. Research has proved that people buy investment advice to avoid responsibility. So follow Napoleon Hill's advice, "Whatsoever you want, O Discontented Man, step up, pay the price, and it is yours."

Understand Diversification of Assets

Whoever coined the phrase "Diversity is the best insurance against adversity" should get a star in his crown. Putting all of their eggs in one basket and watching it may work for people who are in one of the investment fields, but rarely does it work for anyone outside of that occupation.

There are as many ideas about diversification as there are investors. The ideas I will share with you come from a decade of manipulating portfolios to match temperaments, objectives, and circumstances.

The Ideal Portfolio

This portfolio is designed for the mythical "ideal" investor, a person I've yet to meet. However, it provides a starting point so we can plug in our own strong points and arrive at a customized portfolio for a new dentist as well as one five to seven years from retirement.

Precious metals and long-term gov't. securities	15%
Stocks and bonds	35–45%
Real estate	35–45%
Speculative investments (once you have $100,000 in investable monies)	5%
Total	100%

Certainly, long-term government securities and precious metals should be held to some degree as a hedge against inflation and as a secure investment. After all, the government owns the only printing press. Basically, these investments form the insurance part of your portfolio and should not be traded. To be a successful precious metals trader or an excellent commodities person, you have to be willing to take a good deal of time away from treating patients. As you will see when we continue to discuss portfolios, this "insurance" will be a lesser part of the overall portfolio as you approach retirement.

Stocks and bonds should also be "read" to include cash or cash equivalents, including "emergency" money for three to six months and/or your "opportunity" money, as I like to call it. It is no fun saving for emergencies. You will see as the ages go up that the diversification within the stock and bond realm also changes. Money market funds and Treasury bills make up the "cash equivalent" to go with cash in interest-bearing accounts.

Age 30 to 39
20% aggressive growth
50% growth
15% moderate grade bonds
15% cash or cash equivalents

Age 40 to 49
10% aggressive growth
50% growth
25% moderate and high grade bonds
15% cash or cash equivalents

Age 50 to 59
40% growth
15% growth and income
20% high-grade bonds
10% moderate-grade bonds
15% cash or cash equivalents

Age 60 and older
25% growth and income
60% high-grade bonds with staggered maturities
15% cash or cash equivalents

The real estate of your portfolio includes the home you live in and your office building, if you happen to own one. Particularly with regard to real estate, as you get within five to seven years of retirement, you will need to begin thinking about shifting your assets so you will not be caught in a cycle at the wrong time. For example, if your portfolio is loaded with real estate and interest rates begin to move higher, it may be more difficult for you to sell. If you do sell, you may have to become the "bank" and finance the property yourself. During times of high inflation, you do not want to be saddled with fixed-income investments—especially when interest rates ease further upward.

Real estate should begin to move from 35% to 45% of your portfolio to approximately 25% to 30%, and when you actually hang up the drill, even less. You should not have any more real estate than you can comfortably leave to travel and do the things you want with your time. In most instances, this means only your permanent and vacation homes. You want to avoid being tied down to income properties. A few dentists who have enjoyed investing in real estate, and either like to fix the plumbing or have excellent management services, continue to hold large portfolios of real estate. But when the practitioner dies, the sale of these properties becomes the responsibility of the spouse.

Finally, speculation is like playing the horses. We all like to have a little fun. If your game was real estate, then you probably bought the house on the "wrong" side of town and sold it when that area became the vogue. Or you bought penny stocks or long shots in the market and either lost it all or made enough to buy a boat or pay for an extravagant trip. If you have enjoyed this and can isolate these funds from your other secure monies for retirement, there is no reason to stop when you retire. Retirement should not mean giving up the things we enjoy. But because of the time value of money, it is necessary to be more cautious with your retirement funds.

Understanding the Time Value of Money

In the past few years, the time value of money has become a hot topic to the average investor. Astute investors have understood this from the beginning. If a picture is worth a thousand words, then Fig. 7–3 should bring the point home quicker than two thousand words. It pays to begin to save and invest at an early age and to be concerned about the return on your money. It is said that Albert Einstein, after his great insight of $E = Mc^2$, was asked to name the greatest invention of mankind. Without blinking his eyes, he replied, "Compound interest." Whether he said it or not, it is one of the facts of life that works very well for the astute investor.

The following example will help you understand why it is not only necessary to start saving early, but why it is important to be concerned with the interest rate your money returns to you.

$10,000 saved for 20 years at 10% in a deferred compensation plan will equal $67,275. On the other hand, at 11% this same

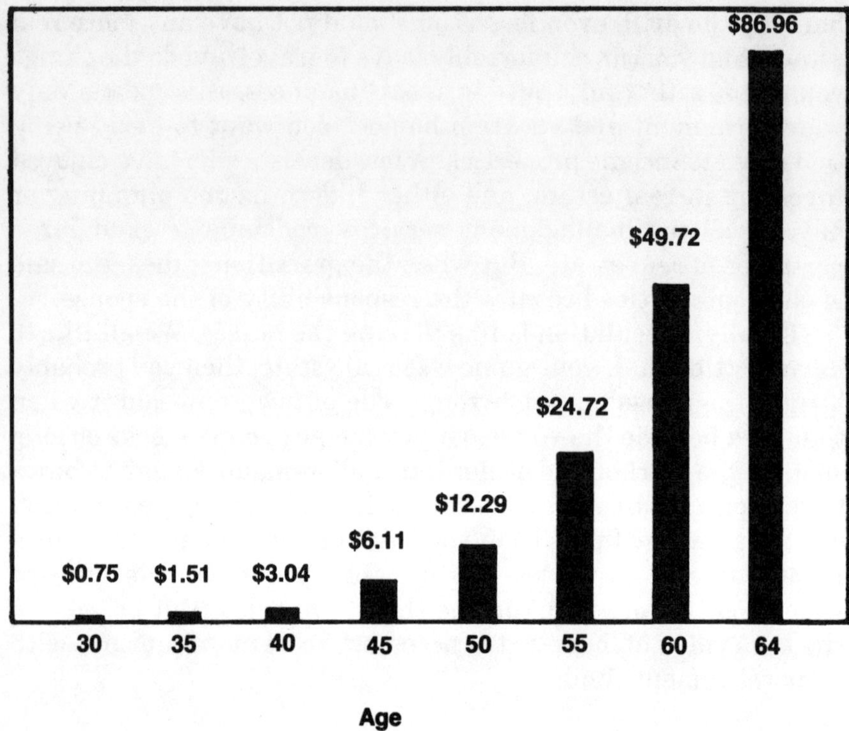

Figure 7–2 Amount to invest for each $100 return expected at age 65, assuming 15% compound/year return

investment would yield $80,623.11—a difference of $13,373.11. Not bad for just a little extra time involved looking for the right investment. What a difference one percentage point makes!

How many of you have been told that an overwhelming amount of money would be needed to retire? Although the sum may be larger than you imagined, it is seldom overwhelming. Many of these figures are arrived at honestly, but usually by someone who has something to sell. The larger the total, the

---

The appendix has problems that can be worked with any financial calculator, such as the Hewlett Packard HP12, Casio, or Texas Instrument Business Analyst II. The College of Financial Planning suggests the Texas Instrument calculator and, because it is the least expensive, the problems are written for it; however, they can be solved on any financial calculator. The problems are the most commonly asked questions dealing with retirement planning and should be worked to familiarize yourself with one of the best "tools" of investing—a financial calculator.

more you buy, especially insurance. Starting early is important, as shown by Figs. 7–2 and 7–3.

The common rule of thumb for a retirement income is that it should be 60–70% of present income. But that does not take into account travel plans and maintaining your current lifestyle. The older we get, the less we want to travel and, because of infirmiaties, we will not be as active. However, I think you should plan to have an income similar to what you have today, assuming the children have been educated.

There are two methods of assessing retirement income and how much will be needed to allow for a carefree retirement: capitalization and programming. Essentially, the *capitalization method* allows you the use of the interest on your investments; the corpus remains the same except when you purposely invade the principal. The *programming method* allows you to eventually use all your assets and leave nothing to your heirs. Personally, I think the programming method is an exercise in futility and would recommend the capitalization method. Perhaps a little of both can be used in conjunction to allow a nicer lifestyle. It is no longer considered taboo for you to invade the principal to have a

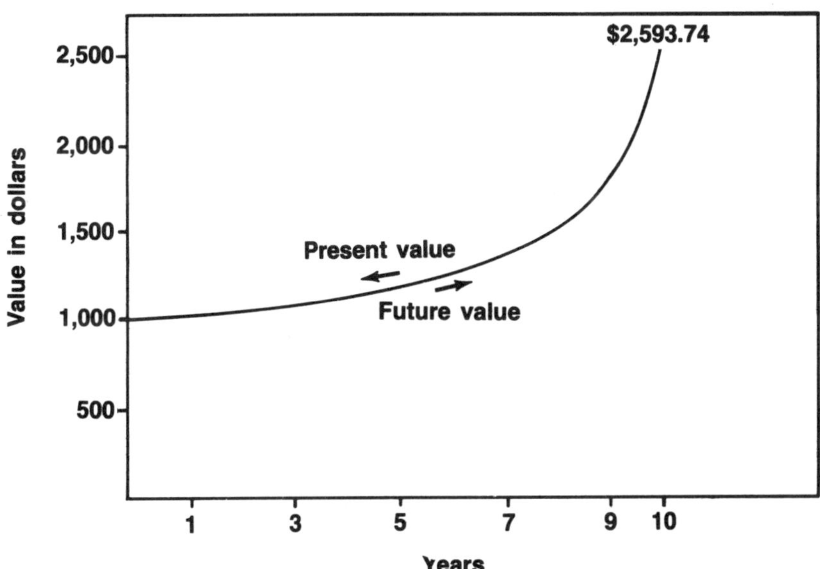

Figure 7–3 Value of $1,000 at 10% interest accumulated for 10 years

nicer lifestyle. It is your money and you should plan to use it as you and your spouse see fit.

There are two ways to look at the capitalization method: inflation protected and noninflation protected. The secret in the inflation-protected method is to decide what you think the inflation rate will be. The problem is worked assuming a 12% return on investments and a 6% inflation rate:

$$\text{Inflation Protected Purchasing Power} = \frac{\text{Yield on Investment} - \text{Inflation Rate}}{1 + \text{Inflation Rate}}$$

$$\frac{0.12 - 0.06}{1 + 0.06} = 0.05660$$

Divide the amount of money you think you will need each year by 0.05660; the quotient, when invested, will allow you to receive an inflation-protected income for the rest of your life. If you think you will need \$50,000, then \$50,000/0.05660 = \$883,392. By placing \$883,392 plus \$50,000 (for the first year) in an investment earning 12% interest and assuming inflation during the rest of your life does not exceed 6%, you will be able to enjoy \$50,000 in today's dollars for the rest of your life. By 1999, the corpus may have grown from \$933,392 to \$2 million. Although you may be receiving in excess of \$100,000 each year, it will still be \$50,000 in today's dollars.

Looking at the same problem from a noninflation-protected method, simply divide the \$50,000 you need by the interest you can get on your money, and the quotient will tell you how much you must invest to receive \$50,000 per year:

$$\$50{,}000 \div 0.12 = \$416{,}666$$

If you are able to live, pay taxes, and save on this amount, you will not be as hard-hit as someone who needs every cent to make ends meet. There is a considerable difference in the two figures!

Understand Being Your Own Annuitant

With tables of life expectancies for "one and two lives" (Tables 7–2, 7–3), you can easily see how you can become your own annuitant. In fact, you can plan how to invade your principal and figure out for yourself how it would work (Table 7–4). For example, if you look at the life expectancy on a "two lives" table and you are a male age 66 and your wife is age 63, you have a combined life expectancy of 22.7 years. If you could invest this money at 11%, you could draw it out over 23 years. That is a half year longer than statistics say you should live. Of course, we do not want to try to cut it that close. But it would be a good idea for you to compile several of your own scenarios and see how they work out.

Table 7–2
LIFE EXPECTANCY
TWO LIVES

		Age of Male												
		60	61	62	63	64	65	66	67	68	69	70	71	72
A	51	31.3	31.1	30.9	30.7	30.5	30.4	30.2	30.1	30.0	29.9	29.8	29.7	29.6
	52	30.6	30.4	30.2	30.0	29.8	29.7	29.5	29.4	29.3	29.1	29.0	28.9	28.8
g	53	30.0	29.8	29.5	29.3	29.2	29.0	28.8	28.7	28.5	28.4	28.3	28.2	28.1
	54	29.4	29.1	28.9	28.7	28.5	28.3	28.1	28.0	27.8	27.7	27.6	27.5	27.4
e	55	28.8	28.5	28.3	28.1	27.8	27.6	27.5	27.3	27.1	27.0	26.9	26.7	26.6
	56	28.2	27.9	27.7	27.4	27.2	27.0	26.8	26.6	26.5	26.3	26.2	26.0	25.9
o	57	27.6	27.3	27.1	26.8	26.6	26.4	26.2	26.0	25.8	25.7	25.5	25.4	25.2
	58	27.1	26.5	26.3	26.2	26.0	25.8	25.6	25.4	25.2	25.0	24.8	24.7	24.6
f	59	26.5	26.2	25.9	25.7	25.4	25.2	25.0	24.7	24.6	24.4	24.2	24.0	23.9
	60	26.0	25.7	25.4	25.1	24.9	24.6	24.4	24.1	23.9	23.8	23.6	23.4	23.3
F	61	25.5	25.2	24.9	24.6	24.3	24.1	23.8	23.6	23.4	23.2	23.0	22.8	22.6
	62	25.1	24.7	24.4	24.1	23.8	23.5	23.3	23.0	22.8	22.6	22.4	22.2	22.0
e	63	24.6	24.3	23.9	23.6	23.3	23.0	22.7	22.5	22.2	22.0	21.8	21.6	21.4
	64	24.2	23.8	23.5	23.1	22.8	22.5	22.2	21.9	21.7	21.5	21.2	21.0	20.9
m	65	23.8	23.4	23.0	22.7	22.3	22.0	21.7	21.4	21.2	20.9	20.7	20.5	20.3
a	66	23.4	23.0	22.6	22.2	21.9	21.6	21.3	21.0	20.7	20.4	20.2	20.0	19.8
	67	23.0	22.6	22.2	21.8	21.5	21.1	20.8	20.5	20.2	19.9	19.7	19.5	19.2
l	68	22.7	22.2	21.8	21.4	21.1	20.7	20.4	20.1	29.8	19.5	19.2	19.0	18.7
	69	22.3	21.9	21.5	21.1	20.7	20.3	20.0	19.6	19.3	19.0	18.7	18.5	18.2
e	70	22.0	21.6	21.1	20.7	20.3	19.9	19.6	19.2	18.9	18.6	18.3	18.0	17.8

Example: A married couple (male 66, female 57) can expect to live another 26.2 years (jointly, not each).

Table 7–3
LIFE EXPECTANCY
ONE LIFE

Present Age	Number of Years Expected to Live: Male	Female	Present Age	Number of Years Expected to Live: Male	Female
26	45	52	56	19	24
27	44	51	57	18	24
28	43	50	58	18	23
29	42	49	59	17	22
30	41	48	60	16	21
31	41	47	61	16	20
32	39	46	62	15	20
33	38	45	63	14	19
34	37	44	64	14	18
35	36	43	65	13	17
36	35	42	66	13	16
37	34	41	67	12	16
38	32	40	68	12	15
39	33	39	69	11	14
40	32	39	70	10	14
41	31	38	71	10	13
42	30	37	72	10	13
43	30	36	73	9	11
44	29	35	74	9	11
45	28	34	75	8	10
46	27	33	76	8	10
47	26	32	77	8	9
48	25	31	78	7	8
49	24	30	79	7	8
50	24	30	80	6	8
51	23	29	81	6	8
52	22	28	82	6	7
53	21	27	83	5	6
54	21	26	84	5	6
55	20	25	85	5	6

Example: Having obtained the age of 65, a male can expect to live another 13 years and a female 17 years.

Source: *Statistical Abstract of the United States, 1976*

Table 7–4
PROVIDE YOUR OWN ANNUITY

Withdrawn Per Year	Growth per Year 3%	4%	5%	6%	7%	8%	9%	10%	11%	12%	13%
4%	46										
5%	30	41				Initial Fund Lasts Indefinitely					
6%	23	28	36								
7%	18	21	25	33							
8%	15	17	20	23	30						
9%	13	14	16	18	22	28					
10%	12	13	14	15	17	20	26				
11%	10	11	12	13	14	16	19	25			
12%	9	10	11	11	12	14	15	18	23		
13%	8	9	9	10	11	12	13	15	17	21	
14%	8	8	9	9	10	11	11	13	14	17	21
15%	7	7	8	8	9	9	10	11	12	14	16
20%	5	5	5	6	6	6	6	7	7	8	8
25%	4	4	4	4	4	4	5	5	5	5	6

Here is an example to mull over. You have a retirement fund of $400,000. You have $300,000 invested at 10%, from which you receive $30,000 a year. You decide to take the other $100,000 and invest it at 10% but withdraw it at 15%, or $15,000 a year. You could count on receiving a total of $45,000 a year for 11 years. That extra $5,000 might make a real difference in your ability to travel and have the retirement you've always dreamed of. It probably would be worth it. I know it would be for me.

Summary

Investing is directed toward the accumulation of capital. To be a successful investor, one must be knowledgeable of many factors, including inflation, interest rates, timing, economic cycles, liquidity and marketability, diversification, and the time value of money. Although these terms may seem intimidating to the beginner, the concepts are straightforward and easily grasped by anyone willing to make the effort.

Investment success is greatly more the result of determination than of luck. The secrets to investment success dwell in such simple things as understanding the basics, sticking with a plan, and anticipating the passage of time.

CHAPTER

8

Stocks and Bonds

Stocks

The choices in stock are numerous and constantly proliferating. In this section we will concentrate on investment ideas that will serve you well as you move toward a more comfortable life and retirement. Most successful investors keep their portfolios simple and their risks moderate. Your biggest obstacle could be yourself; you must decide which of the many investment formats to use. Indecision is a decision not to do anything. You must have and follow a clear game plan.

There are two choices in deciding which approach to take in stock selection: fundamental and technical. I think that fundamental analysis is best for the long-term investor and technical analysis is best for the trader.

Fundamental analysis is a study of the company in which you want to invest. It derives estimates such as net worth per share, current assets, and current and future earnings and dividends. When purchasing a stock with fundamental information, you choose to buy when it is perceived to be below its value, thus allowing yourself a profit. Much information of this sort is found in *Value Line Investment Survey,* which is the largest stock service of its kind today.

Technical analysis deals with supply and demand, and the relationship of price and volume. Technicians are far more interested in historical price movement than value. For the type of investing we will be concerned with, either in individual selection or in a choice of mutual fund, both fundamental and technical material should be used: technical information for the timing of our purchases and fundamental information for value.

Much has been written on fundamental analysis, but perhaps the "Bible" of fundamentalism, *Security Analysis,* was written by Benjamin Graham and David L. Dodd (McGraw-Hill, publisher). Although it was written a few years ago, it still covers the subject with unequalled thoroughness. Any stock investor should read that book, just as we were compelled to study *Gray's Anatomy* in dental school.

Your choice in purchasing common stock is to benefit from stock ownership in two ways: dividends and capital appreciation or capital gains. If a company is well managed, the price of the stock will continue to rise and the overall yield will substantially increase during the initial investment time. However, nothing is forever, and no stock is without an adverse move. Therefore, your thinking must be flexible. Today, there is no "buy and bury" phenomena, not with the pendulum swings in our economy.

There are certain points of information that you should understand about an individual stock to make your investment decision. Most of the categories can be found in *Value Line Investment Survey* or in *Standard and Poor*'s stock service. Almost every county library in the nation takes these periodicals. Therefore, it is not necessary to subscribe to start educating yourself to smarter investing.

Price-Earnings Ratio (P/E Ratio) The price-earnings ratio is usually calculated by dividing the current price by the latest 12 months' earnings per share. By comparing these P/E ratios within a segment of the market, say, the chemical industry, you are able to see how well this one stock matches up with the other competing stocks. It is always wise to check a market segment's average P/E ratio as you begin to research one particular company. If the P/E ratio of the particular company you are interested in has a much higher-than-normal ratio, then you should begin to think it might be overvalued; conversely, a lower P/E might indicate undervalued. However, this is not a total view of a company. Although the P/E ratio does help you with an easy comparison, it only is expressing what is known about price and earnings. As a rule when purchasing stocks, the lower P/E ratio stocks will tend to give you a better long-term run. Therefore, you should limit your purchases to stocks with a P/E ratio below 13, the historical average. Growth and income stocks with P/E ratios in the 7 to 12 range will generally do well in time. Generally, the stock price should be in the lower half of the past 10 years' P/E ratio range.

Dividend Increase Always pick an income-producing stock that has increased dividends in at least 8 of the past 12 years without a decrease and that shows a dividend increase of 100% during that time.

Financial Stability Using the *Value Line*'s "Company's Financial Strength," it should range in the A, A+, or A++ category for income and growth.

Ownership When investing in smaller companies, always look for a substantial ownership by management because it has a vested interest in seeing that the stock improves. This concept can be best understood by looking at our government. If it were run as a business, the board of directors would have been fired years ago.

Dividend Payout The dividend payout should not rise over 65% of earnings. This figure can be found in *Value Line* as "Percentage of all Dividends to Net Profit." You must be sure that the company will be able to pay a dividend. When you are concerned with income, you should also check to see if the record of dividend payouts extends into the 20-year range.

Debt Structure Long-term debt should not be more than 25% of capitalization.

Earnings Growth and Predictability This is probably the most difficult area to pinpoint. Research in recent years shows that past earnings growth rates are of little value when evaluating future growth, or even in predicting the direction of change. Earnings growth estimates, found under "Annual Rates of Change" in *Value Line,* will help you evaluate the problem. When dealing with growth stock, the percentage earned on net worth should be higher than 16% for the company to have a sustained growth rate.

Safety Rating of *Value Line* For consideration as a growth stock, the safety rating should not be below 2; for an income stock, 1 or 2 is adequate.

Because there are so many different stock selection methods, it would be inappropriate for me to suggest that one has all the answers to all your needs. As soon as one emerges into the forefront, another tackles it from behind. Check the list of Additional Readings on p. 250 to find books that will help you better understand the market.

Bonds

Every portfolio should include some bonds, whether it be a deferred compensation portfolio, retirement portfolio, or investors just "getting their feet wet." You should understand that bonds are debt. At certain times in the economy, you should not be lending a great deal of your money. The length of time a debt instrument should be purchased has a direct correlation with where you think the interest rates are going during that time.

Understanding the yield curve offers one of the best basic tools in deciding which maturity will give the highest yield with the least amount of risk. When a fixed-rate security is being priced, one of the important things for those making the offering is to decide where rates will be in the future. Rates are largely influenced by two factors: current demand (short term) and inflation/deflation expectations (long term). By understanding the yield curve, you can decide which bond is best for you. Compare the yield curves on currently available U.S. securities (from several months to 30 years out) with what corporate choices are available and make a better decision.

There are four basic types of yield curves with which you should be familiar:

1. **The normal or positive curve** (Fig. 8–1). This curve is a gradual upward slope and shows there is a steady increase in yields as maturities lengthen. The idea is that rates

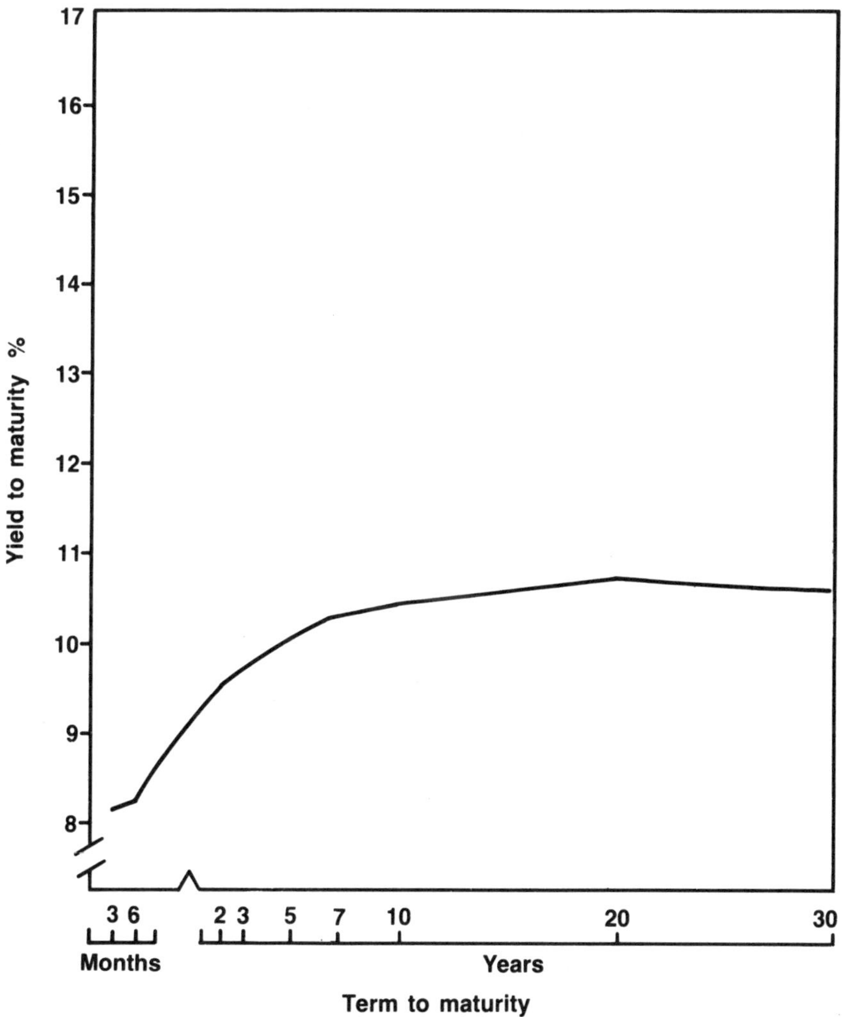

Figure 8–1 The normal or positive yield curve

will rise over time, so an investor should get more interest to induce him to commit his money over a long period.

2. **The negative yield curve** (Fig. 8–2). This is seen when interest rates are particularly high. Short-term instruments actually offer higher rates than long-term investments when a negative yield curve prevails. The concept of the negative yield curve is that interest will certainly decline over time from current levels. For the investor, it is gen-

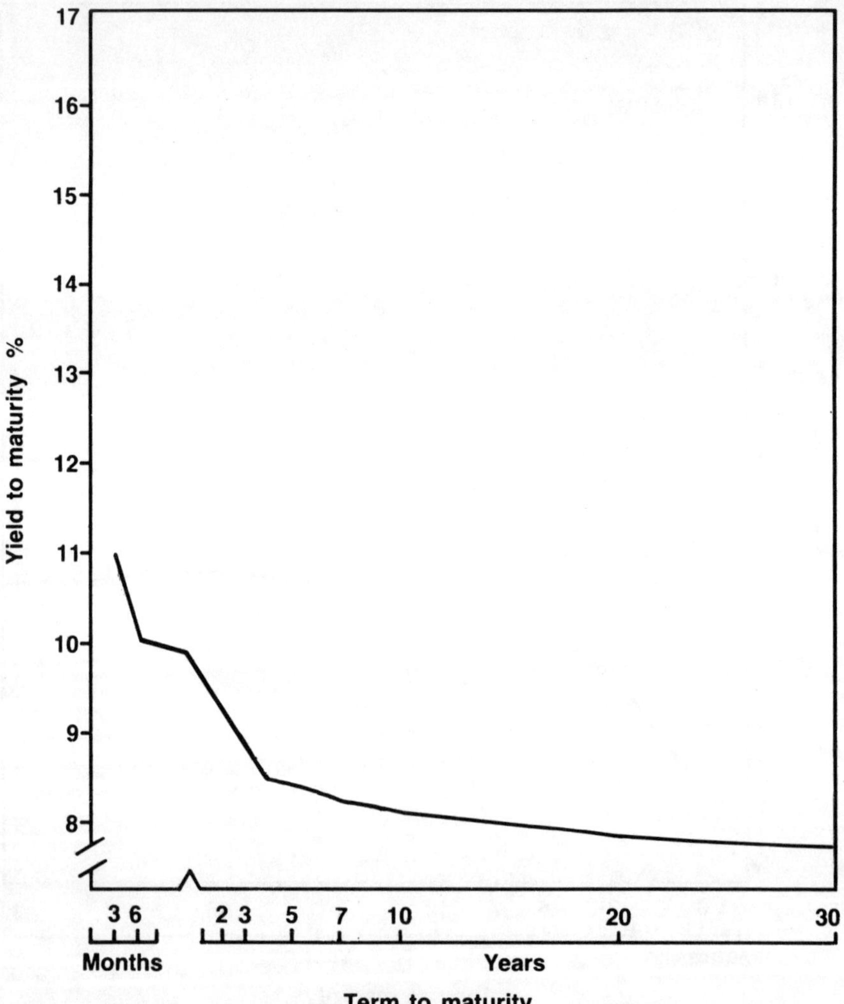

Figure 8–2 The negative yield curve

erally a good idea to buy medium maturities when the yield curve is negative. If interest rates decline, the investor will have locked in a relative attractive rate.

3. **The flat or horizontal curve (Fig. 8–3).** This curve is most commonly seen during a transition in the economy. Under the flat curve, short-term yields are only slightly higher than long-term yields. It is a good bet to assume that a flat yield curve means that even the experts do not know what

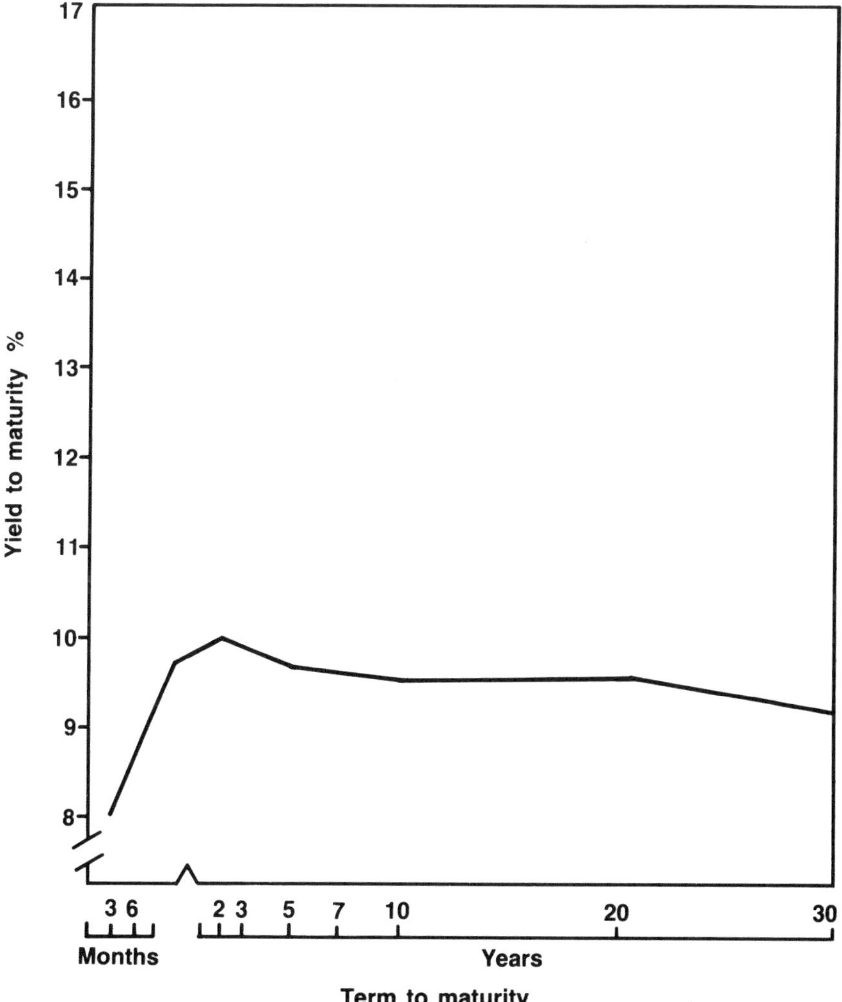

Figure 8–3 The flat or horizontal yield curve

to expect. Take a cue from the experts during a flat yield curve—keep your options open. Stay with very short maturities. A money market fund is a good idea when the yield curve is flat.

4. **The humpback or camel curve** (Fig. 8–4). The humpback curve is indicative of relatively low short-term rates followed by higher intermediate-term rates over the long

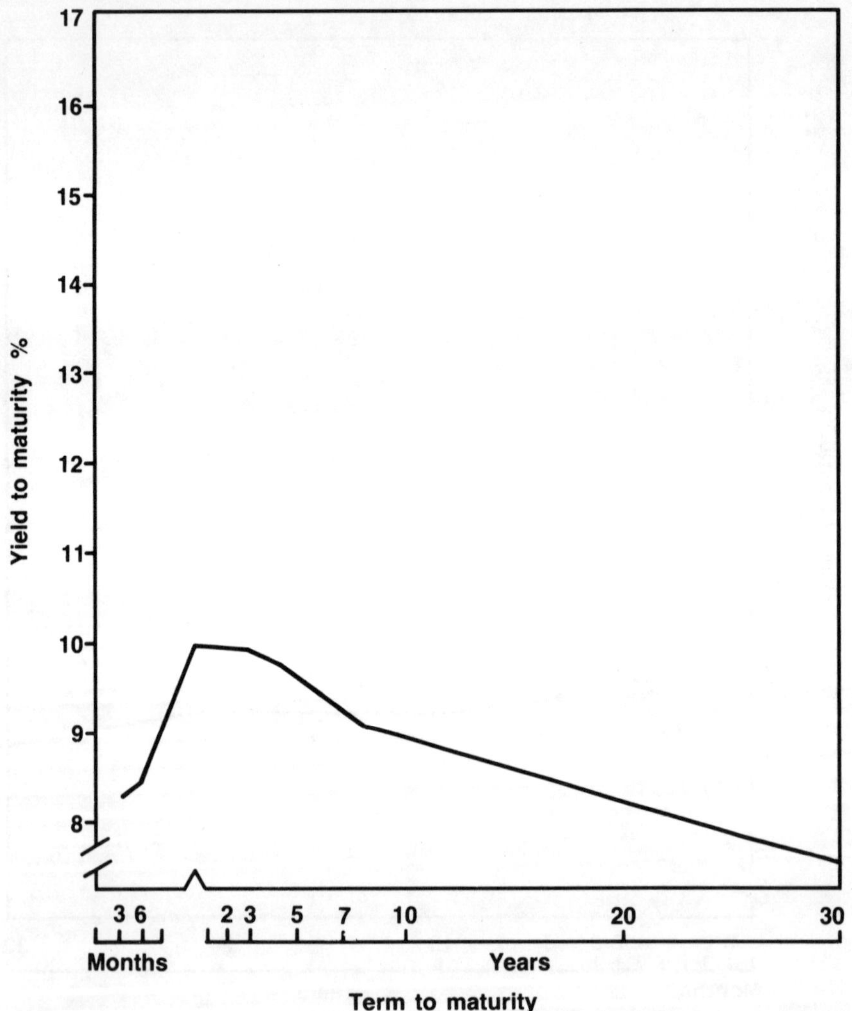

Figure 8–4 The humpback or camel yield curve

term. In this situation, it is a good idea to be no further out than three to four years.

Bond yields are often misunderstood. There are five that you should be aware of when talking to a broker so that you are sure you understand exactly what you are paying for. You do not get any credit for "But I thought you meant . . . ."

1. The **coupon or nominal yield** is the yield that is stated on the bond.
2. The **actual yield** is the yield based on what you paid for the bond.
3. The **current yield** is the yield based on the current price of the bond. It is higher when there has been a decline in the price and lower when there has been a rise in bond prices.
4. **Yield to maturity** is figured when a bond is held to maturity. This is an important tool used by professionals. Following are five easy steps to determine the yield to maturity. Here, you will be able to see that the spread between the selling price of the bond and face (par) value can give you capital gains treatment taxed at a lower rate.

    a. Subtract the current bond price from its face value.
    b. Divide the quotient by the number of years to maturity.
    c. Add all the annual interest payments to redemption.
    d. Add the face price and the current price and divide by two.
    e. Divide the annual interest payments by the face price.

5. The **discount yield** is most often used on issues of less than one year, such as Treasury bills that are discounted. It is essentially just the opposite of yield to maturity.

Risk is an important aspect of debt. Many of us do not think of debt as risk. But you are in fact risking that the principal and interest will not be repaid, that the interest rates will move higher and leave you without the ability to sell the bond before maturity, and that you will receive what you paid for the bond. Another important risk pointed out in the late '70s is that inflation can severely erode purchasing power. The yield curve can help you avoid some mistakes. At 4% inflation, the reduction on a $1,000 bond would be $324 in 10 years, leaving only $676.00 in purchasing power. This is why I do not think that you should purchase bonds with maturity dates of more than 7 to 10 years. If you guessed wrong on inflation rates, your purchasing power could be near zero. There are exceptions, such as zero coupon bonds for deferred compensation plans, but in general stay away from long-term bonds unless you fully understand the vagaries of the bond market and are willing to trade bonds.

Taxation is always an important consideration, and I will discuss that aspect of selection in the section on tax-free bonds. Another important consideration is the difficulty of compounding. Seldom does the interest rate offered on new bonds stay the same during the length of time you own the bond. Therefore, you have a difficult time reinvesting the interest you receive to achieve compounding at the same rate. This problem is one successfully addressed by the zero coupon bonds. I remain an enthusiast for the zero corporate and government bonds for children's education and deferred compensation plans.

In real estate, you have heard that location, location, and location make the successful investment. In my opinion, in individual bonds, quality, quality, and quality make the successful investment. I still find dentists who call a broker and are more interested in the amount of interest on the debt than the quality of the debt. The ratings by Standard & Poor and Moody are similar. If you find the rating significantly lower with one of these services than the others, check it out thoroughly. Because these firms do not rate all debt offerings, I suggest you keep your investments in bonds to those rated A or better with these services.

Junk bonds are ideal investments in a bond mutual fund; however, for the average investor, buying individual junk bonds is asking for trouble. When buying junk bonds, knowledge is power. Although quite rewarding for the knowledgeable inves-

Standard and Poor	Moody	Quality
AAA	Aaa	Highest
AA (+)	Aa	Excellent
A (+)	A	Good
BBB (+)	Baa	Acceptable

tor, it's like walking in a mine field for the uninitiated. Anything lower than BBB or Baa should be considered speculative.

The bond market has almost any type of bond available, from debentures to zero coupon bonds. The important technical point is whether the debt is considered unsecured. I say "technically" because the investment in time and money to retrieve your principal would be enormous. Frankly, you would almost have to go the same route if it were secured. If it is secured, as in mortgage bonds, a specific property is placed as collateral. An unsecured and uncollateralized bond is subject to the ability of the corporation to pay the interest and repay the debt. That is why the financial strength of the company is important.

In corporate issues, stick with quality, medium (7- to 10-year) maturity dates and you will minimize your trouble with risk, inflation, or any of the other criteria set forth. Do not overlook discounted bonds as a way to receive a more favorably taxed capital gain at maturity.

Government Issues

The U.S. Government issues securities that span the loan period from as little as 13 weeks to 30 years. Many people in the investment business believe Government issues are the best all-around investment. One investment counselor recently confided to me that if dentists would just put their money in government notes and roll them over every 2 years, they would have an excellent return—in fact, better than most of the stock brokers, shelter experts, and Ouija board consultants have been able to do for them.

Treasury bills are issued in 3-month, 6-month, and 1-year maturities. *Treasury notes* are medium-term obligations with a maturity from 1 to 10 years. Unlike Treasury bills, Treasury notes are not bought at a discount but have interest paid twice yearly to the holder. *Treasury bonds* that have maturities from 10 to 30 years are most commonly sold in the 20- to 30-year range and may, like some corporate and tax-free bonds, be callable at par value no more than 5 years to maturity. Interest rates tend to be stable and are not subject to the whims of the market as seen in stock, commodities, and future markets.

Government agencies have more than 100 different issues, such as the Federal Land Bank and the Federal Home Loan Bank. These issues generally pay slightly more than the Treasury series and often match the yields of the highest grades of corporate bonds. The only catch with these bonds is that in odd lots they might be a little harder to sell. But if you have diversified correctly, you will not be selling these except in extreme emergencies.

If you write to the Federal Reserve of Richmond, Virginia, you will receive a booklet on how to buy T-bills, notes, and bonds from the Reserve system, thereby avoiding the commission on the purchase that banks charge. Uncle Sam pays the charge. There are some excellent books on bonds that I suggest you read thoroughly before you begin investing in bonds so that you understand all the vagaries of all the bond markets. Consult the Additional Reading section on p. 250.

Zero Coupon Bonds

Most of us think of J.C. Penney as the retail store where many of our children's clothes were purchased. But you should remember J.C. Penney as the first company to issue the zero coupon bond. In 1981, it issued an 8-year bond which, when held to maturity, would yield 14.86% (1989). From that initial foray into a new area, zero coupon bonds have become an excellent investment vehicle, primarily because they are simple to understand. The corporate and government zero coupon bonds have been excellent investments for children's education and for deferred compensation plans. The most attractive aspect of a zero coupon bond is that the return on investment is known in advance, because the compound rate of return is figured into the price of the bond. There is no reinvestment risk as is found in a full coupon.

Be aware that not all brokerage companies charge the same commission. The bonds appear so inexpensive that most purchasers do not bother to compare similar bonds offered by other brokerage houses. When an investment becomes popular, you have to assume that someone will take advantage of the average investor. In addition, zero coupon bonds should generally be held until maturity. When interest rates are volatile, zero coupon bond prices vary widely. Therefore, they become riskier.

The zero coupon bonds that are made by buying long-term Treasuries, removing the interest coupons from the principal portion of the bonds, and selling the two pieces separately are sold under the names of TIGRs, CATs, Lions, and other "animals" by the various brokerage houses. This innovation was brought about by the investment firm of Merrill Lynch, whose zero treasuries go by the name TIGR (Treasury Investment Growth Receipts). In February 1985, Uncle Sam got into the act by offering STRIPS, Separate Trading of Registered Interest and Principal of Securities. STRIPS are safer than the brokerage offers because they come directly from the government, but the tradeoff is a slightly lower interest rate, generally 0.02 to 0.03 of a percent.

Although STRIPS are the safest, zero coupon bonds offered by corporations are the riskiest. Many corporations have entered this "fashionable" market to raise funds. At some point they will have to come up with a very large amount of money or the bonds may be in default. What lies ahead? There are so many variations on zero coupon bonds, such as growth and income hybrids and zero coupon bonds coupled with junk bonds, that only a fortune teller could see into the future.

Tax-Exempt Bonds

Tax-exempt bonds, or municipals, offer an excellent investment for those of us in the proper brackets. However, I often see dentists who would do better with General Motors bonds than municipal bonds. Municipals are debt issues of states, local governments, and some public authorities. A debt issue is free from federal and state taxation if you buy the bond in the state in which you reside. Debt issues from the District of Columbia, the Virgin Islands, and Puerto Rico are also exempt in all 50 states.

It is necessary that you understand the equivalent yield when you are deciding what to purchase (see Table 8–1).

$$\text{Taxable Equivalent Yield} = \frac{\text{Tax-Exempt Yield}}{100 - \text{Tax Bracket}}$$

Table 8–1
TAX-FREE YIELD

Tax Bracket	7%	8%	9%	10%	11%	12%
	is Equivalent to a Taxable Yield of					
25%	9.33	10.67	12.00	13.33	14.67	16.00
26%	9.46	10.81	12.16	13.51	14.86	16.22
28%	9.72	11.11	12.50	13.89	15.28	16.67
30%	10.00	11.43	12.86	14.29	15.71	17.14
33%	10.45	11.94	13.43	14.93	16.42	17.91
34%	10.61	12.12	13.64	15.15	16.67	18.18
38%	11.29	12.90	14.52	16.13	17.74	19.35
42%	12.07	13.79	15.52	17.24	18.97	20.69
45%	12.73	14.55	16.36	18.18	20.00	21.82
48%	13.46	15.38	17.31	19.23	21.15	23.08
49%	13.73	15.69	17.65	19.61	21.57	23.53
50%	14.00	16.00	18.00	20.00	22.00	24.00

Be sure to incorporate your state and federal tax into your tax bracket—do not just use the federal bracket unless you are purchasing tax-exempt bonds of your own state.

There are as many "sizes and shapes" of tax-exempt bonds as there are corporate bonds. *General obligation bonds* are considered the safest because they are backed by the full taxing power of the issuer. *Limited tax bonds* are repaid by a specific tax; *revenue bonds* are paid from the revenue of a particular project. There have been some toll roads that have never produced a dividend because the use was too low.

Following are 12 ideas to help you purchase tax-exempt bonds.

1. Try to buy in your own state.
2. Keep the maturity date below 10 years.
3. Understand the ratio of tax-exempt to taxable securities:

$$\frac{\text{Tax-exempt AAA State Bond (25 yrs)}}{\text{Treasury Bond (25 yrs)}}$$

Traditionally, the ratio has been 72. If the ratio is below 72, in the range of 65, municipals are not a good buy; if the ratio is above 72, in the 80 range, you should consider buying.

4. Be sure to adhere to quality, quality, quality.
5. Unless you know the town and its officials well, stick with state and large well-known authority bonds which have marketability.
6. If possible, buy from your broker's inventory. You can often get a good buy.
7. Consider buying bonds at a discount. Even with a capital gains tax, you may make a sizable profit.
8. Understand the bond buyer ratios, overall and competitive. *The Bond Buyer Newsletter* provides the overall price on all municipals and those that are competitive with the same quality.
9. If you have a choice, buy your bonds in December because bond-swapping during this month tends to reduce prices.
10. Consider unit trust only if you are planning to keep the bonds seven or more years.
11. Consider using a bond fund with only your state's bonds in it or a national mutual fund.
12. For a higher yield, use mutual funds that purchase and manage junk bonds. Fidelity and Vanguard, among others, have these funds, usually known as high-yield municipal funds.

Summary

Through the act of purchasing stock, one becomes the owner of a fractional part of a corporation. It behooves the stock purchaser to be informed about that company's business and management, about its history and, to whatever extent possible, its future.

Such information is gained through the use of various analytical techniques, including examinations of price/earnings ratio, dividend history, financial stability, dividend payout, debt structure, and safety rating.

When you acquire a bond, you have loaned money to a corporate or governmental entity. Bonds, therefore, are debts that are owed by borrowers to the holders of the bonds.

Bonds are structured in many different ways. It is important that you understand precisely what is being offered when you are contemplating the acquisition of a bond.

The value of bonds fluctuates with interest rates and the confidence of purchasers. The key word with bonds is *quality*. The conservative investor is well advised to acquire only those bonds that are rated A or better by one of the rating services.

CHAPTER

9

Mutual Funds

In my opinion, the mutual fund is perhaps the most efficient, responsive, and powerful investing tool for the individual dentist. Mutual funds began overseas, but the mutual fund we know today had its start in Boston in 1924. The Roaring Twenties hardly noticed the small mutual fund. But in 1940, the Investment Company Act made mutual funds one of the most regulated investment vehicles ever offered. The '40s through the '60s can be classified as the childhood of mutual funds. There were a lot of awkward times; most of the funds were extremely conservative and the high load or sales commission made it almost impossible to turn a big profit. When the market fell in the '60s, many mutual funds dropped like a stone.

The mutual fund industry began to develop different ways to help the investor; the market fund, one of the ideas spawned, changed the way Americans invested. At the beginning of the '80s, $75 billion were invested in money market funds. In just two years the involvement expanded to $206 billion.

An important benefactor of the mutual funds has been the Internal Revenue Service. Federal approval of such individual retirement programs as the IRA and Keogh have been valuable to the industry. (Today, there are more than 1,350 funds!) With this help, it was not long before you could buy mutual funds that traded domestically or internationally in options of every kind: common, preferred, over-the-counter stocks; sector funds; stock funds; start-up companies; long-term, short-term, and intermediate-term bonds; government bonds; corporate bonds; tax-exempt bonds; junk bonds; high-yield bonds; convertible bonds; mortgages; certificates of deposit; commercial paper; and precious metals. You could even buy a mutual fund that invested in mutual funds!

As in other investments, determine what you want: the degree of risk you can stand, the kind of return and growth you want, and when you want it. Know your tax position and make shrewd, calculated guesses for next year, the year after, and at retirement. Be as specific in all that as you can. Today, the array of available funds lets you select from within extremely fine tolerances. These developments have provided the individual investor with the kind of control—in some cases, virtually instantaneous fingertip control—that has made the mutual fund today's most important investment tool. Let's look at three different types of funds; the names will help you get the point.

A prospectus for Atilla the Fund might propose that it "assumes higher-than-average risk in search of long-term capital gains" and that its approach is "aggressive and venturesome." This fund invests almost entirely in stocks of relatively small, emerging growth companies. It is a fund for the few, the bold who have patience.

The objective of the Aunt Gertie Fund is to ". . . earn income through prudent investment of its capital in fixed-income securities such as bonds, dividend-paying common stocks, and government obligations." This one is a cup-of-tea-by-the-hearth type of fund.

The last fund, the Good Old Dentist Fund, says it wants to achieve ". . . high current income at a reduced rate of volatility with some growth." It primarily invests in common stocks and includes some that have call options and are traded on organized exchanges. Currently, the fund is making money on expired call options, net short-term gains from the sale of securities in its portfolio when options are exercised, and net profits from sales, dividends, and interest. No thrills, but plenty of good income and some capital gains.

Today, mutual funds are available through insurance companies, brokerage houses, banks, and the mutual companies themselves. I only purchase no-load and low-load funds, and deal directly with the mutual fund company. The value of your portion of the mutual funds fluctuates directly, relative to the value of their portfolio of stocks. At the end of every trading day, the market value of the fund is calculated and published in the newspaper in the form of the Net Asset Value, or NAV.

The NAV is the price (market value) of a single fund share on that day. NAVs are determined by dividing the total value of the fund porfolio (less its liabilities) by the total number of shares outstanding (owned) that day. For example, today the value of a fund is $975,000 and there are 100,000 shares outstanding. The NAV would be $9.75. Tomorrow the portfolio appreciates to $1,000,000, and the NAV increases to $10.00.

Modern mutual funds make their money from the management fee, which ranges from 0.5% to 1% of your investment, prorated and deducted before the NAV is reported. Some are lower; a few are higher. Federal law prohibits the use of the management fee for distribution and marketing costs. Because some of these fees have skyrocketed in recent years, many mutual funds that started as no-load funds have switched to a format called the low-load fund. These funds charge from 1% to 3% and their main intent is to keep you onboard.

A similar device, that I do not favor, is called the Contingent Deferred Sales Commission. This is charged to you at the time you leave the fund and is normally based on a sliding scale, the fee decreasing the longer you stick with the fund. You might be required to pay 5% the first year; but in five years, the fund might dwindle to zero.

There are four basic groups of mutual funds: money market mutual funds, growth mutual funds, growth and income mutual funds, and bond mutual funds.

The *money market mutual fund* is interested in current yield and price stability. These investments are made in short-term instruments that mature in less than a year. Therefore, there is little fluctuation in their value. Most money market mutual funds maintain an annual single-share value of $1. Risk is commensurately constantly low. Yields are closely related to short-term interest rates. During the first half of this decade, money market funds went as high as 17%.

Investment instruments include bankers' acceptances, time deposits, repurchase agreements, certificates of deposit, and commercial paper. The fund makes money on these investments in two ways: interest paid by the user (seller) and profit realized through buying the paper at a discount and selling it back at face value.

The second group of mutual funds is the *growth fund,* which has a certain amount of risk, a low income, and high growth as its criteria. Growth funds buy common stocks of aggressive companies on the move. Often, these companies are brash young world-beaters with more future promise than deliveries. Profits are plowed right back into research & development and expansion and debt service, so dividends are not the point. Growth funds make money by recognizing the product of genius coupled with excellent management, then buying in and staying in. Growth company buys are not for today but must be given time to mature and pay off. In the past 10 years, aggressive growth mutual funds have shown a total average return of slightly more than 510%!

The third group of mutual funds is the *growth and income funds.* They strive for a decent current return, coupled with an acceptable capital appreciation. The growth and income mutual fund sits on the fence quietly growing. It's not the type of fund that makes good cocktail party talk. However, in the past 10 years (1975 to 1985), Fidelity Equity Income managed a more than respectable 24+%. Not bad, no matter what type of fund you are talking about. In the past 10 years, the whole group beat the cost-of-living index by 240.9%

The fourth group is the *bond mutual funds.* These are for people who want immediate income rather than capital appreciation. Fixed-income funds invest primarily in bonds, which, as you know, are loans to companies or branches of government. Some fixed-income mutual funds buy only high-grade, low-risk bonds; others go in for higher-risk, lower-grade bonds, often referred to as junk bonds. The yield a bond pays reflects the prevailing interest rate at the time of its issue. The bond's price (value) may fluctuate in respone to changes in those prevailing rates. If the rates rise over what the bond is paying, the bond's price drops. If the rates decrease from what the bond is paying, the bond goes up.

Yields on high-grade corporate bonds have almost always exceeded the rate of inflation in the past 25 years. But at the same time, their total return has fluctuated widely. In 1967, for example, the average return was −4.4%, an all-time low. In 1982, on the other extreme, the average return was +48.5%, a 50-year high.

"Family" Planning

There are several large mutual fund companies such as American Capital, Fidelity, and Vanguard that furnish logistical support—diversity, low risk, professional managment—and allow you to be your own quarterback. In many ways, it pays to invest in a family of funds. This strategy gives you the ability to keep up with your funds easily because they are in one place and to divide your capital, for example, between blue chips and high-yield bonds, if that would please you. In addition, there is usually no charge for all-in-the-family switching. You can switch by letter or phone. The newest twist is the ability to use the "touch-switch" method. This allows your telephone to become a computer terminal. The Fidelity family of funds contains more than 30 such funds. In the example that follows, I used five of their funds to show what you might do for yourself.

1. Fidelity Cash Reserves provides high income and preservation of capital. Its investment objective is ". . . to seek the highest yields available from short-term money market instruments, both foreign and domestic, when consistent with preservation of capital and liquidity."
2. Fidelity Thrift income provides high income through its investment objectives to ". . . earn a high level of current income by investing primarily in high and upper-medium grade fixed-income obligations, with an average maturity of 10 years or less."
3. Fidelity Equity-Income's investment objective is to ". . . invest in income-producing equity securities and to achieve . . . dividend yield that exceeds the composite yield of the S&P 500 and has the potential for capital gain."
4. Fidelity Freedom Fund is designed for capital appreciation in tax-qualified plans. Its goal is to aggressively manage a portfolio of common stocks to provide the appreciation.
5. Fidelity Magellan has always been an aggressive fund designed for capital appreciation. It has one of the most enviable records in the mutual fund industry. It invests in common stocks or securities convertible into common stocks for its desired appreciation.

Table 9–1 shows $400,000 invested in different combinations of four of the Fidelity Funds over a 5-year period (1978–1982). Of course, the results shown here do not guarantee that they will perform this well in the future, but it does show management's ability.

Table 9–1
INVESTMENT SCHEDULE

	Capital Gains Received in Cash	Dividends Received in Cash	Value of Principal
100% Cash Reserves	$ —0—	$188,564	$400,000
100% Thrift Trust	—0—	211,056	385,156
100% Equity Income	151,796	159,232	595,640
100% Magellan	537,088	77,428	1,356,60 4
25% Cash Reserves	$ —0—	$ 47,141	$100,000
25% Thrift Trust	—0—	52,764	96,289
25% Equity Income	37,949	39,808	148,910
25% Magellan	134,272	19,357	339,151
Total Received	172,221	159,070	684,350
50% Cash Reserves	$ —0—	$ 94,282	$200,000
50% Thrift Trust	—0—	105,528	192,578
Total Received	—0—	199,810	392,578
50% Cash Reserves	$ —0—	$ 94,282	$200,000
50% Equity Income	75,897	79,615	297,821
Total Received	75,897	173,897	497,821
50% Cash Reserves	$ —0—	$ 94,282	$200,000
50% Magellan	268,544	38,715	678,302
Total Received	268,544	132,997	878,302
50% Thrift Trust	$ —0—	$105,528	$192,578
50% Equity Income	75,897	79,615	297,821
Total Received	75,897	185,143	490,399
50% Thrift Trust	$ —0—	$105,528	$192,578
50% Magellan	268,544	38,715	678,302
Total Received	268,544	144,243	870,880
50% Equity Income	$ 75,897	$ 79,615	$297,821
50% Magellan	268,544	38,715	678,302
Total Received	344,441	118,330	976,123

How To Select a Mutual Fund

Selecting a mutual fund need not be confusing. I have found that using these twelve guidelines will help you select a mutual fund that will best suit your needs.

1. Understand your objectives and what you consider your risk versus reward ratio; then choose one of these groups of funds: aggressive growth, growth, growth and income, or income.
2. Choose no-load or low-load funds, never more than a 3% load.
3. Look at the three-, five-, and ten-year results. When you rate the results, remember that three- and five-year results are the most important because you want current information.
4. Find out who manages the fund and how long he or she has been managing it. A simple phone call to the company will get you this information.
5. Order a prospectus for several funds you are considering.
6. Carefully consider the fund's stated objectives. You cannot tell a book by its cover. Sometimes the name has little to do with the fund's objective.
7. Research the BETA or volatility of the fund. If the BETA is 1, the fund will tend to move with the New York Stock Exchange composite average. If the BETA is 1.10, the fund will tend to move 10% or more up, or down, than the New York Stock Exchange Composite.
8. Research the Alpha of the fund. This measures nonmarket-related variability—how well the manager has succeeded in meeting the goals that were set. The measure works best with a diversified portfolio and is really not significant with "sector" funds such as gold, or only utility funds.
9. R^2 is the coefficient of determination. This determines the percentage of each fund's total risk that is caused by the market. If this is high, the fund is more likely to act in all ways similar to its Beta reading.
10. Find the yield of the fund. Usually, the lower yield means the stocks are bought for the fund for capital

appreciation. The average aggressive growth stock had a yield of 1.4% in 1984.

11. If you are having a difficult time deciding which is an aggressive growth fund and which is a growth fund, base your final decision on the Beta or volatility.
12. Judge continual growth. If you have done your homework and pare those funds from your holdings that do not perform, you will have a portfolio designed for growth.

Summary

Mutual funds are devices by which investors may benefit from the ongoing expertise of professional investment managers. Generally speaking, mutual funds are structured in such a way as to satisfy the needs and wants of particular investors. Some funds are designed for those seeking growth and appreciation; other funds are for those seeking income and security. As in all investment matters, the first imperative is that investors know themselves and their objectives.

The value of a share of a mutual fund varies daily with the value of the stocks and other investment instruments contained in the fund's portfolio. Mutual funds are an efficient and powerful investment vehicle and warrant the serious consideration of every dentist-investor.

CHAPTER

10

Options, Warrants, and Commodities

Writing call options as opposed to purchasing call options on stock that you own can be an excellent way to improve the return on your money. Many very conservative stock owners increase their yield significantly by this technique.

Options on major stocks have been listed since 1974, with some of the more recent option offerings, such as financial futures options, more exciting but a lot more speculative. Stay away from financial futures options in your retirement account. An option lets an investor control a large amount of stock for a given time.

Option trading has a whole language of its own, (puts, calls, striking price, in-the-money calls, etc.), and I would think you would find it very difficult to understand what your broker is talking about unless you do some reading. Start with a book such as Max Ansbacher's *The New Options Market.* Other information in layman's language can be obtained from the Chicago Board Options Exchange Marketing Services, 400 La Salle Street, Chicago, IL 60605 (1-800-535-CBOE). They have a particularly good booklet entitled "Understanding the Risks and Uses of Listed Options." If you want to read a service with specific recommendations, try *Value Line Options and Convertibles,* published four times monthly. You can probably get a copy of this from your library.

Remember, don't invest in something you don't understand! It takes good stock selection and constant monitoring, but selling options can boost income by 15% or more. I frankly think that selling options is investing, but buying options is more speculative.

The best way to attain safety plus income is to concentrate on stable stocks that pay sizeable dividends and whose option cost (known as the *premium* in option lingo) is not large. Another rule is to always write "close-to-the-money" calls, which means that you are writing (selling) a call very near the current price of the stock. The higher quality stock you can write calls on will prove to be the best bet. Higher-quality stocks tend to move slowly in price, either up or down, and their general potential can be more accurately projected. This is important because you are trying to add extra income to your stock's dividends, not be speculative. All profits with all options are short term, but this should not matter if you are writing them in a retirement plan.

Once you have decided to start using options, be persistent. In rising markets you will be writing calls, and in a falling market you will be writing puts. You may find that you are spending a good deal of time reading and understanding options. But once you get the hang of it, you'll find it fascinating and rewarding. This type of investment requires constant monitoring, so you and your broker should have an excellent understanding with each other. The expertise for making judgment calls is moderate to high, especially as it relates to timing. Once you understand options, you will find the conservative strategy is rather easy to follow, involves a minimum of risk, and can increase the return on your retirement funds considerably.

Warrants are just long-term options. Some even have no expiration date. Because of their volatility and the fact that they do not pay any dividend, I think they are inappropriate to use in conjunction with retirement funds.

While commodities are fascinating, they are also high-risk investments—or should I say gambles? Because you have to be right on the market all the time and the total loss of capital is probably more real here than any other area of investing, I would not want to have you invest your money in this highly volatile medium.

It is always important to understand other people's biases in recommending certain types of investments. Remember my slogan: "Nobody loves my money like I do." It will keep you out of trouble.

Summary

Other investment vehicles that are available include options, warrants, and commodities. An option is a device which allows an investor to control a large amount of stock for a given period of time. A warrant is much like an option only for a longer, or indefinite, period of time.

Options and warrants are investment vehicles that require constant monitoring. It is essential that you be informed about this type of investment before entering the options market.

Dealing in commodities involves more risk than would normally be prudent for a retirement portfolio. Such investments, therefore, are not advised for the readers of this book

CHAPTER

11

Real Estate and Precious Metals

Real Estate

Real estate has rightfully been called "America's Gold" because in no other country has real estate been available to everyone. In most instances, a family's home has been the largest part of their net worth. More Americans own homes than own stock. In the '60s and '70s, real estate was one way to build wealth easily through inflation. During the '60s the average home price grew at approximately 8% to 9% a year; in the '70s it grew at an even faster pace, doubling in value in less than 6 years (see Fig. 11–1).

Most dentists own their own home and many own the building in which their practice is located. This ownership has allowed many of their net worths to grow at a rapid rate. But nothing lasts forever, and this bonanza will not continue, at least at its historical pace. Commercial real estate will probably outpace homes in the next 10 years, but investors will not be allowed the luxury of throwing their money down and watching it grow.

Some astute real estate investors believe the market for single-family homes will remain soft for much of the next 10 years. When a variable-rate mortgage is used, an investor loses to rising monthly payments and, subsequently, the sales price. The homes that will be best for investment are smaller homes that are easily rentable and duplex apartments.

Many investors use the following four formulas when making decisions about purchasing rental property. It is important to know which yield is relevant to your particular situation—especially when talking to the realtor presenting the property. Let's take an example and see how the four formulas calculate yields on the real estate investment

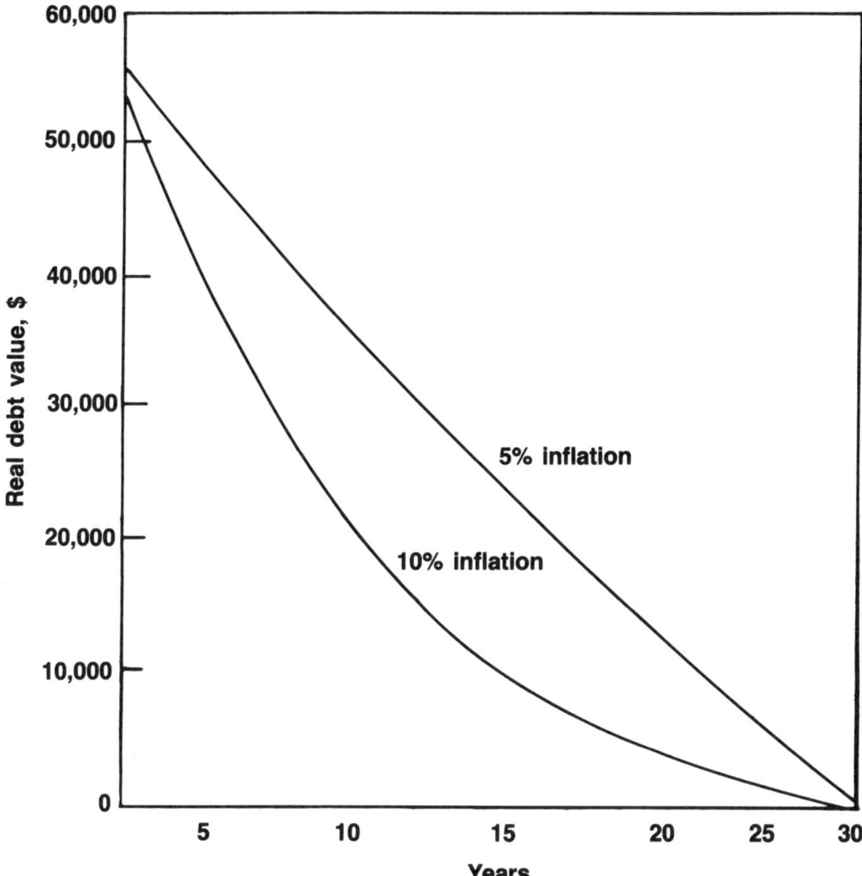

Figure 11–1 Mortgage value versus inflation

A 50% bracket investor buys an 8-unit apartment house for $240,000. He put up $40,000 and has a 20-year mortgage on the balance. Annual payments are $20,400 ($16,000 interest and $4,400 principal). Annual income from the building is $34,000; expenses are $10,000. After depreciation the first year, net taxable income is $3,600.

Purchased price	= $240,000	Mortgage interest	= $16,000
Cash payment	= $ 40,000	Net taxable income	= $ 3,600
Net income	= $ 24,400	Tax bracket	= 50%
Mortgage payments	= $ 20,000		

1. **Broker's yield** is used by brokers when they represent yield on properties. It is simple net income as a percentage of purchase price:

$$\text{Broker's Yield} = \frac{\text{Net Income}}{\text{Purchase Price}} = \frac{34{,}400 - 10{,}000}{240{,}000} = 10.17\%$$

2. **Yield on equity after mortgage payment** concerns the investor's return on initial cash outlay. It is net income less mortgage payments as a percentage of cash down payment:

$$\text{Yield on Equity after Mortgage Payment} = \frac{\text{Net Income less Mortgage Payments}}{\text{Cash Down Payment}} = \frac{34{,}400 - 20{,}400}{40{,}000} = 10.0\%$$

3. **Yield on equity after mortgage interest** is calculated by assuming that principal payments on mortgage increase the investor's equity. Hence, they are added to the investor's profit:

$$\text{Yield of Equity after Mortgage Interest} = \frac{\text{Net Income less Interest}}{\text{Cash Down Payment}} = \frac{24{,}400 - 16{,}000}{40{,}000} = 21.0\%$$

4. **Yield on equity after mortgage interest, including tax savings,** reflects the significance of tax benefits of investing in real estate, including equity buildup of principal payments:

$$\text{Yield on Equity Mortgage Interest Including Tax Savings} = \frac{\text{Net Income less Interest plus Tax Effect}}{\text{Cash Down Payment}}$$

$$= \frac{24{,}400 - 16{,}000 + 0.50\ (3{,}300)}{40{,}000}$$

$$= \frac{10{,}200}{40{,}000} = 25.5\%$$

An investor should always judge performance by return on the equity accrued to the property since he owned it, not the return on down payment. If the return gets too low, he can shift to another property. It never ceases to amaze me how many professional persons are talked into buying a property with a negative cash flow. Careful investors buy properties with a positive or break-even cash flow as well as appreciation potential.

It would be an excellent idea for a dentist interested in owning real estate as an investment to follow a successful investor around for a week. Such things as leaving too much equity in individual properties, holding properties too long, and not thinking of exchanging properties but selling them would be stopped. Too often, dentists form unneccesary "local" partnerships. I recommend limiting your real estate investments to single-family homes and duplexes—partnerships should be left to public and large private offerings.

It only takes a little time with a pro to shape up a poor investment track record. It would be worth paying someone to teach you in a hands-on atmosphere. You would learn how to check out properties much better than taking a realtor's word for it. Full-time real estate investors will show you how to use a "housing engineer" (structural engineer) to evaluate a building, and when to consider using a program such as the National Association of Realtors "Home Protection Program." If you look around your town or ask a few realtors, you will come up with someone. And you'll be really surprised at how delighted they will be to share some of their ideas with you.

You should always look at four areas when purchasing former rental property. These can be your checklist to be sure you have not overlooked anything.

1. **A copy of the leases.** It's necessary to see who is obligated for what length of time and what rent and services are offered. Things such as "any repair bill under $50.00 must be assumed by the rentor" will make many tenants take better care of the disposal and toilet and avoid nonsense repair calls.

2. **A copy of the mortgage.** You should know whether the mortgage is assumable and what problems might arise with this mortgage.

3. **A copy of the past three years' tax returns on the property.** If the validity of the worksheets is questioned, verification will be found on the tax returns. It is not probable that the current owner would try to fool the IRS. If he did, you could offer to sell the property back or call his hand.
4. **A survey of the land.** You should know what you are buying and be sure the property is as represented.

Like so many endeavors, the first purchase as an investor is the toughest—financially and psychologically. Once you have established a track record, you have nothing to worry about. You know you can do it; better yet, the banks know you can do it. Reading books like Robert Allen's *Nothing Down* and *Creating Wealth* and Peter Pace's *The Complete Book of Real Estate Math* will help you understand how to use different techniques to attain the same goals. A 20% down payment is not always necessary, nor are you always required to obtain a mortgage from the savings and loan. But at the same time, tape a note on your bathroom mirror that says "Happiness is a positive cash flow!"*

Precious Metals

No investment seems to be as emotional as gold. You either love it and think it should be held as part of a portfolio, or you feel it is un-American and, therefore, owning it is against motherhood, apple pie, and the flag. In reality, precious metals are a hedge against inflation for most investors. Therefore, they should be part of your portfolio, like long-term government securities that are held for security against the day that we have deflation. The two investments offset each other.

An ounce of gold costs about $250 to mine when all the mining companies average their costs. Therefore, you could consider that no miners want to sell their gold below their cost. In fact, copper has sold for less than the cost of mining and, for short periods, so have most other metals. If $250 is theoretically the break-even point, then gold sold within a range of 20% of that point is considered a good buy. Within the 5% to 10% range it is considered an excellent buy. As a pure investment, gold is not so

*Chapter 12 gives additional ideas on real estate investing.

good because it does not pay dividends or interest and there is always the chance of being swindled. On top of that, there are fees for storage. It should be held primarily as an insurance against inflation. But like other insurance policies, you should decide how much you can afford to own.

For conservative investors, the 1970s were unsettling. Many dentists had most of their assets in bonds and certificates of deposit, known as "certificates of depreciation" as inflation raged on. Coupled with the fact that the U.S. government stopped its gold auctions in 1979, the price of gold began to move upward. The auctions tended to be a deterrent to gold rising because the government was selling between 500,000 and 1,500,000 ounces.

Although jewelry is enjoyable to wear and to give as gifts, you should understand that the workmanship affects price. For example, the price of a gold bracelet could be 100% or more higher than the actual cost of the gold. One-of-a-kind gold antiques can hold their unique value; a bracelet in mass production will not. If you buy an object just to own gold, you're choosing the most expensive way to own it.

Four gold coins are actively traded and worthwhile: the $20 U.S. gold piece, the Mexican peso, the Austrian corona, the Canadian maple leaf.* The $20 U.S. gold piece trades with a much larger premium (about 25% to 30%) than do the others, which have a premium in the range of 2% to 8% above the price of an ounce of gold on any trading day. *Barron's,* the financial newspaper obtained at any newsstand, publishes the prices and premiums of these and other coins weekly.

Rare coins are excellent as investments if you are willing to take the time to become an expert as in any other areas of "collectibles." The bullion content in a gold coin is easily known, but the collector's part of the value depends on many things, such as condition and number available to purchase. Gold should also be held in stock form. I believe that 50% of your gold holdings should be in stock, preferably through a mutual fund. There is

---

*The South African Kruggerrand has been one of the most popular coins in America; however, with the strife in South Africa, the Kruggerrand may lose its popular appeal. But it should not be sold into bad press, for gold is gold. It will always have a strong secondary market.

nothing wrong with owning gold in bullion form, but I prefer to limit gold possession to that held in coins and in stock.

Generally, silver should be priced in a 40:1 ratio with gold. If gold is selling for $320 an ounce, then silver should be very near $8 an ounce. This ratio can be important when you plan on purchasing more precious metals for your portfolio. However, supply and demand is equally important—perhaps even more so than the historic ratio. You can judge for yourself which metal you should purchase.

Silver can be purchased in pre-1964 U.S. coins known as "junk silver," and many "Gold Bugs" feel that you should have a bag of junk silver for each member of your family. The premium on junk silver and silver dollars is in the range of 9% to 10%. This is considerably higher than owning gold in the 1-oz. troy bar, which has a premium of about 4%. Other than the physical ownership of silver, it should also be owned in mutual funds or in individual stock, and in the ratio of 50% metal and 50% stock.

Generally, I think it is important to own gold and silver in a 2:1 ratio, two ounces of gold for every one of silver. But this is no firm rule, just a ratio with which I feel comfortable. Becoming obsessed with precious metal ownership is just as bad as other obsessions. Costly at best.

Summary

For many dentists, real estate holdings are a significant part of their net worth. Most dentists own their homes and many their offices. The value of such holdings has risen at a rapid rate during the last couple of decades.

Growth in real estate values are leveling, however, and smaller homes and duplexes appear to be the best route for investors interested in owning rental properties.

As with any investment, investors must be knowledgeable of real estate to be successful. Time spent with realtors and full-time real estate investors will prove rewarding.

Precious metals are a hedge against inflation—nothing more. Since inflation is a reality, some precious metal holdings are prudent. Precious metals should be owned in the proportions of 50% metal and 50% stock.

CHAPTER

12

Tax Shelters

Almost 50 years ago, Judge Learned Hand uttered his famous statement that is just as true today. "Anyone may so arrange his affairs that his taxes shall be as low as possible; he is not bound to choose that pattern which will best pay the Treasury; there is not even a patriotic duty to increase one's taxes." Tax planning is not intended to decrease the government's revenue share but is designed to increase the amount of money the investor has available to achieve his objectives.

The cardinal rule of sheltering is: **A tax shelter should be a good investment before it is a shelter.** Tax shelters can be divided into four different areas to better understand all shelters. The first group is exclusionary types of shelters, like tax-exempt issues such as municipals and their hybrids. In the second group are income-shifting tools such as short-term trusts and spousal remainder trusts. These first two areas have been previously discussed in this book. Third, there are deferred compensation shelters such as the Keogh, pension and profit sharing, and IRAs. The fourth area is "shelter" shelters, such as real estate, oil and gas, leasing, and research and development.

Deferred Compensation

Today, everyone should have some form of deferred compensation. Currently, it is the best tax shelter available. Because of tax law changes, there is little consequential difference between Keogh plans and corporate pension and profit-sharing plans, other than the ability to borrow money from the corporate plans. The size of your retirement plan will be principally governed by the size of your contributions and the age at which your contributions start, as you saw in the discussion on the time value of money.

Top-heavy plans—plans in which one or two people will receive the majority of funds—should always be custom-produced by an attorney and not a boiler-plate or generic product of a brokerage house, savings and loan, or mutual fund. By allowing the use of a boiler-plate plan, you spend more to save money without needed flexibility.

The younger you are, the more a defined-contribution plan will work in your favor. However, if you are in the range of age 50, have not been able to save all that you would like, and suspect a shortfall in the amount of your retirement funds, a crossover to a defined benefit plan is recommended. Different authors put the age for the most effective crossover between ages 49 and 53.

If you are incorporated and have not yet started a retirement plan, you should start with the profit-sharing plan. If you have a bad year and cannot fund a profit-sharing plan, no harm is done—but you must fund a pension plan even if you must borrow to do so. With a profit-sharing plan, you also have the option of using a formula with a percentage of the profits or any amount up to 15%. A profit-sharing plan is more cost-effective because you do not need an actuarial service.

This is perhaps not the place to discuss whether you should incorporate. However, because this book does not intend to address that specifically, I will only say that books such as *Incorporating Your Talents* by Esperti and Petersen (published by McGraw-Hill) and discussions with a knowledgeable tax attorney who is able to review your business records should be the source of this advice.

Incorporation has to be worked at to make it profitable. In my opinion, there are still distinct advantages to being incorporated. But this should be reviewed with someone who understands your objectives, temperament, and circumstances. Too many dental corporations have never taken advantage of the initial reasons they incorporated. They seem to have been formed by those following the leader, and in many instances cost more than they are worth.

Properly organized Keogh plans using the 401K rules will allow for a contribution for the staff of about 10% and for the dentist of around 20%. In a corporate plan, this will rise about 5% for each category, allowing the staff about 15% and the dentist 25%. Because there are so many deferred compensation plans and each case is different, a competent attorney should be consulted. But no boiler-plate plan should be instituted.

Everyone should have an IRA. The money should be allocated according to your philosophy of investment. I believe that no-load mutual funds and families of funds are ideal ways to invest this money. You can use a different fund each year or move your money around in a family of funds according to how you interpret the market. Zero coupon bonds are also popular. This particular method of investing is heavily advertised because once you have started an IRA with, for example, a savings and loan, you will tend to leave it there and add to it yearly. This is not a good strategy, but the investment companies are aware of human nature, so it pays to "set the hook."

Equally important to getting your money into a deferred plan is how to get it out. Presently an IRA gives you no choice but to withdraw the funds during a prescribed time, using a formula based on your age and likely lifespan. Other deferred-compensation plans provide some choices. If you are a key employee in a top-heavy plan, or if the proceeds are in an IRA, the distributions must be in the taxable year in which you, the key employee or IRA owner, becomes 70½ years of age, regardless of whether you have retired.

Because each situation is different, once you have set a retirement date, you should thoroughly familiarize yourself with the alternatives because, as tax law changes occur, you may find that one alternative may be better than another. The 10-year forward averaging that has been so popular, and which may be eliminated by Congress, has been ideal for some, but all choices *must* be considered individually. Some dentists want to maximize the after-tax cash flow from their retirement income; others may be more interested in passing on a larger estate at death. After your own ability to manage the investments, the most pertinent points to consider are:

1. The amount to be distributed from the plan.
2. Your marginal tax bracket during retirement. With a little pencil-pushing, you should be able to estimate what will be needed.
3. Your pretax rate of return on investments. By keeping your money in an IRA, tax deferral benefits are always greater when interest rates are high and, conversely, less when they are low.
4. The longer the distribution period, the more probable the IRA will make enough to offset the taxes.
5. No doubt taxation of Social Security will become progressively higher for those able to have an income other than Social Security benefits.
6. Estate tax considerations.

Many of you will have a sufficient amount in a deferred-compensation plan to warrant having a tax attorney and your accountant look over your plans. Too much may be at stake to leave it to chance.

"Shelter" Shelters

Different tax shelters have different economic benefits. There are tax shelters for every time in your life. The old saw that "Nothing is certain except death and taxes" reminds us that we will need to be concerned about taxes even after retirement. Shelters such as unleveraged real estate give you an income, appreciation, and some write-off, whereas those that are highly leveraged give you little income but plenty of write-off and appreciation.

Do you have what it takes to invest in a shelter? Discretionary income and a reasonable cash flow are a necessity to avoid trouble. Many dentists looking for ways to pay fewer taxes do not have an ongoing cash flow. As soon as they have decreased the tax they owe to Uncle Sam, they immediately want to sell to raise cash to "put out another fire." Do not lose sight of the fact that a shelter should first be a good investment and only secondly a way to reduce taxes. Rarely do you get out of any investment quickly and make a profit. If you are going to lose money on an investment, it is better to lose it on a tax shelter than on stock—the tax law treats you better.

Understanding your risk threshold is also important. Oil and gas drilling is a high-risk investment, whereas the purchase of an existing real estate tax shelter is moderate. Always choose one that will not only make money, but one in which the money is equitably split between the general partner and the limited partners.

The most common vehicle for the "shelter" shelters is the limited partnership. The limited partnership is the ideal vehicle because tax benefits and gains can be passed to the individual investor; in addition, a limited partner has limited liability. For a limited partnership to exist, it is necessary that it not have any more than two of the following:

1. Centralized management. Limited partners have no voice in running the partnership.
2. Limited liability for the limited partner. The general partner is usually a corporation that allows for limited liability. The general partner is required to have a net worth of 10% of the total contributions over $2.5 million.
3. Continuity of life is there only as long as the general partner remains. When the general partner leaves, the partnership is dissolved. Another alternative is to put a limit on the length of the partnership, usually 15 years.
4. Transferability of ownership of limited partners' shares is rigidly controlled by the general partner; only a certain percentage can change hands in a given year.

Certain criteria should be looked at for any investment, particularly a sheltered one. The most important single criteria, after the economics of the shelter and its tax consequences, is to know something about the general partner and his track record. It is never prudent to use a general partner who is learning at your expense. A major point should be to examine the general partner; examine the results he or she has obtained from previous partnerships. Evaluating how much money the general partner is putting into this particular partnership often will let you know how much time he or she will devote to its success.

Generally, I do not think it is a good idea to invest in what is known as a "blind pool." In other words, the general partner is going to see how much money he can raise before he goes to purchase property. Frequently, this creates a situation in which you are paying more for a property than it is worth.

Now that you have worked through all these pointers, before you invest you should decide how you intend to get out. Never get into an investment of any sort without asking yourself, "If I don't like this investment, how can I get out, and what are the financial and legal consequences?" This is never as true as it is in tax sheltered investing.

Check out the shelter broker you are using. I recommend that you use the following list of do's and don'ts when you are making a decision. I do not recommend one of the large brokerage firms for purchasing your shelters; rather, choose a firm that specializes only in tax shelter brokerage. They are generally more knowledgeable than the average brokerage house. They spend time educating you about tax shelters as an investment because they want you for a continuing customer, and they only have one type of investment to sell. Of course, there are exceptions to this rule.

Do

1. Ask for a rèsumé of the broker's experience in the field.
2. Ask the broker to provide a list of previous purchasers for references.
3. Ask the broker which programs he or she has recommended in the past 4 years and how well they have done.
4. Determine which firm did the "Due Diligence" on the offering.
5. Ask the broker for a detailed explanation of the economics and the tax-sheltering aspects of the offering.

Don't

1. Do not be afraid to say "No" if you are uncomfortable with the offering; there will be others.
2. Remember, buy the economics, not the shelter.
3. Do not buy in December because good offerings are gone; only sucker bait is left.
4. Check the offering through the *Stanger Register* or an attorney who specializes in tax-shelter work.
5. Do not forget to check the financial stability of the company.

Oil and Gas Drilling Programs

Approximately 30% of the money put into tax shelters in any given year is put into oil and gas shelters. There are three basic programs with oil and gas investments: developmental, exploratory, and balanced. The developmental program drills in areas with proved reserves; therefore, income usually starts within 18 to 24 months. Although some firms begin a return on money sooner, this is out of the ordinary. An exploratory program has a higher risk, but also the higher reward for taking that risk. The cash flow will usually start within 30 to 36 months. "Wildcatting" is exploratory drilling whose rewards are based on a roll of the dice; the risks for controlled exploratory drilling are somewhat tempered. The third program is balanced, really a combination of the first two types, but not in a 50:50 ratio.

What kind of program should you look for? I recommend a developmental or balanced program. Usually, the best balanced programs are those that are approximately 80% developmental and 20% controlled exploratory. I do not think you should attempt wildcatting unless you have an inside track. The same holds true for private placements. I do not believe that the average dentist involved in a private placement can win. You must have the right connections in oil and gas to make the incredible returns about which you hear.

Once you have considered the available programs, decide on a structure of a drilling partnership. There are four ways to structure a drilling partnership. Two you should consider; two should be avoided.

1. **Functional allocation.** The limited partner pays all the intangible drilling costs, which are deductible. This structure gives you the most write-off the first year. The general partner pays for the completion costs. If you find oil, the general partner will produce and sell it. Usually, the general partner will receive 40% of the revenue; the limited partners will receive 60%. Although the general partner will sometimes invest 15% of the funds from the beginning, this is not always true.

2. **Promoted interest.** In this arrangement, the general partner shares all the costs from the beginning. The only

drawback with this structure is that it does not give you a sizeable write-off. However, many experts in the oil and gas field like this structure best. The general partner usually invests 10% and receives 20% of the revenues from the wells.

3. **Reversionary interest.** This is used essentially by general partners who do not have a track record and are trying to "break in" to the oil and gas business. The general partner will not receive a return on his investment until you have been paid. From then on, the returns are split on a preset formula. I believe a dentist should stay away from any but the most experienced general partner.

4. **Carried interest.** In my opinion, this is the worst structure. The return in dollars and write-off is poor.

I recommend you use a public program registered with the Securities and Exchange Commission. I think most public offerings have excellent management and are more closely scrutinized than a private company. Most programs are sold on the basis of management expertise in the area in which they will drill. Choose either a developmental or a balanced program that is structured as a functional allocation or a promoted interest.

Oil and gas can be rewarding if you have a quality program. You must have the money and the psyche to withstand the risk. Understanding your goals will help you decide whether you want an income fund that has the lowest risk of any of the oil and gas investments; a completion fund, which is essentially in the middle; or a drilling fund, which has the highest risk but the highest rewards. Income funds are not discussed here but have been good for pension plans, with the notable exception of Petro-Lewis. Many dentists have that fund, but the outcome is yet to be seen.

It is essential to diversify your investments in this field. If you are going to invest $15,000, you should diversify that money into three different partnerships. Understand that when you look back on it with your 20/20 hindsight, you may see that one had a remarkable track record, one was above average, and one was a "dog." Don't blame your tax shelter broker or yourself. If you had only chosen one program, you might have gotten the "dog!"

Real Estate Shelters

More than 60% of the money invested in tax shelters every year is put into real estate. No wonder. We are educated to understand the tax losses and equity buildup of home ownership, thanks to the generosity of the federal tax laws. Most countries do not allow their citizens the luxury of writing off their interest on their federal taxes. Real estate will always be a good investment, but not the unbelievable one it was for many in the 1970s. In my opinion, the '80s will be cyclical in the real estate market; to win you must have more experience. No longer will you be able to put your money down and be assured of coming out a winner every time.

Single-family homes and duplex apartments will continue to be good investments, but you will need to study real estate mathematics to move into the success circle. One excellent way to understand real estate is to take the courses leading to becoming a realtor. It is not necessary to actually become a realtor, but exposure to the courses provides insights from the other side. Many books on real estate are also valuable information sources.

If location, location, location is Number One in real estate, then economics, economics, economics has got to be Number Two. Too many investors stop when they think they have picked the spot. There are unsuccessful buildings in great real estate towns. A market analysis will help you understand the risk involved. Do not try to invest in one of the cities that is a "hit" today. You must have a 5- to 8-year head start.

I recommend that you start thinking about investing in national limited partnerships such as Equitec and JMB-Carlysle. They, and other successful national partnerships, have returned 18% to 20% after-tax return on the invested funds to participants in the 50% bracket. Because the market will be tougher for many investors, and because you can get varying degrees of shelter, I recommend you get your feet wet in some national partnerships. Both Equitec and JMB have toll-free numbers you can contact that can put you in touch with the regional representative. Although these are offered through brokerage houses, I think you will get more time from the regional representative and, consequently, more understanding.

I like national limited partnerships for dentists in the areas of apartments because more than 20% of the population lives in apartments. Existing shopping centers and office buildings are good investments because much of the risk is behind the investor. The major syndicators give you a larger view and strategy, they seek AAA properties, and they will diversify across the nation. The financial sophistication and management are usually ahead of local efforts at starting a partnership. The offer of liquidity is possible through large limited partnerships. On a local level liquidity might not be possible, regardless of the price of the property. You may find yourself invested with a group who can not or will not buy you out. There are now companies who do nothing but purchase investors' interest in real estate limited partnerships.

Leasing

Leasing as a tax shelter is easy to understand because most of us have leased something. Today, it is one of the hottest areas of tax sheltering, especially for those in high-income brackets. It involves two entities: a lessor (in this case, the limited partners) and a lessee (the one leasing the equipment). Large companies lease equipment because it is to their advantage not to tie up large amounts of cash. Frequently, the lease payments are no higher than the loan payment and, because it can be expensed, it gives them more flexibility in what they do with their capital.

Essentially, as a result of the 1981 Economic Recovery Tax Act, the government controls the useful or depreciable life of most equipment. The most common depreciation terms are 3, 5, and 10 years. The limited partnership uses the lease payments to cover the bank financing; the majority of the tax benefits are received through depreciation of the equipment. Payout is usually designed to pay the partnership loan during the first lease. If the equipment is leasable after the initial lease, the partners make money during the second lease period and at the sale of the property at the end.

In the past, container leasing has been an excellent tax shelter investment. These containers are those you see on flatbed railroad cars and ships. Not only has the demand been strong, but the price of containers has significantly increased over the past 10 years, allowing the initial investment to be recouped when the container was sold.

Liquidity is not as available as it is in real estate and oil and gas, although some partnerships will try to accommodate your needs. Try to purchase a limited partnership that will have a reasonable life in the 5- to 8-year range, will be usable afterwards, and will have a slight income in the 7% to 8% range. If structured properly, the write-off will be substantial.

Other Shelters

Other shelters such as cattle breeding and feeding, horse farms, and research and development only amount to 5% or 6% of the tax shelter market. I believe dentists should avoid these. Only the knowledgeable should use those types of shelters—there is plenty of money to be made in oil and gas and real estate. Leasing allows for large write-offs for those in the high brackets with a return on investment at the end of the lease period.

Talent Scouts and Other Ideas

Not everyone likes to spend time with investments. If you think you could spend your time to better advantage, then one of my recommendations would be that you find someone to do it for you. There are firms which specialize in bringing you and the right investment advisor together. For instance, you can meet with one of these talent scouts and if, after several talks, you agree on what your goals are, he or she will find an investment counselor who fits your criteria. Beyond that, the scout will monitor the firm for you on a quarterly, semiannual, or yearly basis to be certain the performance is still the best for your criteria.

This has become big business. It is an ideal way to have your money invested if you are not interested in managing it yourself. How do these talent scouts get paid? They usually have a link with a large brokerage house, and the trades are made through that particular company.

Another idea is to use information from *Pension and Investment Age,* 740 Rush Street, Chicago, IL 60611. This periodical rates the performances of trust departments of banks on a quarterly basis. By taking a newsletter like this, you can find which banks perform best overall. As in purchasing one of the 1,350 mutual funds available on the market today, it is not important to be in the Number One bank all the time. In a recent issue, over 20 banks had a 5-year return on their commingled equity accounts of over 20%. That's not bad, considering what most investors get on their self-managed accounts.

Remember the old maxim: "It's better to have your money working for you than you working for money."

Summary

A tax shelter is a device that, as the term suggests, "shelters" income from taxation either permanently or for some period of time. Tax shelters have been designed to encourage investment in certain areas. Through the prudent use of tax shelters and the consequent tax savings, investors may increase the money they have available to attain their objectives.

The first rule of any tax shelter is that it must be a sound investment. Shelters that lose money are worse than taxes.

Tax shelters exist in four broad categories: (1) exclusionary types such as tax-free municipals, (2) income-shifting devices such as Clifford or Spousal Remainder trusts, (3) deferred compensation mechanisms such as Keogh plans and IRAs, and (4) "shelter" shelters such as limited partnerships in real estate and oil and gas programs.

For those who find the demands of financial management onerous, seeking the services of an investment counselor is well advised. Talent scout firms specialize in directing clients to those counselors who are best suited to assist clients in meeting their objectives.

SECTION IV

FINANCIAL PLANNING FOR DENTAL FAMILIES

Until now, you've been reading *my* views on planning for a solid financial future in retirement. This final section presents the subject from the view of the professional financial planner.

Financial planning has become a new profession because of the important need to implement and monitor our entire game plan. Although anyone can be his own financial planner, I believe that professional experience gives the investor an important edge. If your financial plan is properly implemented, it will need annual fine-tuning. As your circumstances change, your financial plan should be manipulated to reflect that change. You should remain flexible and in tune with the changing political and social climates that dictate modifications in your investments.

CHAPTER

13

Roundtable Discussion

In this chapter, financial planners have been invited to answer questions about financial planning for the professional. The respondants are Richard Whitehead and Barbara Naylor of Whitehead Financial Advisors, Atlanta, GA; Roberta Jean Smith of the Matrix Group, Santa Monica, CA; H. Jack Free of H. Jack Free Advisory Corp, Summerville, S.C.; and J. Randall Hedlund of Financial Management Consultants, Overland Park, KS.

Jackson: *What is the biggest deterrent today that limits a dentist from attaining a comfortable retirement?*

Naylor: The biggest deterrent limiting anyone, especially the professional, is the attitude that today's needs are more important than tomorrow's. As a dental wife, I have labeled this the "philosophy of entitlement."

Many doctors and their wives feel "entitled" to a higher and higher standard of living. They have paid their dues in the struggling, early years of a practice and now, with the financial rewards coming in, they feel entitled to earmark those funds to fulfill their dreams. It becomes a vicious cycle of more, bigger and better, and with no regard to the future.

Fortunately, with foresight and early financial planning, they could have both. They could see their dreams come true and be comfortably positioned for retirement.

Smith: Lack of planning and/or bad financial advice are major deterrents. As a matter of public policy, the tax code has several options to encourage retirement building through tax-deferred retirement vehicles. Every person with personal service income can start an IRA. Unincorporated individuals should consider Keoghs; professional corporations should look to Qualified Retirement Plans. A combined Money Purchase Pension and Profit-Sharing Plan in early stages of professional development followed by a Defined Benefit Plan during middle and latter periods is ideal.

A twofold planning device, retirement plans offer ideal tax shelter and wealth-building opportunity. As a first-choice tax shelter, they allow minimum risk for return. As a wealth builder, they allow controlled investment management.

Hedlund: A comfortable retirement requires a combination of good planning, reasonable effort, some willingness to defer immediate gratification to accumulate for future needs, and a modicum of good luck. Today dentistry is a more competitive field. This may affect the earning potential of dentists in general and some practitioners in particular. However, the biggest deterrent to a dentist's retirement is no different from that of most other people: a combination of inertia and a limited time and knowledge of the alternatives available.

Free: Failure to recognize the basic principles as you go through a period of learning, earning, and *yearning*. You must understand that you need to save a part of every dollar to build an income-producing estate for your later years. Once this point is fully recognized and the desire is there to provide a comfortable retirement for yourself and your family, everything else becomes secondary.

Jackson: *When should a practitioner start planning for his or her retirement?*

Hedlund: It is never too soon and it is never too late to start planning for retirement.

Planning can start when the dentist is in his early 30s if the income is unusually high or if there are extra dollars from some other source. Early retirement is often well within reach when the planning starts this early. For most people, specific planning starts some time after age 40. The practitioner is entering his or her highest earning years, and investable dollars should be plentiful. Also, the children are in or nearing college, and the end of their financial support is in sight. If planning is delayed until the 50s, accelerated planning is necessary and early retirement is usually out of the question. If planning is delayed until the 60s, it is really more a matter of stretching whatever dollars happen to be there than it is planning and implementing a long-term strategy.

Smith: Because young people rarely perceive themselves as older people, most people in their 20s and 30s do not plan for retirement. Of course, the sooner a retirement plan is started, the longer you have to accumulate a substantial amount of money and to lower your risk of not reaching your retirement earning stream.

Initially, retirement funds should be viewed as a tax shelter, the conservative element of tax minimization technologies, rather than as a retirement planning vehicle. As people pass their 35th birthday, they become more responsive to retirement goals and the specifics of later life cycle planning. At that point, what was once a tax shelter becomes the cornerstone of future security.

Free: Mental planning really starts with the answer to the first question. To begin with, the dentist must recognize that he is going to have this in front of him. I recommend cash flow projections at the onset of the dentist's income. It may not be possible for a dentist to allocate funds for retirement as soon as he starts to practice. For example, he may want to purchase a mid-range home and furniture, and arrange his lifestyle to accommodate for saving for the education of his children. Often a second home can be enjoyed and later be used as an investment. But this planning starts by spending less for the cost of living than the dentist earns. For some, the problem is not a high cost of living but a *high living cost*. I think it is probably wrong to start with an IRA or Keogh plan or any retirement planning until the dentist knows that he will be able to manage the mammoth expense of educating his children.

Although charts show that an IRA plan started 10 years earlier than normal can result in a substantial sum for retirement, I believe it is folly to create financial problems by borrowing to educate children because you have placed a priority on setting money aside for your retirement.

Recognize what you need to do, set your goals, and then place priorities on your needs so that each goal is met. Obviously, the goals for a single person will differ from those of a person with a family. Spending habits, the size of the family, and the amount of your income will influence your timing of the implementation of a retirement plan.

Jackson: *What do you consider the most important element in financial planning?*

Smith: Without doubt, clients' goals drive the planning process. Planning is a meaningless bag of tricks if not based on clearly defined and stated goals. Goals are future states, a describable set of characteristics to occur within bracketed time periods, for example, 5, 10, or 15 or more years. "I wanna get rich" is *not* a goal. "I want to spend three months traveling in the Far East when I am 47 years old" is a goal.

Part and parcel of the planning process is defining the risk premiums the client is willing to assume when goals are being funded. Trade-offs can then be rational, based on goal priority and willingness to assume risks.

Whitehead: Apart from starting with a good game plan that recognizes and quantifies a client's objectives, investment advice is the most critical element in financial planning. The most important elements in good investment advice are sound portfolio design, performance monitoring, and progress reporting. Performance compared to objectives is more important than performance alone. It permits investors to understand where they are and, therefore, avoid unnecessary risk, which is the biggest threat to any financial plan.

Hedlund: Financial planning combines a broad range of skills and knowledge, from an understanding of investment vehicles and tax laws to an understanding of the overall economy. However, the most important element is the ability to make common-sense decisions, given incomplete or conflicting information and a lack of time to exhaustively research every alternative.

Free: The most important element of financial planning is to look at assets as a future source of income. Luxury items such as expensive automobiles, mink coats, diamond rings and exotic vacations are nice to have, but they must be considered as the cost of living (or high living cost). Assets such as stocks, mutual funds, or investment property are different. A million dollars in equity that might be positioned in securities or real estate at 10% annual return will provide an unlimited annual income of $100,000. If the assets are properly monitored, the principal could increase even while providing an annual income of $100,000. Those who have inherited assets are already aware of the tremendous value in not spending the principal. Of course, those people who have no desire to leave anything to children or charity would differ with this view. If you are motivated to build an income-producing estate and adopt a plan and timetable to do so, choose other professionals to help you through the important steps. The first step is to recognize the need to have an income-producing estate of a specified amount of money, adjusted for expected inflation, by a certain date.

Jackson: *What types of investments would you consider inappropriate for a retirement account?*

Hedlund: Generally investments with a high degree of risk are inappropriate for retirement accounts. These would include commodities, research and development partnerships, speculative stocks, oil and gas drilling, and almost anything purchased on margin or with borrowed money. Investments most appropriate for retirement accounts are interest-bearing ones, for example, CDs or bonds which provide a high degree of security and presently an unusually high yield. A distinctly second choice would be real estate and other forms of equity, but only those that are relatively stable in income-generating potential or market value.

Smith: Aside from any investment prohibited because of unrelated business income rules, I consider high-risk, speculative investments inappropriate. Although venture capital deals may seem inappropriate for the cornerstone of future financial security, this mismatch is not my main reason for disliking speculation in retirement accounts.

Instead, my recommendations are based on the "highest and best use" concept often used in real estate. Outside of tax deferral, ordinary income commands the highest tax and, respectively, a lower after-tax return; within tax deferral, ordinary income commands the highest return for the least amount of risk. The effects of compounding pretax interest are hard to beat. Only a minority of a retirement portfolio should be in nonincome-producing assets (no more than 25%). Under no circumstances should a retirement plan include a whole life insurance policy.

Free: Inflation is the greatest risk for the long-term investor. Therefore, I never recommend a fixed-dollar investment such as a mortgage, savings account, certificate of deposit, fixed-dollar annuity, or corporate or government bonds as permanent investments. These investments are good for the short term. In my opinion, you should recognize that you will be dealing with 5% or 6% inflation and taxes of over 40% a year. You will need to earn 15% or more on your money to have any growth after taxes and inflation. Money can be made with the fluctuation of interest rates affecting the value of bonds, but this calls for a managed account with a view toward appreciation of principal rather than to long-term yield. Your principal is ten times more important than the income on the principal. Therefore, you should protect your principal from erosion by inflation or taxes. All fixed-dollar investments are eroded by inflation.

Jackson: *Where can an investor find a good tax shelter?*

Whitehead: Lots of places. First, you need to know what a tax shelter is and why you are looking for one. Most common tax shelters are those that allow you to reduce your taxes through deductions and credits. Frequently, people let that be the sole criterion for making the investment, rather than its economic ramifications. They take on too much risk in the name of tax deductions. We explain to people that tax shelter investing is a way to control a valuable or potentially valuable investment with little or no money out of your own pocket. With this type of investment, we hope to increase a person's net worth after the tax shelter is eventually sold. The purpose, therefore, is to increase wealth without incurring inordinate risk, rather than reducing taxes.

Jackson: *How can dentists protect themselves against salespeople? How can they avoid being taken advantage of?*

Whitehead: You can avoid dealing with salespeople by dealing with fee-only advisors who are objective and not compensated with commissions. If unable to find a fee-only planner who meets the criteria, you should have an independent planner not aligned with one of the major financial products firms.

Hedlund: Do not respond to "hype" or "sellers' puff," the unsubstantiated and often irrelevant facts or opinions about the product. The salesperson will give you what you respond to. If you react positively to the "fluff," that is what you will get.

Ask the salesperson to explain specifically what you are buying. A brief explanation of the general concept is fine, but almost every investment can be broken into a few relatively simple components that are understandable. Get to the specifics.

Do not be overly influenced by who else is "in" the deal or "sure to go into it" unless you really know them and their ability to analyze the deal.

If you are not interested, say so quickly and quietly. An explanation is not always necessary. This will save time. If you really are interested but have some reservations, state your objections clearly and specifically. Listen to the response. If the response is evasive or manipulative, it probably means that your objections are valid. If the response is relevant, your objections may be eliminated or the risks acknowledged. If you still want to make the investment, at least you are going in with your eyes open.

Ask the salesperson for a description of the specific risks of the investment or, alternatively, for what kinds of people or situations it is not well suited. If he or she cannot answer the question, do not trust the assurances that it is a good deal. Do not be afraid to pass up a good deal. The risk of that is *much* less than the risk of buying a turkey.

Smith: The self-serving answer to this question is: establish an ongoing advisory relationship with a fee-only financial planner and refer all salespersons to that advisor.

If you do wish to retain an advisor, do some homework. First consider taking some courses on portfolio management from the local university to learn risk assessment. Second, habitually read articles in *Barron's* that have question-and-answer interviews with money managers and describe investment fraud and failures. The interviews give insight to professional thought processes, and the fraud articles reveal the many ways you can be bilked.

The objective of this homework is to collect a series of standard screening questions, sorted by type of investment. Before speaking with any salesperson, have at least three questions in mind. Interrupt the sales pitch to ask the questions. Appear knowledgeable and control the conversation. If the salesperson just wants the commission, he or she will probably move on to an easier sell. Always request a prospectus. Be very skeptical if the salesperson downplays the prospectus or sends a summary instead of the actual disclosure document.

Jackson: *Where does the dentist get the help needed to design and monitor a portfolio?*

Whitehead: To find an appropriate advisor, you must first know what you are looking for: a good independent financial planner. To find one, you could contact the International Association for Financial Planning, the Institutue of Certified Financial Planners, or the National Association of Personal Financial Advisors.

You can also educate yourself by reading books, newsletters and magazines and by attending seminars. Seminars give you two things: factual information and the opportunity to talk to others in the audience, as well as the speakers, about where to find these experts.

Some characteristics of an advisor are:

1. A person who is an independent financial planner
2. Someone not affiliated with an insurance company or stock brokerage firm, thereby allowing the advisor the independence to make decisions and to conduct his or her own research

You need to determine the advisor's educational and professional qualifications and, particularly, experience. The advisor should have professional designations such as the CFP or CHFC. He or she should be a member of the Registry of Financial Planning Practitioners, the most highly qualified financial planners in the International Association for Financial Planning.

The optimum qualifications of an advisor would include an experienced, independent CFP, member of The Registry, who is knowledgeable about all types of investments and makes changes as needed, and who comes well recommended.

Jackson: *How important is diversification and what should be included in the diversified portfolio?*

Free: Diversification is very important. For many years, I have recommended a family of mutual funds. If you invest $1,000 in a common stock mutual fund, your investment will probably be spread in 50 or more individual companies chosen by a professional security analyst. Although this does not minimize the risk in the stocks, it does minimize the risk when compared to investing $1,000 in a single stock. A family of mutual funds allows you to transfer or change all or part of your holdings to another mutual fund with a different degree of risk such as bonds, utilities, municipals, money market fund, or balanced fund. Each time you move all or part of your holdings to another mutual fund, you immediately get diversification.

Owning and following a family of mutual funds should be an educational process. Once you understand how and why these funds work, you can see the advantage of owning a similar portfolio of real estate through a limited partnership. It is tough to be diversified when you invest in individual properties, unless you have a substantial sum of money. I do not discourage individual ownership of properties, but it does take more time to manage these properties than you may have available.

Hedlund: Diversification is very important. Because you cannot guarantee perfect decisions or the ability to anticipate all possible future outcomes, diversification is your main strategy for safety.

A well-diversified portfolio will combine a mix of fixed-dollar investments (bank accounts, CDs, corporate or municipal bonds) and equity-type investments (stocks, mutual funds, real estate, tangible assets). The mix depends on factors such as age, size of portfolio, expectations for inflation, and tax laws. Generally, the percentage of the investment portfolio in fixed-dollar assets is roughly equal to the investor's age.

Smith: "If you're sure, keep it pure. If you doubt, spread it out." Few rational investors are "sure" about the outcome of an investment. Diversification is the most important factor in portfolio design. Even a portfolio of all high-risk investments is less risky in total than any one included investment, if appropriately diversified.

How a well-diversified portfolio is structured depends on the business cycle stage and other macroeconomic factors such as Federal Reserve Board monetary policies. In disinflationary times, the portfolio should be weighted to financial assets, but the distribution should always include real assets as well as stocks and bonds.

Stocks should include 12 issues diversified over market tier, industry, Standard and Poor rating, and location. Bonds should include a mix of treasuries, munis, and corporates spread over 5 to 20 years, but with a weighted length of maturity (or call) not to exceed 10 to 12 years (or generally the point where the yield curve flattens out). If the amount of investable dollars does not allow for adequate diversification, at least $100,000, no-load mutual funds diversified by investment objectives are preferred. Real assets should include real estate, oil and gas, precious metals, either as individual investments or limited partnerships.

Jackson: *Can the average dentist who has been "financially planned" successfully manage his or her own investing?*

Hedlund: Yes, assuming that the average dentist has the time and the interest to do so. Financial planning is something that you do for yourself. A financial planner is a professional who can help in the process, but the impetus must come from you. Financial planners are no smarter than their clients but they (planners) do the same thing (manage finances) all day, every day, and they can get pretty good at it.

If financial planning is done well, there should not be a need for a lot of frequent "fine-tuning" or major decisions. The daily operations should go relatively simply unless major items are still being decided or implemented.

There will still be the need for an occasional visit with a professional to ensure that the planning is still on track at the time of a major decision.

Smith: Yes, but you must be willing to invest the time to stay informed and monitor individual investments. As a fee-only financial advisor, I believe any of my clients—successful, intelligent people—could manage their portfolios after I have written their financial plans. However, my clients value their time highly, earn more money working in their profession than they would from managing their investments. In other words, the opportunity costs are too high for self-managing their portfolios.

To decide whether to self-manage or hire a professional advisor, you should estimate your hourly wage as a practitioner, then assess how you want to spend your free time. On average you should expect to spend at least 10 hours a month seeking out and monitoring investments and be willing to invest in a personal computer, software, and financial periodicals, approximately $10,000. If your preferred quality of life would be tainted by such time commitment and capital expense, you should retain an advisor who charges less than your imputed hour wage.

Jackson: *Many dentists use gold in their professional practice. Do you think that precious metals are a good investment for dentists?*

Hedlund: Not particularly, although dentists may have a slight advantage over other investors because of their familiarity with the commodity.

If you are worried about a doomsday scenario, where we are reduced to a barter economy and a survivalist mentality, precious metals are an effective protection. However, raw metal is not as easily marketable (because of the potential for adulteration) as gold coins or other certified forms of bullion. If worried about the possible return of runaway inflation, gold mining stocks are better than bullion. There are no storage costs and they are more easily marketable. They also provide some dividend income while you are holding them.

If you are not particularly worried about the doomsday scenario or runaway inflation, there are other investments that will probably help you better achieve your financial objectives in a more stable economic environment.

Smith: Whether to add or decrease precious metals depends on several factors: what percentage the gold inventory represents of your asset base; whether inflationary or disinflationary trends prevail; and tolerance of the investor.

If inflation is accelerating, you may want to add precious metals holdings, probably through stocks or no-load gold mutual funds, given that your inventory is in the hard asset.

Alternatively, in disinflationary times, you may want to short gold, assuming your gold inventory then represents too high a percentage of your holdings. Depending on your willingness to assume risk, shorting may be accomplished through commodities, naked puts on ASA, or selling short a NYSE stock like Homestate Mining.

Jackson: *What are the most common mistakes practitioners make when entering the investment market?*

Hedlund: I am not sure "mistakes" is the best term to describe what happens when neophytes enter the investment market. In general, a new investor has an unrealistic expectation of how the marketplace operates. Some common misconceptins would include:

- Someone has all the answers and I have to find that person.
- All the information I need is available if I just work hard enough at gathering it.
- The future can be determined perfectly if I only have enough information.
- I can eliminate all luck from my decisions.
- I will never make an investment mistake.

Investment decisions are like any other decisions we make in our lives. The more decisions we make and the harder we work at them, the better the decisions will be. But there will always be mistakes and both good and bad luck. It also helps to take some of the ego out of the decision-making process.

Smith: There are several common mistakes:

1. Not having a master portfolio design to systematically allocate assets into investment categories over time. Rational investing is systematic and disciplined, done according to plan.

2. Failure to sell based on targeted returns. To force discipline, the new investor should place sell orders at percentage loss or gain (10%, 15%, 20%) when purchasing stock.

3. Failure to assess the risk/reward tradeoffs. All projected returns should be benchmarked against the risk-free rate of return, typically the 6-month T-bill rate. The greater the spread between the risk-free yield and the candidate investment, the greater the risk and probability of losing the capital invested. For example, if five-year Treasuries yield 10.8% and six-month T-bills yield 7.24%, the investor is assuming a 3.56% risk premium. Very speculative, venture capital deals anticipate 40% rates of return, a 32.76% risk premium. A well-managed mutual fund could yield 18%, a 10.76% risk premium.

4. Trusting investment judgment of colleagues and friends.

5. Failure to read prospectuses. In considering a limited partnership, for example, a minimum review includes (1) sources and uses of proceeds, (2) track record and financial strength of the general partner, (3) "Risks and Conflicts of Interest" sections.

6. Generally underestimating the amount of time and knowledge investing requires.

Free: You must segment your objectives into those that are short term, intermediate, and long term. Once you have defined your objectives, you must determine the cash flow commitment for each segment. Different investments are required for each objective, and a long-term strategy is necessary. For example, if you decide you must earn 15% or more each year on an investment to stay ahead of inflation and taxes, but fall short of that mark the first year, you should not become discouraged. Do not abandon a good long-term investment before it has time to mature. Above all you should be patient.

* * *

You can see that the financial planners who participated in the roundtable discussion are more than tuned to professionals and their needs. But in a sense it is only *common* sense. Just stopping to take stock of your circumstances, objectives, and temperament will be your first step forward to a more secure financial future.

Richard W. Whitehead and Barbara O. Naylor of Whitehead Financial Advisors, Atlanta, Georgia, have provided the financial scenarios of three dentists which are presented in the next three chapters. The discussions and analyses of these three families are representative of the kind of solid, thoughtful analysis and planning provided by competent financial planners.

The financial plans of the three dental families you will read about in Chapters 14, 15, and 16 are typical of professional families. You can learn a lot by studying these families and how they have planned their financial futures. These families may not be like you in age, lifestyle, or annual income, but having an inside look at how others have done it will help you plan your future.

CHAPTER

14

The Turner Family

Dr. James Turner is a 47-year-old solo practitioner of family dentistry. He lives with his wife, Cynthia, and two children, Mark and Lisa, in a midwestern community of 50,000. Twice a month, the family gets away to their lake cabin, only 75 miles from their home.

Dr. Turner's active and growing practice annually grosses $190,000; he believes it will continue to grow for another 5 to 7 years. The business is incorporated, and Dr. Turner has established a profit-sharing plan to which he makes maximum contributions each year. This year his salary is estimated to be $77,910.

Cynthia Turner, also age 47, has never worked outside the home, although she enjoys filling-in at the office when Dr. Turner is short-staffed. She has been active in civic and volunteer work as well as school activities with their children.

Mark Turner, age 20, is a junior at an eastern university majoring in electrical engineering. During high school, Mark worked part-time for a local manufacturing company. He works there full-time during the summer to earn money for his education. He is paying one-third of the cost of his education from savings, earnings, and student loans.

Lisa, age 16, is a high school junior and is very active in school activities. She plans to major in education at the state university.

Dr. Turner has taken a moderate approach to investing and money management over the years. Although he has dealt with the two local stock brokerage firms, Dr. Turner has no active trading accounts. He subscribes to several investment newsletters that provide his most reliable source of investment ideas and recommendations. Although Dr. Turner does not think he has to be overly conservative in his investments at his age, he wants to obtain more diversification. He will accept some risk of principal as long as the expected return is commensurate with the risk. He considers $15,000 in money market funds adequate for emergencies (see Table 14–1).

Table 14–1
DR. JAMES TURNER
FINANCIAL STATEMENT

Assets		**Liabilities**	
Cash Assets			
Cash & checking account	$ 1,000	Auto note (Ford)	$ 3,500
Money market fund	15,000	Home mortgage	60,000
Total cash/cash equivalent	$ 16,000	Lake home mortgage	47,500
		Total liabilities	$142,500
Invested Assets			
Growth stock portfolio	$ 40,900	**Net Worth**	$443,125
Municipal bond fund	12,600	**Total Liabilities & Net Worth**	$585,625
Krugerrands	10,200		
Corporate bonds	20,000		
IRA	6,425		
Keogh/profit-sharing plans	100,000		
Total invested assets	$190,125		
Personal Assets			
Residence	$125,000		
Lake home	65,000		
Automobiles	12,000		
Professional practice	142,500		
Personal property	35,000		
Total personal assets	$379,500		
Total Assets	$585,625		

Dr. Turner's Goals

Dr. Turner's long-range plan is focused on retirement at age 62. He wants to build his personal net worth and retirement plan balances so that he and Mrs. Turner can maintain their standard of living in retirement.

The family's short-term goals are to take a trip to Europe when the children graduate in 2 years and to provide for Lisa's college education.

Investments

Dr. Turner has built his stock portfolio with solid blue chip stocks, for example IBM, 3M, AT&T, and McDonalds. Growth has been satisfactory with few big losers. The compound rate of return during the past 3 years has been 9.0%, including dividends of 3.5%. The Krugerrands have declined by more than 50% in the past 5 years. The mutual fund of AA rated or better municipal bonds yields about 6.5%. In the past 18 months, the corporate bonds which pay 9.5% have appreciated about 30% and the municipal bond fund has increased by 17%. The money market fund yield is now about 8.0%.

Cash Flow

Dr. Turner's salary of $77,910 (see Table 14–2) is supplemented by dividends and interest of $5,425. After state, federal, and FICA taxes, the family has a discretionary income of $55,417 per year. They contribute $8,500 toward Mark's education, about two-thirds of the total cost. The family had been investing about 10% of their income until Mark entered college. Investments have been suspended until the children's educations have been completed. After Lisa graduates, they expect to resume making personal investments at a substantial level. Currently, their standard of living consumes $46,917, about $4,000 per month.

Table 14–2
DR. JAMES TURNER
CASH FLOW AND TAXES

	Cash Flow	Taxable Income
Income		
Salary	$ 77,910	$ 77,910
Dividends		
Stock portfolio	1,430	1,230
Municipal bond fund	820	—
Corporate bond fund	1,900	1,900
Interest	1,275	1,275
Subtotal, income	83,335	82,315
Deductions		
IRA	2,250	2,250
Personal exemptions (4)	—	4,160
Itemized deductions		
Taxes, state (5% top marginal rate)	3,900	3,900
Other	—	1,700
Interest, mortgages	—	875
Other	—	180
Contributions	—	2,300
Miscellaneous	—	450
Less: Zero bracket amount	—	(3,540)
Subtotal, deductions	(6,150)	(12,275)
Net Income	$ 77,185	$ 70,040
Less: Federal income tax	(18,976)	
FICA	(2,792)	
Discretionary Income	$ 55,417	
Less: College expenses*	(8,500)	
Investments	—	
Cost of Living	$ 46,917	

*Son pays balance of expenses from savings, earnings, and loans.

Retirement Plans

Dr. Turner's primary personal financial goal is to be able to retire in 2000, at age 62, with no diminishment in his standard of living. Of course, the family's lifestyle and the cost to maintain it will change, particularly with regard to their children, who should cease to be a financial responsibility 8 or 9 years before retirement.

Any retirement planning must account for inflation; however, one important expense in the Turners' budget is mortgage payments on the residence and lake cabin, both of which are fixed payments. Furthermore, because the house will be paid for by the year 2000 and the cabin shortly thereafter, this monthly expense of $1,167 can be deleted from the Turner's retirement income requirements.

The Turners' present cost of living, less the mortgage payments, is $32,917. The Turners have estimated that inflation will average 7% until their retirement; therefore, their annual income needs will then be about $90,878. Because this is the amount they will need to spend, income taxes must be considered. Although top marginal federal tax rate for the Turners is 42%, their total income taxes divided by the total income produces an effective tax rate of 27.4%.

If the inflation rate projected by the Turners proves to be as high as 7%, then it is hard to imagine their being in a lower tax bracket in retirement. Even with lower top marginal rates, as proposed by Congress and the Reagan Administration, and a switch to more tax-exempt bonds in their portfolio, the Turners will have an effective combined rate of at least 25% for state and federal income taxes. Therefore, their retirement assets must produce at least $121,090 to permit them to maintain their 1985 standard of living (see Table 14–3).

Retirement Analysis

The entire analysis of retirement funding rests on several very important assumptions: investment rates of return, ability to meet future savings goals, and inflation. Even a slight deviation can dramatically affect the feasibility of a comfortable

Table 14–3
DR. JAMES TURNER
FINANCIAL INDEPENDENCE/RETIREMENT COMPUTATION

I. Income Required to Maintain Standard of Living		$ 46,917
Adjusted income requirement*		$ 32,917
Income required in 2000 (age 62) with 7% inflation		$ 90,919
Before-tax income required†		$ 121,090
II. Capital Required in 2000 with 8% Return		$1,513,625
III. Capital Available	8%	10%
Personal investments‡		
1. Present value $ 99,700		
Value in 2000	$ 316,268	$ 416,467
2. Future additions: 1991–2000, $17,500/yr	273,796	306,796
Retirement plans		
1. Present IRA/Keogh balances = $106,425		
Value in 2000	337,760	444,558
2. New contributions		
a. Profit-sharing plan: 1985–90, $13,500/yr; 1991–2000, $15,000/yr	442,812	524,411
b. Pension plan: 1991–2000, $10,000/yr	172,100	192,843
Subtotal	$1,542,739	$1,885,075
Practice value (2000) @ 5% appreciation, after tax	236,995	236,995
Total capital available	$1,779,734	$2,122,070
IV. Surplus/(Deficit)	$ 266,109	$ 608,445
V. Income Available @ 8% Return	$ 142,379	$ 169,765

*Mortgage payments deleted: $1,167/month.
†Assuming effective federal and state tax rate of 25%.
‡At indicated growth rate.

retirement. Rates of return, if not achievable with certainty, are manageable. Continued saving requires discipline and adequate earnings. Although the Turners have no control over inflation, they should be able to adjust the components of an investment portfolio to maintain a favorable increment of return in excess of the rate of inflation. For example, if the Turners achieve a 9% return with 5% inflation; or a 15% return during an inflationary period of 11%, they should be able to meet planning goals. Because investment returns relative to inflation have historic precedence, a soundly managed portfolio may be expected to meet reasonable goals if risk is also properly managed.

The Turners want to accumulate enough capital so their retirement income will not require consumption of principal. Recognizing the impact of inflation and the burden of no reduction of principal, Dr. Turner will need to accumulate just over $1.5 million dollars to fund his retirement.

This objective appears to be achievable. Reasonable rates of investment return have been used for the analysis, and the required level of additional investments seems reasonable, barring unforeseen setbacks. In fact, the most conservative assumption made is the 8% rate of return on invested capital in retirement—only 1% over Dr. Turner's inflation estimate. If he is able to meet his growth objectives, a conservative retirement portfolio should be able to realize returns of 2% to 4% above inflation—if the assets are properly managed.

This analysis should provide Dr. Turner with a proper perspective for making investment decisions. He has expressed a willingness to accept greater risks if potential returns are commensurate with the risk. It does not appear that he needs to make any risky investments in search of higher returns because he doesn't need to "go for it." He can isolate his risk, taking to small amounts for therapeutic reasons.

Social Security benefits have not been included in this calculation. Because Dr. Turner's retirement is still 15 years away, it would seem unwise to include this benefit as an integral part of the plan. However, if Dr. Turner were to retire in 1985, at age 62, he would be eligible for maximum benefits of $7,126, which would equal 21.6% of the Turners' retirement income requirements.

Although it would seem unlikely that this benefit could be expected to produce 21% of Dr. and Mrs. Turner's income requirements in the year 2000, some comfort may be found in keeping this resource in mind as an additional cushion if it is needed. Fortunately, it appears that the Turners will be able to meet their needs from their own resources.

Two *rate-of-return assumptions* were made for the asset

accumulation period until retirement to illustrate the power of compound return and the importance of each "percent" of investment performance. By increasing his rates of return by only two percentage points in the next 15 years, Dr. Turner may generate an additional $342,336. This represents an extra 22.2% above the lower accumulation estimate of $1,542,739 (excluding the value of the practice, which is not subject to investment management).

Looking at this return differential another way, the lower estimate will exceed their basic need by only 1.9%. The larger investment accumulation total would exceed the basic requirement by 24.5%! Although the practice brings in another 15.7%, even without considering the value of the practice, the lesser accumulation would produce after-tax spendable income of $123,419 versus a need of $121,090. The larger accumulation would produce a yield of $150,806.

This exercise demonstrates the importance of obtaining the maximum value for the practice and carefully managing the investment portfolio so that extra percentage points of return can be received. Total portfolio monitoring and management should be able to increase the rate of return without increasing risk. The key to good portfolio management is proper portfolio design, monitoring, and minimization of losses.

Planning and Investment Recommendations

The first steps to be taken are administrative and do not require the investment of one dollar.

Education Funding for Lisa. The Turners are paying for their children's education with after-tax dollars. A fundamental strategy used in all education funding programs is to shift taxable income to the student who will be taxed at a lower rate. Consequently, less capital is required to produce the same amount of spendable after-tax income. The most popular strategies in the past have involved gifts to minors, interest-free loans, and Clifford trusts.

In 1984, interest-free loans were eliminated as a viable strategy by a change in the tax laws that imputed an interest rate to all loans in excess of $10,000. As a result, parents are deemed to have received interest equal to a rate set periodically by the federal government. Income taxes must be paid even though no interest is received and the children receive no offsetting deduction. Consequently, this strategy is no longer practical.

Gifts to minors require an irrevocable transfer of capital to the child. Thereafter, earnings in the custodial account are taxed to the child. Given enough time, this is a good way to accumulate for a child's education. Unfortunately, it involves the irrevocable transfer and ultimate consumption of funds earned by the parents in their higher tax brackets. The appeal of the method is that a small, steady transfer of capital over time can produce a meaningful treasure chest for the child, and all earnings after the transfer are taxable to the child. It is not an appropriate vehicle for funding near the beginning of college because the transfer of capital may be so large as to entail a taxable gift and a relatively minor amount of income will be taxed to the child instead of the parents, that is no meaningful shifting of income from higher to lower brackets.

Clifford trusts have been popular for many years because the earnings in the trust are taxed to the child, but the capital reverts to the parents after the minimum trust period (10 years). These are awkward vehicles because they must be established well in advance of the child's need (at age 11) if they are to pay for college and not continue beyond graduation. They also require a substantial amount of capital, usually $40,000 or more, which most families do not have when their children are young. The expense of establishing the trust and the administrative hassles and expense should not be overlooked.

Another caution concerning the use of family income-splitting through gifts to minors or trusts is that the Reagan Administration has proposed that all earnings received by children younger than 14 that are attributable to capital received from their parents are to be taxed to the parents. This limitation seems to find favor in Congress.

The Turners may find their solution in another strategy that is becoming increasingly popular: the Spousal Remainder Trust. Under such an arrangement, one spouse makes a gift to his or her spouse through a trust vehicle. During the term of the trust, a child can be named income beneficiary and receive the income that will be taxed at the child's lower rate. At the termination of the trust, the corpus passes to the spouse as his or her sole property.

Under the Spousal Remainder Trust, no gift tax is paid for the transfer to the spouse under the unlimited marital deduction for transfers between spouses and there is also no minimum term for the trust.

However, like a Clifford trust, the assets are tied up for a specified time, gift taxes may be incurred because of the gifting of income during the term of the trust, and there are administrative procedures and expenses. In addition, this approach has no solid support from the courts. IRS challenges to Clifford trusts have received many court decisions favoring the taxpayer. Spousal Remainder Trusts are too new for a similar accumulation of favorable court decisions.

The Spousal Remainder Trust may prove beneficial for the Turners because they have the capital to fund a trust for Lisa who is older than 14 and, therefore, the family would not be subject to the restrictive Administration tax proposals; the term of the trust can be less than 10 years; and an estate planning side benefit can be accomplished.

Because Mrs. Turner has few assets in her own name, her estate is underfunded with regard to her Unified Credit for gift and estate taxes. This means that she can leave a taxable estate of up to $400,000 ($600,000 in 1987) without paying estate taxes. Conversely, Dr. Turner's estate exceeds the $600,000 limit and any excess left to heirs other than his wife would be subject to tax. Therefore, it makes sense to reduce his estate by making gifts to Mrs. Turner so the children can benefit from the Unified Credit available to each parent.

To put the Spousal Remainder Trust into perspective, certain economic effects must be considered. If Lisa's college expenses at State are to average about $7,500 per year from 1987 to 1991, the total cost would be $37,385 (allowing for inflation of 8.5%), for which Dr. Turner would have to earn $66,878, pre-tax. His state and federal combined marginal tax rate is 44.9%. By transferring $50,000 into a Spousal Remainder Trust for six years and investing the funds in a portfolio of high-yielding corporate bonds at 11%, the family can generate $33,000 of income for Lisa's education. Assuming she earns more than $2,370 per year, Lisa's income taxes would be less than $700 per year. Dr. Turner's tax on this amount of income would be $2,470 per year—$1,770 more. Therefore, for a cost of $750 to $1,000 to establish the trust, the family could save about $10,620 in income taxes during the period from now until Lisa graduates from college. Dr. Turner would also have $50,000 less in his estate, and that could save his heirs at least $18,500 in estate taxes.

Increase Contributions to Qualified Retirement Plans. Currently, Dr. Turner has only a profit-sharing plan to which he can make a maximum contribution of only 15% ($11,686 this year). By adopting a Money Purchase Pension Plan (which, like a profit-sharing plan, is also a defined-contribution plan), he can increase his total contribution to 25%. He expects his practice income to continue to increase in the next 5 to 7 years and should be able to introduce a pension plan without reducing his salary.

This analysis assumes that Dr. Turner will need to keep more income to pay for Lisa's education and would postpone establishing a pension plan until she graduates. At that time, if his practice income and salary have increased at his estimated rate of inflation of 7%, he will be earning $116,920 per year in 1991. Under the present retirement plan guidelines, he could contribute $29,230 to a combination of pension and profit-sharing plans. This calculation, based on annual contributions of an additional $10,000 from 1991 until retirement, indicates that Dr. Turner could increase his retirement net worth by from $172,000 to $192,000, which would be more than 10% of the total.

A more aggressive retirement program could be built around the adoption of a Defined Benefit Pension Plan. Defined Benefit Plans differ from Defined Contribution Plans (profit sharing) in that they define the amount of contribution as that required to accumulate the intended retirement benefit. By adopting such a plan just 10 years before retirement, Dr. Turner could certainly contribute much more to his pension plan than under the

Defined Contribution Plan limits (25% of compensation up to a maximum of $30,000/year).

Another advantage of Defined Benefit Pension Plans is that they tend to favor the older participants. In virtually all dental practices, the dentist could realize a greater personal percentage of the total business contribution compared to the other employees than he could realize under a Defined Contribution Plan.

Because Dr. Turner's needs for additional retirement assets do not require that he contribute more to a pension plan than can be accommodated by a Money Purchase Pension Plan, we do not think it appropriate to incur the greater administrative expense of adopting and administering a Defined Benefit Plan. It requires actuarial calculations and expense, which are not required in a Defined Contribution Plan. We also do not want to overlook the importance of balancing today's lifestyle with tomorrow's security. Because Dr. Turner seems able to provide adequately for his retirement with the addition of a modest pension plan, a more ambitious Defined Benefit Plan would reduce his current available salary.

There is an interesting, yet misunderstood and underutilized, retirement plan that might be ideal for Dr. Turner and many other dentists: a Target Benefit Plan. This pension plan is subject to the Defined Contribution Plan limitations but uses a Defined Benefit formula for allocating the plan contribution among plan participants. Thus the percentage of the total contribution is skewed toward the older, more highly compensated employee—in this case, Dr. Turner. Looking at it another way, if Dr. Turner chose a plan with annual contributions of only $10,000 for himself, he could probably reduce the contribution made on behalf of his younger employees through the adoption of a Target Benefit Plan.

For those who choose to fund such a plan to the maximum of the defined contribution limits, a Target Benefit Plan has added advantage over a Defined Benefit Plan. Under a Defined Benefit Plan, contributions are set by a formula that has a modest, built-in interest rate. If plan investments exceed the internal rate of the formula, subsequent contributions must be reduced. Because no such reduction is required of a Target Benefit Plan, if plan investments do better than the internal formula rate, amounts accumulated in participant accounts may produce a larger benefit than could be realized in a Defined Benefit Plan. The absence of accumulation limits in a Target Benefit Plan could permit a dentist like Dr. Turner to increase his total retirement benefit and total share of the plan assets compared to that which could be accomplished under either Defined Benefit or Money Purchase Pension Plans.

With the two administrative techniques described above being given their proper consideration, we can turn our thoughts to investments.

Present Investments. Although Dr. Turner's personal and retirement plan investments belie his expressed willingness to take risks, they also speak well for his prudence. His brokers have presented several real estate and oil & gas income limited partnerships in the past decade, but Dr. Turner did not want to take the time to evaluate these offerings to the degree such large investments require. Because the brokers were armed only with their firm's sales literature, he refrained from getting involved. He also wisely rejected all telephone solicitations, especially those touting get-rich-quick schemes in precious metals, commodities, and offshore ventures.

Perhaps Dr. Turner's investment decisions were on the cautious side because he lacked the time to properly manage his portfolios and found the other advisory resources in town to be inadequate. Nonetheless, now that we have quantified his goals and their attainability, he can be more purposeful in creating a new portfolio strategy.

Portfolio Design Considerations

If Dr. Turner is to steer a dependable course toward retirement, his portfolio should be designed to recognize balance, diversification, taxation, liquidity, and risk. He must also be aware of domestic and international economic conditions and trends.

In fact, the task is so enormous that we empathize with Dr. Turner's concern about ever being able to move beyond his present careful approach. If he has been impressed by the benefits of adding just 2% to his overall rate of return, he must take the next step to reach higher, more sustainable rates of return. The main elements missing in the Turners' investment program are full-time management and performance monitoring.

Dr. Turner has taken one step in that direction by investing in mutual funds. These investments represent the employment of strategic asset management. Dr. Turner should seek full-time management for all his assets in the form of mutual fund managers, independent investment advisors, and product specialists.

Every mutual fund represents a stated investment objective adhered to by a full-time professional staff. Most independent investment advisors also manage assets according to a particular objective. The keys to using the people are determining what strategies the investor wants to use, reviewing the records of performance of the managers, deciding the timing of the investments, and then *monitoring* their performance and adjusting.

One perfect example of the lack of full-time management, monitoring, and adjusting is the presence on Dr. Turner's balance sheet of Krugerrands. They may have been appropriate in inflationary times, but no critical decisions were made to cut the losses and reposition those funds. Not only did the coins lose value, but they produced no income—thus compounding the loss. Minimizing losses is a central ingredient in total performance. For example, an investment that grows steadily at 9% will double in eight years. If a more aggressive, but volatile, investment loses 50% in three years, it must grow by 32%/year for five years to equal the 9% investment.

Dr. Turner should also hire some advisors/managers who practice market timing, a form of technical analysis that permits an investor to take defensive measures to protect against losses when economic or market trends turn negative. This means moving back and forth between stocks and money market funds, depending on price trends.

Market timing can be a two-edged sword. Many investors have learned about whipsaws the hard way. Whipsaws are losses caused by selling below the purchase price (real loss) or buying back in at a price above the previous sale price (opportunity loss). Observations of the records of market timers indicates that the more frequent the buy/sell moves, the more likely an investor is to incur whipsaws and diminished performance. Less-sensitive timing services should be selected to help investors like Dr. Turner avoid the major downturns in the market and otherwise enjoy the rewards of an investment with more aggressive growth potential—one the investor would not feel secure in selecting without downside protection. Many growth mutual funds, when coupled with relatively inactive (± 1 move per year) market timing services, have achieved annualized rates of return in the 15% to 20% range over long periods.

Dr. Turner should consider the current major macroeconomic trends. The United States economy has entered a period of healthy growth that may be sustainable for many years. Inflation has abated, and many economists forecast moderate rates for several years. Interest rates have declined dramatically in recent months, and it is predicted that bank lending rates, which have exceeded the banks' cost of money by historic margins, may soon begin to return toward normal spreads. Add to this the force of the Reagan Administration's tax reform proposals that seek to discourage borrowing by limiting interest expense deductions and encourage saving and investing by lowering the top tax rates.

The overall effect of such economic shifts would seem to favor equity investments. These same forces would also seem to favor financial instruments—stocks or bonds rather than direct asset ownership, such as precious metals or real estate. Whatever trends the economy follows, the ownership of stocks or bonds makes management, monitoring, and adjustment easier. Because change is inevitable, the more flexibility Dr. Turner can retain, the better he will be able to guard against losses and steer a positive investment course.

Portfolio Design

Dr. Turner's personal portfolio is worth $98,700. After setting aside his $15,000 money market emergency fund, only $83,700 remains to be invested. He will not be adding to his portfolio until Lisa graduates from college and may shift more than half into a Spousal Remainder Trust that would further restrict his choices and keep a premium on liquidity. The constraint of diversification requires the extensive use of mutual funds to reduce the price risk of a small portfolio of individual securities. A shift toward equities seeking tax-favored, long-term capital gains is appropriate with a balance of 65% equities to 35% debt.

Corrective measures should start with deletions and adjustments to the present portfolio. On the equity side, the Krugerrands should be the first to go. Next, the common stocks should be liquidated to make room for two growth mutual funds. The stocks should be eliminated because the number of holdings is too small to provide adequate diversification. Because one of the guiding principles is avoidance of losses, the price risk of even one stock in a portfolio of less than ten stocks cannot be accepted.

In the debt area, the money market fund should be converted to a tax-exempt money market fund which provides superior after-tax yield. The corporate bonds should be eliminated in favor of shorter-term Treasury bonds as we approach the bottom of an interest rate cycle which could see the bonds give back some of their recent appreciation.

This emerging portfolio is more equity-oriented. The convertible preferreds provide a nice yield while offering the prospect of common stock-related appreciation. The Treasuries are a defensive position in which to wait out the next interest cycle for a possible switch to stocks.

The division of the stock holdings into two growth funds gives ample diversification. Steady performing funds that offer reasonable protection during down cycles in the market are recommended. There is no need to incur the price risk of aggressive growth funds.

It is no accident that real estate is absent from this portfolio. This darling of the past decade has been avoided because real estate flourished in a highly inflationary period. Now that the economy has entered a period of relatively low inflation, real estate prices may stagnate. The enactment of any of the proposed anti-real-estate tax reform measures may also depress the price of real estate.

Dr. Turner's portfolio is too small for individual properties, and leveraged purchases should be discouraged. The public real estate partnerships are too high priced with returns no greater than could be obtained in any number of liquid, less risky alternatives.

The new portfolio is totally liquid, totally manageable, and exceeds Dr. Turner's growth requirements by as much as 5%. With such potentially attractive returns from a relatively low-risk portfolio, we see no need to take any gambles.

Retirement Portfolio

The retirement plan commitment to equities has been slightly decreased, while a new balance favoring fixed-income issues by a ratio of 55:45 has been proposed. This strategy adjustment was made to reduce Dr. Turner's susceptibility to an increase in interest rates. The profits in many of the utility stocks were taken; only those bonds with maturities of less than seven years were retained. Issues with nuclear power elements were removed, and the ratings quality was increased without sacrificing much yield.

Corporate bonds were eliminated, and the maturities of the remaining debt issues were shortened. In the long run, the portfolios should favor equities over debt; but with the high yields currently available, Dr. Turner will want to continue receiving returns that exceed his requirements. The convertible bonds and Treasuries will probably be converted to stocks when it is advantageous to do so—probably some time in the next two years when another economic cycle is completed. In the meantime, Dr. Turner will hedge his equity bets by augmenting dividends with option premiums and keep his stock powder dry in debt issues.

When Dr. Turner resumes making personal investments, it would be advantageous to add to his growth mutual fund accounts. By the same token, his profit-sharing contributions may be made to his option income mutual fund. A program of steady contributions of, say, $1,000/month would permit a very sound dollar cost-averaging approach to the growth of that account (see Table 14–4).

Table 14–4
DR. JAMES TURNER
PROPOSED PORTFOLIO DISTRIBUTION

Type Investment	Amount	Percent	Expected Return
I. Personal			
Equity			
Growth mutual funds (2)	$50,000	50.6%	17.5%
Convertible preferred stocks	15,000	15.2	8.5
Total equity	$65,000	65.8%	15.4%
Debt			
Tax-exempt money market fund	$15,000	6.3%	4.5%
Limited-term municipal bond fund	12,500	12.6	7.2
Short-term treasuries	6,200	15.2	8.3
Total debt	$33,800	34.1%	6.2%
Total portfolio	$98,800	100.0%	12.2%
II. IRA			
Debt			
Money market fund	$ 6,425	100.0%	7.5%
III. KEOGH			
Equity			
Utility stocks	$ 8,000	12.6%	9.5%
Growth and income fund	12,000	18.9	15.0
Option income fund	11,750	18.5	18.0
Total equities	$31,750	50.0%	14.7%
Debt			
U.S. government securities	$15,000	23.6%	12.4%
Certificates of deposit	16,750	26.4	7.8
Total debt	$31,750	50.0%	10.0%
Total portfolio	$63,500	100.0%	12.4%

DR. JAMES TURNER–Cont.

Type Investment	Amount	Percent	Expected Return
IV. **Profit Sharing**			
Equity			
Utility stocks	$ 8,000	21.9%	9.5%
Option income fund	9,000	24.7	18.0
Total equity	$17,000	46.6%	14.0%
Debt			
Convertible bonds	$11,000	30.1%	11.0%
U.S. government securities	8,500	23.3	12.4
Total debt	$19,500	53.4%	12.75
Total portfolio	$36,500	100.0%	12.7%

CHAPTER

15

The Mitchell Family

Dr. William Mitchell, a 55-year-old solo practitioner, and his wife Lucille live in a community of 60,000 just south of the Mason-Dixon line. Their three children have graduated from college and are financially independent.

Dr. Mitchell's practice grosses $195,000 per year and has been stable in recent years, with fee increases approximately equal to the rate of inflation. His general practice was one of the first to be incorporated in his state 13 years ago. Dr. Mitchell's salary and bonus have just reached $100,000 per year. He has made substantial contributions to his pension and profit-sharing plans, which will reach $25,000 this year.

Lucille Mitchell, 53, has made a career of her volunteer work with a local hospital and its little theater guild. She is also active in organizing tennis tournaments at the country club.

The Mitchells are prominent members of their community and leaders in civic affairs. They enjoy entertaining and purchased an elegant home a few years ago to accommodate their active social life. They enjoy getting away to their condominium on the Gulf of Mexico which they purchased seven years ago. They are also active participants in the Gulf social community.

An innovative investor, Dr. Mitchell found local investment offerings lacked the tax benefits he learned about from several of the publications he subscribes to and the seminars he has attended. Dr. Mitchell was receptive to solicitations from out-of-towners who offered more aggressive investments. He takes pride in being a sophisticated investor and often speaks of how few taxes he has been paying.

Avid tennis players, the Mitchells belong to the country club and can be found there during the week as well as on weekends.

They plan to retire to their condominium where warmer weather will permit them to play year round and participate in the outdoor social activities of the tennis and country club. Dr. Mitchell is in good physical condition and expects to die with his sneakers on.

Because he and Mrs. Mitchell are beginning to seriously contemplate retirement, they are also beginning to question the worth of some of their investments. The audit of their gold mining investment in Nevada has them particularly worried (see Table 15–1).

Dr. Mitchell's Goals

Dr. Mitchell has long wanted to retire at 62, but recent discussions with his accountant have caused him to shift his sights toward age 65. In retirement, he and Mrs. Mitchell want to play tennis whenever they wish and enjoy and active social life.

Investments

An experienced financial planner has only to take one look at the Mitchells' financial statement to begin asking some very pointed questions. The oil and gas program has been less than a resounding success and will probably not even repay the partnership note secured by Dr. Mitchell's letter of credit. The movie deal, which seemed like a sure thing, has not returned a nickel, and after three years is not likely to.

The cruelest questions were about the Nevada gold mine—an audit by the IRS is inexorably leading toward disallowing the deductions taken several years ago. The IRS has contended that the investment was not entered into for a profit and the 3:1 write-off, which saved Dr. Mitchell about $23,000 in taxes on his $15,000 investment, is about to cost him a bundle in back taxes and interest. Dr. Mitchell is hoping that the IRS will permit him to retain a deduction for the amount of cash he paid, $15,000. According to his accountant, Dr. Mitchell's best hope for such a settlement stems from the enormous backlog of tax shelter cases being attacked by the IRS, not from the facts of the case. The IRS

Table 15–1
DR. WILLIAM MITCHELL
FINANCIAL STATEMENT

Assets		**Liabilities**	
Cash Assets			
Checking account	$ 2,900	Home mortgage	$ 163,500
Money market fund	7,200	Condominium mortgage	56,600
Life insurance cash value	20,100	Rental property notes:	
Total cash/cash equivalents	$ 30,200	Duplex	55,800
		Office building	61,000
Invested Assets		Credit cards	5,300
		Limted partnerships:	
Mutual funds:		Gold mine note	30,000
Aggressive growth	$ 13,800	Oil & gas letter of credit	20,000
International	9,600	Apartment payments	15,000
Krugerrands	12,100	Total liabilities	$ 406,600
Rental properties:			
Duplex	73,000	**Net Worth**	$ 648,900
Office building	94,500		
Pension plan	63,500	**Total Liabilities & Net Worth**	$1,055,500
Profit sharing plan	98,800		
IRA	5,500		
Limited partnerships:			
Oil & gas	30,000		
Movies	10,000		
Gold mine	45,000		
Apartments	55,000		
Dental practice	140,000		
Total invested assets	$ 650,800		
Personal Assets			
Residence	$ 240,000		
Condominium	80,000		
Automobiles	20,500		
Personal property	34,000		
Total personal assets	$ 374,500		
Total Assets	$1,055,500		

is allowing out-of-pocket settlements as an expedient in dealing with an inventory of more than 64,000 cases, of which over 22,000 are docketed in the U.S. Tax Court.

The gold mine partnership is a classic case of an abusive tax shelter. The general partner formed several partnerships to reenter abandoned mines and extract gold and silver using new mining methods. Interest in these ventures increased substantially with the rapid escalation in the price of the metals. The investment was structured as a leveraged investment from which Dr. Mitchell and the other investors were able to deduct three times their cash contribution by adding a recourse note. The deductions were based on advance payment of exploration and development expenses.

Unfortunately, because the general partner never commenced operations on any of the several mining partnerships it formed, the IRS has disallowed the deductions. Another matter of great distress is Dr. Mitchell's $30,000 note. At the time he made the investment, the salesman assured Dr. Mitchell that it would be paid off by the mine's success and "Anyway, the general partner would never attempt to collect!" Although no real mining expenses were actually incurred, the note exists and its presence makes Dr. Mitchell nervous. The irony is that part of the IRS's contention that the venture was not entered into for profit is based on the presence of the notes that were not called on by the general partner. If he is fortunate to retain a deduction for his out-of-pocket costs, Dr. Mitchell will still be looking at a tax bill plus interest of more than $24,000. Although the interest will be deductible in the year paid, it is small solace to Dr. Mitchell, who sees a big chunk of cash being lost in paying the IRS as well as the bank for his oil and gas letter of credit.

While we are on the subject of abusive tax shelters, let's be more specific about the definition and penalties associated with these abominations. Simply stated, an abusive tax shelter is any transaction that is entered into "primarily for tax avoidance" and the IRS determines that the price paid for the property acquired substantially exceeds the fair market value of the property or other tax-loss benefits are not accompanied by a commensurate burden of economic risk.

The IRS is now adding a penalty to taxpayers who are deemed to have invested in an abusive tax shelter. The penalty is assessed as a percentage of the underpayment of tax attributable to the abusive shelter. If the property valuation exceeds the correct valuation by 50%, the penalty is 10% of the underpayment. If the overvaluation is 100% to 150% of the correct value, the penalty is 20%. And if the overvaluation exceeds 150%, the penalty is 30%. Of course, interest is due, too, from the original date of filing the tax return.

A new section of the tax code also imposes interest penalties for abusive shelters. If a person made an abusive shelter investment years ago which has been overturned by the IRS, the interest rate is increased by 50% for any interest payable after January 1, 1985. Consequently, we believe a taxpayer whose CPA says he will probably lose an IRS audit of an abusive shelter should post a bond equal to the tax and interest due so the heavy interest penalties can be avoided or minimized.

Readers should also note that the IRS is cracking down on overvalued charitable contributions. The penalty is 30% of any tax underpayment. The IRS is also looking at the investor as a possible criminal for conspiring to defraud the Treasury of tax revenue by participating in abusive shelter schemes. It is assessing penalties of 5% of any underpayment for "negligence and intentional disregard of the rules." More serious penalties, including heavy fines and jail sentences, could be the reward for investing in a shelter suspected to be abusive going in.

The IRS is not fooling around. Be careful. Invest in solid tax shelters if you need them, but watch out for shady deals. It isn't fun and games anymore.

Dr. Mitchell learned the lessons of tax shelter dangers the hard way. Fortunately, he has benefited from his decisions to invest in real estate tax shelters. He has realized sound tax benefits from his personal ownership in the duplex and office building. Each has appreciated in value, and the prospects for further appreciation are good. The only drawback to the duplex is the negative cash flow; however, the next round of rent increases should bring him up to breakeven on cash flow.

The two apartment partnerships in which he invested also provided good tax benefits. Dr. Mitchell will have completed his investment payments next year and one of the apartments is being considered for sale by the general partner.

Elsewhere on Dr. Mitchell's balance sheet, we see evidence of impatience and aggressiveness. His mutual fund investments represent a desire for big gains. The Krugerrands are a common mistake—they produced no income and have declined in value by more than 50%.

Fortunately, Dr. Mitchell has been more conventional in the investment of his pension and profit-sharing investments. Perhaps it was the presence of four employees in the plans which introduced some caution, but he has benefited by using the trust department of one of the major banks in the region. Many people have despaired over the poor performance of bank trust department investment portfolios. In Dr. Mitchell's case, the bank is one of the top performers in the industry; therefore, he has realized nice returns from certificates of deposit and commingled funds that invested extensively in corporate bonds, U.S. Treasury obligations, and commercial paper. The bank's equity fund, which purchased blue chip stocks and high-yielding utility stocks, has also performed very well.

Cash Flow

Dr. Mitchell's salary and bonus of $100,000 are supplemented by $5,225 in rents, dividends, and interest (see Table 15–2). When he can eliminate the $75/month that he pays to cover his duplex expenses, his income is $105,225. After paying $15,402 in state, federal, and FICA taxes, he has discretionary income of $86,673.

Payments of $11,450 on his partnership obligations should end in 1986, thus increasing available funds for investment. Currently, Dr. Mitchell is making about $8,500 of new investments which he expects to go mainly to growth mutual funds. The oil and gas programs will add another $2,500 per year after he settles with the bank over his letter of credit. Because the bank is unwilling to renew the letter of credit for another year, Dr. Mitchell may need to dig in to pay the partnership about $20,000 to relieve him of his obligations under his leveraged 1982 investment.

The Mitchells' present cost of living is $66,723, or $5,560 per month. Of this amount, $2,310 is for mortgage payments on their home and their condominium.

Table 15–2
DR. WILLIAM MITCHELL
CASH FLOW AND TAXES

Income	**Cash Flow**	**Taxable Income**
Salary	$100,000	$100,000
Dividends		
Mutual funds	700	500
Interest	575	575
Rental income		
Duplex	(900)	(7,600)
Office building	1,350	(3,725)
Limited partnerships		
Oil & gas	0	1,700
Movies	0	(350)
Gold mine	0	0
Apartments	2,600	(4,200)
Subtotal, income	104,325	86,900
Deductions		
IRA	2,250	2,250
Personal exemptions (2)	—	2,080
Itemized deductions		
Taxes, state (7% top bracket)	5,000	5,000
Other	—	2,900
Interest, mortgages	—	26,900
Investments	—	4,700
Other	—	2,800
Contributions	—	2,200
Miscellaneous	—	1,700
Less: Zero bracket amount	—	(3,540)
Subtotal, deductions	(7,250)	(46,990)
Net Income	$97,075	$ 39,910
Less: Federal income tax	7,610	
FICA	2,792	
Discretionary Income	86,673	

DR. WILLIAM MITCHELL–Cont.

Less: Investment payments	
Apartments	(8,250)
Oil & gas, gold mine	(3,200)
New investments	(8,500)
Cost of Living	$ 66,723

Retirement analysis

Dr. Mitchell has revised his retirement plans and now intends to enter a concentrated program of responsible investing and saving so he can retire at age 65. With the help of his CPA, Dr. Mitchell now recognizes that he may fall short of his retirement capital goal of $2,000,000. According to his CPA, Dr. Mitchell should be able to reach his goal based on the reasonable assumption of receiving returns of only 4% or 5% in excess of inflation in the remaining 10 years of his active career. Dr. Mitchell must hire a competent investment advisor to help him make the correct investments, and he must be disciplined in following a pattern of steady but unspectacular investing. Dr. Mitchell needs no more losses or surprises, just steady, solid growth.

Given the IRS audit and his worthless investments, Dr. Mitchell may find that he has precious little cash to reinvest. Considering possible cash payments approaching $50,000, the foolishness of his past investments is abundantly clear.

Nevertheless, Dr. Mitchell's situation is not hopeless. As the table indicates, depending on how well his investments perform in the future, the goal can be reached. Furthermore, he has three additional cushions. First, we have assumed modest investment returns and that no principal will be consumed in his retirement. These are very conservative assumptions. If Dr. Mitchell is able to locate a good investment advisor, the kinds of investment returns that are produced by many sources would permit him to exceed his retirement income needs on a smaller capital base.

The value of his house has not been included in our computation, but it is reasonable to assume that additional cash could be received from the sale of the residence. Because the Mitchells wish to move further south to a warm, year-round climate, they will not need to retain their present home. Even if they upgrade to a nicer condominium in Florida, it is reasonable to assume another $100,000 to $150,000 would be available for investment at that time.

Finally, Social Security income was not included in the computations. Even though that source of income may be altered in the 10 years until the Mitchells retire, it should still provide a meaningful contribution. As much as 20% of their income could be received from Social Security; however, it is too uncertain and, therefore, is excluded from our computations. Dr. Mitchell needs all the motivation he can summon to accumulate his retirement nest egg. We do not want to undermine his resolve by including too many elements that might make his predicament seem less urgent (see Table 15–3).

Table 15–3
DR. WILLIAM MITCHELL
FINANCIAL INDEPENDENCE/RETIREMENT COMPUTATION

I. Income Required to Maintain Standard of Living			$ 66,723
Income required in 1995 (age 65) with 7% inflation			$131,257
Before-tax income required*			$175,010
II. Capital Required in 1995 at Indicated Yield		8%	10%
		$2,187,625	$1,750,100
III. Capital Available‡			
Personal Investments:		8%	10%
1. Present value†	$258,000		
Value in 1995		$ 556,996	$ 669,175
2. Future additions:	$19,950/year	312,128	349,747
Retirement Plans		10%	12%
1. Present value	$187,800		
Value in 1995		$ 487,097	$ 583,269
2. Future addition:	$25,000/year	438,280	491,365
Subtotal		$1,794,501	$2,093,556
Practice value§		140,000	140,000
Total capital available		$1,934,501	$2,223,556
IV. Surplus/(Deficit)		$ (253,124)	$ 483,456
V. Income Available @ 8% Return		$ 154,760	$ 178,684

*Assuming effective federal and state tax rate of 25%.
†Excluding oil and gas, gold mine, and movie deals.
‡At indicated growth rate.
§Assuming after-tax value approximately equal to current value.

Planning and Investment Recommendations

Dr. Mitchell has a straightforward challenge to seek solid investment managers to put his portfolios to work. He needs to seek rates of return somewhat higher than needed by Drs. Turner and Stevens. Still, because he has 10 years in which to accumulate his retirement capital, he can accept greater price volatility than he could in retirement. This means he could select a money manager with a track record of higher rates of return than the bank's trust department, but with larger price fluctuations along the way. With the prospect for at least two more complete business cycles before retirement, we believe Dr. Mitchell can be somewhat more aggressive in managing his money.

Dr. Mitchell must seek greater returns from his qualified retirement plans because they represent his largest single block of present and future capital. Because there is some question about how much cash he may actually have to invest personally, he must concentrate on managing his planned assets.

Changes in Present Portfolio

Because the tax shelter investments, other than real estate, have proven to be worth less than he paid for them, if not outright liabilities, Dr. Mitchell must reduce the value at which he carries them on his balance sheet. We recommend some nominal value, for example, for the movie deal, so they will not be forgotten. The Krugerrands should be immediately liquidated to provide cash for his shelter liabilities. The value obtained can begin earning income in his money market fund until it is required for payment to the banks or IRS. The aggressive growth fund should also be repositioned to seek more manageable returns and to protect against any losses in a down market. The international fund should be retained for its strategic advantage in a period when the U.S. dollar may begin to decline compared to foreign currencies. Because the cash value in his life insurance policy is also a good source of cash to pay the banks or the IRS, we recommend that Dr. Mitchell borrow at the favorable 6% rate rather than liquidate assets, for example, real estate, which should be expected to grow at a rate well in excess of 6%.

Portfolio Design Considerations

Dr. Mitchell has very little liquid capital he can reposition. To permit him to gain the most advantage from repositioning plus the addition of as much as $20,000 per year after he has paid off his real estate notes, he should concentrate on growth mutual funds—not the aggressive type, but the next echelon that seeks long-term capital gains with less downside risk in declining markets.

Dr. Mitchell may find a market timing approach helpful because he seeks above-average gains. Many investment advisors publish market timing newsletters or actually manage money according to technical guidelines. Dr. Mitchell might rely on one of their services to guard against market declines by taking a defensive position in money market funds when stock prices are declining. This strategy has proven beneficial when used in conjunction with growth-oriented mutual funds.

Dr. Mitchell does not need more tax shelters. He has reduced his top marginal tax rate down to the 38% level, below the point that he can obtain meaningful tax savings from any additional investments. He should stick with liquid, growth-oriented mutual funds.

His pension and profit-sharing plans are the vehicles for his financial salvation. He can accumulate more than $1,000,000 at a 12% rate of return. We believe he needs to focus on seeking a greater growth rate due to his questionable ability to see his present personal assets grow to over $600,000.

We believe it is possible to achieve growth in his plans of over 15% per year, and expectations of returns in the 18–20% range are not just dreaming. There are many money managers with long track records of returns in excess of 20% per year.

To illustrate the power of adding just a few percentage points of return to Dr. Mitchell's retirement plan growth rates, consider this: a 15% rate of return would add over $250,000 to his account in ten years, and he could fund his entire retirement objective with a rate of return of 19%!

Many managers do not accept amounts of less than $1,000,000 to manage, but there are managers all over the country who can help Dr. Mitchell. They may be invisible to most of us, but a concerted search through money manager rating services and stock brokerage firms can turn up firms that will be glad to take on accounts of $50,000 or more—just the type that Dr. Mitchell needs.

We think Dr. Mitchell needs to be more attuned to the economic trends, especially interest rate trends. Having seen substantial gains in the value of his corporate bonds and U.S. Treasuries, he should know that a managed portfolio of fixed-income securities can produce very nice yields and capital gains, too. By using the market timing techniques we described above, we believe a fixed-income portfolio can generate the kinds of returns he needs with much less risk than might be found in the stock market.

Do not take the advocacy of fixed-income securities and comments about stock price risks as an indication that the stock market is bad. On the contrary, the major concentration of Dr. Mitchell's plan investing should be equity oriented. Dividend-paying equities like convertible preferred stocks and utility stocks should play a major part of his program. Dr. Mitchell should put more than half his planned assets with managers of common stock portfolios. Two carefully selected and carefully watched managers should receive $50,000 each with the balance being allocated to a fixed income manager, a growth and income mutual fund, and a government securities fund.

Annual contributions should maintain the equities' favoritism and be allocated to reward performance. Dr. Mitchell could practice market timing of his own by putting new contributions in defensive money market accounts until favorable market signals initiate their release to the stock or fixed-income managers.

If he would feel more comfortable leaving his other employees' assets with the bank trust department, he can accommodate all participants by permitting them to earmark their accounts and let them choose. As a result, he would be in a position to pursue a more aggressive personal course without introducing imprudent risks into the others' accounts (see Table 15–4).

Table 15–4
DR. WILLIAM MITCHELL
PROPOSED PORTFOLIO DISTRIBUTION

Type Investment	Amount	Percent	Expected Return
I. Personal			
Equity			
International mutual fund	$ 15,000	5.3%	15.0%
Growth and income fund*	30,000	10.6	15.0
Rental properties	167,500	59.0	10.0
Apartment partnerships	55,000	19.4	9.0
Other partnerships	500	0.2	0
Total equity	$268,000	94.5%	10.6%
Debt			
Money market fund	$ 15,700	5.5%	7.5%
Total portfolio	$283,700	100.0%	10.4%
II. IRA			
Equity			
Option income mutual fund	$ 5,500	100.0%	15.0%
III. Pension and profit sharing			
Equity			
Managed stock accounts (2)	$100,000	53.2%	17.5%
Growth and income fund	10,000	5.3	15.0
Total equities	$110,000	58.5%	17.3%
Debt			
Managed fixed-income account	50,000	26.6%	15.0%
Corporate bond fund	10,000	5.3	12.0
Money market fund	17,800	9.5	7.5
Total debt	$ 77,800	41.4%	12.9%
Total portfolio	$187,800	100.0%	15.5%

*Including $18,000 from insurance policy cash value loan.

Chapter

16

The Stevens Family

Dr. John Stevens, age 63, maintains an unincorporated general practice. He and his wife Mary live in an older suburb of a large eastern city. He and Mrs. Stevens have three grown children and are awaiting the arrival of their first grandchild.

Dr. Stevens nets $82,500 (50%) from his $165,000/year practice (see Tables 16–1 and 16–2). The gross revenues have remained about the same in recent years. The value of his practice is estimated to be $99,000; however, Dr. Stevens does not want to rely on its value in computing his retirement income. In retirement, in addition to two trips per year with Mrs. Stevens, he wants to get in a lot of bass fishing and perfect his golf game.

Mary Stevens, age 62, has worked part-time as an interior designer but presently is not working. She likes to travel and is looking forward to doing more after Dr. Stevens' retirement.

Dr. Stevens is interested in retiring as soon as possible, but not later than age 65. He wants to know if it is feasible to do so at this time. A conservative investor, Dr. Stevens does not want to worry about price fluctuations in his retirement portfolio. He does not want to reduce his principal during retirement so he will have an adequate hedge against inflation and the uncertainties of old age. For Dr. Stevens, the ideal portfolio is comprised of high-quality government securities of short to medium maturities. Because Dr. Stevens did not have time to study investments, he relied extensively on his stockbroker, who recently retired and moved to Arizona. The only other source of investment advice he received was from a general-purpose financial newsletter for dentists and *Money* magazine.

Table 16–1
DR. JOHN STEVENS
FINANCIAL STATEMENT

Assets		Liabilities	
Cash Assets			
Checking account	$ 1,000	Credit cards	$ 500
Money market fund	10,000	Auto note	9,000
Certificates of deposit	20,500		
Total cash/cash equivalents	$ 31,500	Total liabilities	$ 9,500
Invested Assets			
Blue chip stock portfolio	$ 30,000	**Net Worth**	$737,500
Municipal bond fund	50,000		
AA corporate bonds	25,000	**Total Liabilities & Net Worth**	$747,000
IRA	13,500		
Keogh	375,000		
Total invested assets	$493,500		
Personal Assets			
Residence	$160,000		
Personal property	50,000		
Automobiles	12,000		
Total personal assets	$222,000		
Total Assets*	$747,000		

*Dr. Stevens did not feel he could count on the value of the practice. He did not want it included in the balance sheet. Practice valued at $99,000 (60% of 1 year's gross).

Dr. Stevens' Goals

Dr. Stevens' only goal is to retire and provide for himself and his wife. Mrs. Stevens would like to help their children financially if the need were to arise and to set something aside for the grandchildren.

Table 16–2
DR. JOHN STEVENS
CASH FLOW AND TAXES

Income	**Cash Flow**	**Taxable Income**
Salary	$82,500	$82,500
Dividends		
Money market funds	850	850
Stock portfolio	1,800	1,600
Corporate bond fund	2,050	2,050
Municipal bond fund	2,900	—
Interest	2,358	2,358
Subtotal, income	92,458	89,358
Deductions		
Keogh	12,375	12,375
IRA	2,250	2,250
Personal exemptions (2)	—	2,080
Itemized deductions		
Taxes, state (6% top marginal rate)	4,000	4,000
Property	—	1,200
Other	—	750
Interest, mortgages	—	—
Other	—	950
Contributions	—	3,500
Miscellaneous	—	400
Less: Zero bracket amount	—	(3,540)
Subtotal, deductions	(18,625)	(23,965)
Net Income	$73,833	$65,393
Less: Federal income tax	(17,024)	
FICA	(4,673)	
Discretionary Income	52,136	
Less: Investment/savings	(9,000)	
Cost of Living	$43,136	

Retirement Analysis

In the five years since their youngest daughter became financially self-supporting, the Stevens have enjoyed a comfortable, but not excessive, lifestyle that they hope to maintain in retirement. They believe they will be able to enjoy two major trips per year within their present level of spendable income of $3,595 per month.

If he waited until 1987, Dr. Stevens would be eligible for an estimated maximum Social Security benefit of $10,123. By taking early retirement at age 63, he will be eligible for a reduced benefit of $7,490. Mrs. Stevens is also eligible for a reduced benefit of $3,240 at age 62. Their combined benefit will be $10,730. In two years, their projected benefit will have increased to about $12,170 based on current estimates of cost of living increases. Compared to the full benefit they would receive if he waited until age 65 to retire, Dr. and Mrs. Stevens' combined Social Security benefit will be reduced about $216 per month, equivalent to about $30,506 of additional capital at an 8.0% yield.

For those taking Social Security fully into account in making their retirement decisions, these facts may be enlightening. The earliest age at which retirement benefits may be received is 62. The benefit is reduced by 0.555% per month for each month prior to age 65 that a person retires. Conversely, for each month beyond age 65 that a person waits to retire, the benefit is increased by 1% per year for workers born before 1917. The delayed retirement credit is reduced for persons born after 1917.

Mrs. Stevens' eligibility to receive a benefit is related to Dr. Stevens' eligible amount. During Dr. Stevens' lifetime, she will be eligible to receive half the full amount he is eligible to receive. After her husband's death, Mrs. Stevens will receive an amount equal to 100% of his full benefit, subject to the early retirement adjustment.

With the Stevens' retirement income projected to be about $41,920 plus $10,730 of Social Security, their effective tax rate will be about 20%. The remaining spendable income of about $42,000 ($3,500 per month) does not quite meet their projected needs.

Although they would have adequate income for a comfortable retirement, it is prudent to provide as much of a cushion as possible. The sale of the practice could provide a very desirable additional amount of capital. Assuming Dr. Stevens could sell the practice for $99,000, another $6,336 per year could be added to their income. This will help protect the Stevens' against inflation, excessive medical expenses, or other unforeseen emergencies. It would also be beneficial to have extra income to compensate for possible future reductions in Social Security benefits.

Finally, Dr. Stevens has achieved one of the most desirable, most important conditions of financial stability: no debt. Other than the small balance on his car purchase note, Dr. Stevens owes nothing. He has maximum flexibility because he has no fixed obligations (see Table 16–3).

Our analysis indicates that Dr. Stevens can retire immediately. The computations are based on an 8% rate of return that seem easily achievable with little risk.

Table 16–3
DR. JOHN STEVENS
RETIREMENT COMPUTATION

I. Income Required at Age 63:		$ 43,136
Before-tax income required*		53,920
Less Social Security income (est.)		(10,730)
Net income required		$ 43,190
II. Capital Required at 8% yield		$539,875
III. Capital Available		
Personal investments	$135,500	
Keogh balance	375,000	
IRA balance	13,500	
Total capital available		$524,000
IV. Surplus/(Deficit)		(15,875)
V. Annual Income Available with 8.0% Yield		
Excluding practice value		$ 41,920
Including practice value†		$ 48,256

*Assuming effective federal and state tax rate of 20%.

†Assuming practice sold for $99,000, less long-term capital gains tax of 20%.

Although it would be possible to raise the yield on the Stevens' assets another 2%, the risk involved would be inappropriate. An extra 2% yield could produce another $1,000 per month, or 25% more than the projected income. This is where the critical investment decisions will be made because the lesser, safer yield seems to meet the needs of Dr. and Mrs. Stevens.

Because risk cannot be completely eliminated, Dr. Stevens should create a diversified portfolio. A totally liquid, income-oriented portfolio can be constructed with a capital base of $600,000. It would be wise to also keep an eye on inflation. Too much emphasis on fixed-income securities could cause the assets to shrink. Therefore, equities are advised to provide an inflationary hedge.

To maintain his income and preserve his asset base, Dr. Stevens must properly design his portfolio, obtain full-time monitoring and management, and minimize his losses. Good portfolio management can provide all these advantages and maintain the value of the assets.

Dr. Stevens has accomplished his primary goal of accumulating enough income-producing assets to retire. However, he is entering a new era of money management in which greater burdens will be placed on him. Because he will no longer receive a salary, new funds must be available to compensate for any losses. Dr. Stevens must now concentrate on income generation and capital preservation. The matter is complicated because Dr. Stevens' most reliable advisor, his stockbroker, has retired and moved away. A new advisor must be found to help manage the portfolio.

The role of portfolio management is so important that if Dr. Stevens is unable to find the help he needs, he might consider purchasing annuities. Through these vehicles, he would turn over the management of his portfolio to an insurance company who will provide Dr. and Mrs. Stevens with a guaranteed amount of income for the remainder of their lives. Although a remainder interest can be built into the annuity contract, it would reduce the payout during their lifetimes. Therefore, for practical purposes, the Stevens would surrender any residual for their heirs and their capital reserve would no longer be available for other possible needs, e.g., medical expenses, nursing home care, or loans and gifts to their children.

Dr. Stevens could purchase a joint and 100% survivor life annuity of $3,600 per month for about $380,000. For about $500,000, he could purchase a similar annuity with a 5% annual increase in the income payout. This would meet the Stevens' retirement income requirements but would leave only $100,000 in available assets for emergencies and their estates.

Annuities also offer some income tax advantages in that payments from annuities purchased with personal funds represent a partial return of principal. Because only the interest-earned portion of the annuity is subject to taxation, about half of the annuity income described above for Dr. Stevens would be excluded from taxation. On the other hand, payments received from annuities purchased with qualified retirement plan money (pension, Keogh) would be completely taxable.

If the annuity concept appeals to Dr. Stevens, he should use it for a partial solution only—possibly $100,000 for a $950 per month joint and 100% survivor life annuity. Keogh plan proceeds would be the preferable source of funds to purchase the annuity. Dr. Stevens should also consider purchasing contracts from several insurance companies to guard against risk of failure of any issuer. Another protection is to purchase annuities only from the largest, most well-known insurance companies. Their rates are usually quite competitive with lesser-known companies.

Another strategy would be to purchase staggered contracts. Annuities with a five-year payout could be coupled with deferred annuities. Decisions about electing lifetime payout or one-year payout from the deferred annuity could in fact be deferred, thus providing greater flexibility for the Stevens', particularly because of their desire to keep a major portion of their capital available for emergencies or their heirs. Dr. Stevens should consult a competent insurance agent who specializes in annuities should he consider this approach to retirement income.

Present Investments Analysis

Dr. Stevens' personal and retirement plan portfolios are fundamentally invested in high-quality, fixed-income securities: certificates of deposits, Treasury notes, and utility stocks and bonds. The yields have become quite attractive in recent years with interest rates reaching unprecedented levels. The bonds purchased over the past five years are now worth about 35% more because interest rates declined in the past year.

His stock portfolio has also performed well. But because of its modest size, it has not played a significant part in his capital accumulation. Still, the presence of $66,000 of high-quality common stocks, e.g., General Electric, IBM, Coca Cola, and Proctor and Gamble, reinforces the importance of buying quality. Dr. Stevens has invested carefully and avoided serious losses—an indispensable ingredient in capital accumulation. The fact that he has reached his retirement objective largely through fixed-income securities gives testimony to the power of gradual accumulation and the compounding of reinvested dividends and interest.

New Portfolio Design

Dr. Stevens' personal portfolio is valued at $135,500. His combined retirement plan assets are worth $388,500, before taxes. Our goal is to provide $43,136 in spendable income for him and Mrs. Stevens without disturbing the principal. Our earlier calculations followed conventional methods and, anticipating a substantial amount of taxable income from his Keogh plan, assumed that the Stevens' would be subject to top marginal tax rate of at least 38% and an effective rate of 20%.

A more dramatic approach is chosen to simplify matters for Dr. Stevens, reduce his tax rate, and lessen the degree of risk. The central element in our strategy is to distribute his Keogh as a lump sum, subject to favorable 10-year forward averaging taxation. We also purchased a life annuity, paying $130 per month with the IRA to greatly simplify that account.

Before creating a new portfolio for Dr. Stevens, we must dispose of most of his present investments while retaining a few. Because we are turning almost 70% of his portfolio over to professional managers, there is no room to retain individual securities. The utility stocks, zero coupon bonds and corporate bonds have served him well, but these should be eliminated because reduced expectations of further interest rate reduction leaves little opportunity for additional profits.

Conversely, the municipal bond fund is a high-quality, limited-term fund that should be retained. A growth and income fund in the same mutual fund family will be a good companion to serve as a conduit for the Stevens' future income.

With all Dr. Stevens' assets now in his personal account, he has just over a half-million-dollar portfolio that is large enough to permit individually managed portfolios. Our objective will be to select the proper asset managers and monitor them closely.

First, we allocated $200,000 to equities, with $150,000 of that amount to be divided between two individual advisors. The balance will be placed in a growth and income mutual fund with an automatic monthly distribution to Dr. Stevens. All dividends from the managed equity accounts are to be reinvested by the asset managers.

The larger allocation of assets is to fixed-income issues, with particular emphasis on municipal bonds. The bulk, $250,000, will be invested in an "immunized" portfolio of individual, high-quality bonds. By purchasing a portfolio with staggered maturities in the next 10 to 15 years, bonds of $15,000 to $20,000 will be redeemed every one or two years. By scheduling the coupon dates, Dr. Stevens will have a steady income flow and his portfolio will be protected against interest rate risk by holding each bond until maturity. As each matures, he can make new investment decisions in accordance with market conditions at the time. As bond interest is received, it can be automatically invested in his municipal bond fund from which he can receive an automatic monthly check in the amount he requires.

Overall, this portfolio should yield about $40,000 in interest and dividends with another ±$15,000 of capital gains to reinvest. Adding in their $10,730 of Social Security income, the Stevens will have more than $51,000 of income subject to only about $6,000 of state and local income taxes due to their major reliance on tax-exempt income. The Stevens' effective tax rate has been reduced to about 12%, their required spendable income has been surpassed, their risk has been reduced to acceptable proportions, total money management (and monitoring) has been provided, and additional appreciation as a hedge against inflation has been generated (see Table 16–4).

Table 16–4
DR. JOHN STEVENS
PROPOSED PORTFOLIO DISTRIBUTION

Type Investment	Amount	Percent	Rate of Return*
I. Personal			
Equity			
Growth and income stocks, 2 managed portfolios	$100,000	19.8%	17.5%
Growth and income mutual fund	50,000	9.9	15.0
Total equity	$150,000	29.7%	16.7%
Debt			
Money market fund	$ 29,000	5.8%	7.5%
U.S. Government securities	50,000	9.9	12.4
Municipal bonds, managed portfolios	250,000	49.6	7.6
Municipal bond mutual fund	25,000	5.0	7.0
Total debt	$354,000	70.3%	8.2%
Total portfolio	$504,000	100.0%	10.7%
II. **IRA**			
Debt			
Joint and 100% survivor annuity	$ 13,500	100.0%	11.4%
III. **Keogh**		(Liquidated)	

*Estimated.
†Including after-tax proceeds from Keogh distribution ($289,300) and sale of practice (79,200).

In Closing

Audience questionnaires from my retirement seminars lead me to believe that the situations of Drs. Turner, Mitchell, and Stevens are fairly representative of dentists in their age groups. There are, of course, extremes on both ends; those with much larger holdings and those with much less. But the good news is that it is seldom too late to initiate a retirement plan. The challenge at 55 is much the same as it was at 35—finding the determination to act, devising a plan, and then working the plan.

We've looked at many areas that must be considered in retirement planning. For some readers, parts of the book were easy and "old hat"; for others, those same parts may have seemed difficult. Such are the inevitabilities of writing to a broad audience. But grasping the fundamentals is essential. As with most things, success in retirement planning requires the acquisition of skills.

You now possess the tools. You've seen the routes taken by others. It's time for you to start down your own path. As the Chinese proverb so accurately states, "The journey of a thousand miles begins with one step."

Take that step, and then the next. You'll get there—to a reward that is rich and much deserved. And take with you my most sincere best wishes.

ADDITIONAL READING

Financial Planning

Personal Financial Planning, 3rd edition. Rev. G. Victor Hallman & Jerry S. Rosenbloom, McGraw-Hill Inc., 1985.

Your Book Of Financial Planning. Loren Dunton, Reston Publishing Co. Inc., 1983.

Personal Financial Planning for Executives. Paul A. Randle and Philip R. Swensen, Lifetime Learning Publications, 1981.

Insurance

The Invisible Banker: Everything the Insurance Industry Never Wanted You To Know. Andrew Tobias, Winden Press, 1982.

Fundamentals Of Risk and Insurance, 4th edition. Emmet J. Vaughan and Curtis M. Elliot, John Wiley and Sons Inc., 1985.

The Life Insurance Game. Ronald Kessler, Holt, Rinehart and Winston, 1985.

Estate Planning

Family Security Through Estate Planning. Arnold Kohn, McGraw-Hill Inc., 1983.

Estate-Planning Guide Including Financial Planning. Sidney Kess and Bertil Westlin, Commerce Clearing House Inc., 1983.

The Tools and Techniques of Estate Planning, 5th edition. Steven R. Leimberg, et al., The National Underwriter Co. Inc., 1985.

Investing

The Intelligent Investor, 4th revised edition. Benjamin Graham, Harper & Row, 1973.

Security Analysis, 4th edition. Benjamin Graham, David L. Dodd, and Charles Tatham, McGraw-Hill Inc., 1962.

Analysis of Financial Statements, revised edition. Leopold A. Bernstein, Dow Jones-Irwin Press, 1984.

The Three Rs of Investing: Return, Risk and Relativity. Austin S. Donnelly, Dow Jones-Irwin Press, 1985.

Stock Market Logic. Norman G. Fosback, Institute for Economic Research, 1985.

The New Options Market, 2nd edition. Max G. Ansbacher, Walker and Company, 1975.

The Dow Jones-Irwin Guide to Put & Call Options, revised edition. Henry K. Clasing Jr., Dow Jones-Irwin Press, 1978.

The Handbook for No-Load Fund Investors. P.O. Box 283, Hastings on Hudson, 1985.

The Quarterly Newsletter of the Handbook for No-Load Fund Investors.

The Complete Hand Book of Real Estate Math. Peter Pace, Reston Publishing Company Inc., 1972.

Nothing Down. Robert Allen, Simon & Schuster Inc., 1980.

Creating Wealth. Robert G. Allen, Simon & Schuster Inc., 1983.

The Retired Investor's Guide to Financial Security. John W. Cookson, Prentice-Hall Inc., 1983.

Long-Range Forecasting: From Crystal Ball to Computer. J. Scott Armstrong, Wiley Interscience, 1978.

Tax Shelters: A Guide For Investors & Their Advisors, revised edition. Robert & Barbara Swanson, Dow Jones-Irwin Press, 1985.

How To Use Your Business or Profession as a Tax Shelter. Judith Cowan Zabalaoui, Reston Publishing Co. Inc., 1983.

The Time Value of Money. Gary E. Clayton & Donald Spivey, Spivey & Associates, 1981.

APPENDIX
Problems for a Financial Calculator

The financial calculator is a must when working on your financial future. These problems are designed for a Texas Instrument Business Analyst II, but can also be worked with a financial calculator from Hewlett Packard or Casio.

1. *Future Value Problems:* Each **different** area of your deferred compensation, whether Keogh, Pension and Profit Sharing or IRA will have two parts. One is what you currently have invested and the second is what you intend to put away yearly from now on.

   Dr. Jones has $97,000 in his Keogh plan. He will put away $10,000 each year for the next 15 years. How much will he have in 15 years if he continues to get a 12% return on his investments. Use these two formulas to determine what you will have one day.

   a. Enter $97,000 Press PV
      Enter 15 Press N
      Enter 12 Press % i

      Press 2nd then FV for an answer____________________

   b. Enter $10,000 Press PMT
      Enter 15 Press N
      Enter 12 Press % i
      Press 2nd then FV for an answer____________________

   a.______________ + b.______________ = total______________

   c. Now substitute some of your deferred compensation "problems" here and master future value.

2. *Present value problems:* These problems are the reverse of the problems in No. 1. You are simply asking "What do I have to start with?"

   a. Dr. Jones establishes a trust for his son. In order to cover anticipated college cost at State, he figures he will need $45,000. Assuming a growth rate of 11%, how much will he have to put in today to have $45,000 in four years.

Enter $45,000 Press FV
Enter 4 Press N
Enter 11 Press % i
Press 2nd then PV for an answer____________________

b. Dr. Beall sold a home in Florida for $275,000 this year. He figured he received a return of 13% on his money. He owned the home for ten years. How much did he pay for the house originally?

Enter $275,000 Press FV
Enter 10 Press N
Enter 13 Press % i
Press 2nd then PV for an answer____________________

3. *Annuity problems:* An annuity due simply means you will collect the money at the beginning of a period, and an ordinary annuity means you would get paid at the end of the period. Here are two examples which will highlight the difference.

a. This problem assumes you will receive the money at the *beginning* of the year.

Bob and Susan Jones are expecting their first annuity payment beginning today. They are expecting to receive $12,500 a year for the next fifteen years. If you could assume an 8% discount (interest) rate, what is the present value of these payments worth in today's dollars.

Enter $12,500 Press PMT
Enter 15 Press N
Enter 8 Press % i
Press Due then PV for an answer____________________

b. This problem assumes you will receive the payment at the end of the first year.

Bob and Susan Jones are expecting to receive their annuity check of $12,500 one year from today. The discount (interest) rate will be figured at 8%. They will receive their annuity for 15 years. How much would they have to have placed in this investment for them to receive the annual payments?

Enter $12,500 Press PMT
Enter 15 Press N
Enter 8 Press % i
For an answer press 2nd then PV____________________

c. Do you see a difference?________ how much?________. Do you understand how important it is to know if you're going to get paid at the beginning of a period or at the end of a period?

4. What interest did I earn?
   Joe put $10,000.00 in a tax-free Zero Coupon Bond five years ago and was sent a check today for $17,623.42. What percent interest did he earn on his investment?

   Enter $10,000.00 Press PV
   Enter 17,623.42 Press FV
   Enter 5 Press N
   Press 2nd then % i for an answer____________

5. Solving for the periods: N
   David M. can't remember how long he invested his money, but he does remember that he put in $10,000 at 11.5 percent interest. Today he received $45,903.75. How many years did his investment grow?

   Enter 10,000 Press PV
   Enter 45,903.75 Press FV
   Enter 11.5 Press %i
   Press 2nd N for an answer____________

6. Real estate problems you ought to know how to solve. (The display on the right side of the page is there simply because the problems involve more than one step and you can follow the steps by looking at the display.)

   a. Figuring out a mortgage payment.
      Dr. Jay Jones decides to buy a $100,000 home with 95% financing. The mortgage will be for 25 years at 13.25%. Taxes will be $940.00 a year and the insurance premium is $508.00. What's Jay's monthly payment, including taxes and insurance. Do you think a toy tooth doctor can afford this?

	DISPLAY
1. Figure monthly payments on property taxes	
940.00 [÷] 12 [=] [STO]	78.33
2. Calculate monthly payment to insurance	
508 [÷] 12 [=] [SUM]	42.33

3. Enter selling price of home $100,000 — 100,000

4. Deduct (and display) amount of down payment
   [–] 5 [%] — 5,000

5. [=] — 95,000

6. Enter [PV] as the mortgage amount — 95,000

7. Enter number of payment periods
   25 [×] 12 [=] [N] — 300

8. Enter interest per payment period
   13.25 [÷] 12 [=] [%i] — 1.10

9. Compute monthly payment to principal and interest
   [2ND] [PMT] — 1089.37

10. Add monthly taxes and insurance
    [+] [RCL] — 120.67

11. Display full payment
    [=] — 1210.03

b. Taking back a second mortgage, then deciding you need the money and having to sell the mortgage at a discount becomes a not too pleasant experience. Here is how to figure what your mortgage would be worth.

   Dr. Sam Jones took back an 11% second mortgage when he sold his home two years ago. The original mortgage was for $40,000 and the original length was ten years. If the present market rate for second mortgages is 13% today, what is the discounted present value of Sam's loan?

DISPLAY READS

1. Enter the amount of the mortgage
   40,000 [PV] — 40,000

2. Enter number of payment periods
   10 [X] 12 [=] [N] — 120

3. Enter interest rate per period
   11 [÷] 12 [=] [%i] — .92

4. What is the monthly payment?
   [2ND] [PMT] — 551.00

5. Enter number of periods remaining to be collected
   [120] [−] 24 [=] [N] — 96.00

6. Enter Market interest rate per period
   [13.0] [÷] 12 [=] [%i] — 1.08

7. What is the mortgage worth today?
   [2ND] [PV] — 32,783.47

You can see by this example that it does not pay to be in the lending business unless you have no choice.

ANSWERS:

1.a. $530,935.88
  b. $372,797.14
  a + b = $903,733.02

2.a. $29,642.89
  b. $81,011.80

3.a. $115,552.96
  b. $106,993.48
  c. yes – $8,559.48

4.a. 12%
  b. 14 years

GLOSSARY

annuitant: The person receiving an annuity.

annuity: A series of payments usually paid for a specific period of time or for life. Commonly used as a retirement vehicle.

BETA: Known as the BETA coefficient, it is the measure of systematic risk associated with mutual funds or stock.

capital gain: A profit derived from the sale of capital assets such as stock; can be either long term or short term.

compound interest: The interest on principal which is increased periodically by interest paid on the previous amount of principal.

certificate of deposit: A time deposit with a specific maturity date usually offered by the banking industry.

Clifford trust: A short-term trust lasting for 10 years and a day. The 10 years and a day lasts from the day of the transfer of property to the trust. It permits income-splitting without giving up the property permanently.

commercial paper: Short-term promissory notes, bills of exchange, or acceptances which are unsecured.

common stock: A certificate which represents an undivided ownership in a company with no set rate of return.

disclaimer trust: A trust which allows the surviving spouse to disclaim assets left to them in order to do estate planning for themselves.

dividend: Payment distributed pro rata among shareholders. Can be a fixed amount such as in preferred stock or a variable amount.

fiscalists: Persons believing in taxation, spending policies, and debt management by the federal government.

fixed income issues: A fixed constant amount of income which does not fluctuate. Usually from bonds, annuities, etc.

Keogh plan: A tax-deferred retirement plan for self-employed individuals.

limited partnership: A business form which allows the general partner to carry all liability for the right to control management. The limited partner has liability limited to the extent of his investment.

municipal bond: Today, this designates a bond issued by a city, a state, or an authority. The dividend is exempt from federal taxation and from some state and local taxes, depending on the place of issue.

mutual funds: An open-end investment company which offers new shares and redeems other ones constantly.

no-load: A mutual fund which does not charge a commission, or load.

pour-over will: A will directing that the remaining assets of a person be added to a trust established in the decedent's lifetime. Typically a pre-established living trust.

power of attorney: A legal instrument which authorizes one person to act on the behalf of another.

price earnings ratio: The ratio of a stock's price to the company's previous 12 months' earnings.

Q-Tip trust: The qualified terminable interest trust allows for the spouse to have all the income from the trust and that no one shall remove the principal of the trust from the spouse during his or her lifetime.

spousal remainder trust: A trust set up for a period of time which allows all the income to go to a third party, usually a child. At the end of the period, the spouse receives the principal or remainder of the trust.

square root volatility: A "rule" which states that all stocks will change in price by adding a constant amount to the square root of the beginning price. Therefore, the lower the price of the stock, the greater its advance.

trust: An arrangement whereby one person (the settlor) transfers real and/or personal property to another person (trustee) to hold for a third person (the beneficiary) of the trust.

Index